ALSO BY DAVID AND TOM GARDNER

The Motley Fool Investment Guide
You Have More Than You Think

THE MOTLEY FOOL INVESTMENT WORKBOOK

DAVID and TOM GARDNER

A Fireside Book
Published by SIMON & SCHUSTER

For our Foolish sister, Mackie

FIRESIDE
Rockefeller Center
1230 Avenue of the Americas
New York, NY 10020

FIRESIDE and colophon are registered trademarks
of Simon & Schuster Inc.

Designed by Irving Perkins Associates, Inc.

Manufactured in the United States of America

1   3   5   7   9   10   8   6   4   2

Library of Congress Cataloging-in-Publication Data
Gardner, David, date.
The Motley Fool investment workbook / David and Tom Gardner.
p.   cm.
1. Portfolio management.   2. Investment analysis.   3. Stock
exchanges.   I. Gardner, Tom, date.   II. Title.
HG4529.5.G372   1998
332.6—dc21   97-43602
                                                          CIP

ISBN 0-684-84401-X

Contents

Preface

The Motley Fool Investment Workbook is a stand-alone interactive guide to taking control of one's own finances.

We wish to emphasize *stand-alone* because while this book brings together concepts from our other books into a single interactive whole, it is by no means dependent on them. It is not a reference work—indeed, it's the very opposite. This book is an entirely new sort of book, a roll-up-your-sleeves-and-get-Foolish interactive learning center. It's designed to take anyone who can read (no pre-existing financial knowledge or interest necessary) through a tour of his own financial landscape. But unlike tour books, this Foolish one teaches you to guide *yourself.*

No tour through one's own financial landscape could be particularly enjoyable without some humor and some jazz accompaniment. That's where the "Foolish" part comes in. We hope you'll find this book written in a manner very different from the standard financial books out there which are, shall we say, a tad Saharan?

Dear reader, you have found an oasis. Get your pencil out, your calculator ready, and let the jazz begin!

— David and Tom Gardner

CHAPTER 1
Getting Started

WHY ARE YOU HERE?

Turn on any investing show on television. (OK, you might never have done this before, but humor us.) Chances are that at some point in the next half hour you'll see a person looking quite knowledgeable make a prediction about the stock market. He or she might say something like, "The market is entering a push-pull phase, as evidenced by the inverse parabolic formation that is occurring in the advance-decline line. The Dow will drop 342 points over the next two months, starting Monday." The interviewer nods gravely and sympathetically. You, of course, are mystified, and so is everybody else (including the interviewer).

Is it any wonder that, for decades, most Americans haven't thought they could handle investing on their own?

The good news is that, despite how intimidating investing might seem, never before have so many been this interested in it and never before has the information been so accessible.

These days a lot of us are successfully directing our own retirement money through things like 401(k) plans and individual retirement accounts (IRAs). And most of us expect that in our lifetimes we'll save enough to buy a house, put our children through school, and cover unexpected expenses. But did any of us think we could expect some Foolish fun along the way, too? Hopefully, you've realized that managing your money can be extremely entertaining and enlightening.

Others, however, have not yet taken to saving and investing—either because the stock market seems indecipherable or because they consider "money watching" a petty, self-interested pastime. Oddly enough, because of their failure to save or invest, they tend to be the very sort who eventually worry most about how they're going to make it to and through retirement. For them, the stock market is a bugaboo. Unlike gaining interest in a savings account, they know, making money through investing in the stock market is not guaranteed. "I could lose it all!" they cry.

While this may be a common worry among those who've never invested in stocks, their catastrophe mentality is equivalent to never crossing the street because they might get hit by a bicycle. Granted, watching financial "experts" on television probably does little to put one's mind at ease; but the first thing we want you to know is that the experts know a lot less than they think. And *you* know a lot more than you'd ever believe.

Thanks to the recent and unprecedented spread of education about money, it's easier and more rewarding than ever before to take a do-it-yerself attitude about your money. It's a revolution, dear Fool, and if you need proof, just look in the mirror. With this book in hand, you're our latest indicator! And what's particularly important to recognize is that our collective interest these days in managing our own money flies in the face of most Wall Street institutions, which have a strong financial incentive to make investing seem like Newtonian physics. After all, much of Wall Street exists to manage other people's money— that's the reason these guys work in skyscrapers, not back alleys. And since the whole way they continue to afford their high rent is by charging you to manage your money, part of their sales job has to be showing you that this is just too difficult for you to do on your own. But as we'll demonstrate in this Foolish guide, investing is not Newtonian physics. The Wise men of Wall Street know that well. It's about time that you did, too.

Professional money management in fact contradicts the normal way things work in business. Most professions exist to translate or reduce complex things into simpler forms that are more accessible and helpful to the rest of us. An accountant sifts through difficult tax laws and reams of financial data to tell a corporation how much it

owes in taxes. A doctor takes advantage of years of research and education to prescribe a drug that will help your hay fever. An engineer makes use of physics and material science to design the office building you work in. Professionals in the investing world, however, generally try to make everything more difficult, because that's how they make their money. They make your investing decisions sound dicey so that you contract *them* to guide you. Convenient, eh?

This workbook is designed to show you that while investing may be hard work, it isn't as difficult as you thought. What do you know about investing? We're already convinced that *you know more than you think*. Everybody knows something about business, and the stock market makes it possible for you to buy shares in companies that are involved in almost any facet of your life.

Do you work with automobiles? Chances are you know which companies make the best parts. Do you play sports? You probably know which companies make the best-selling gear. If you are a doctor, you probably know which pharmaceutical companies are coming out with the best drugs. Successful investing involves, primarily, just looking around you, scratching your head a bit, and saying stuff like, "Uhh, that makes sense."

The Motley Fool Investment Workbook has been carefully designed to provide a roll-up-your-sleeves interactive learning experience. The aim is to have you take control of your financial future. Absolutely no knowledge of any kind about personal finance or the stock market is required.

Quiz #1

Do you know what variable-ratio option writing is?

a. Yes   *b.* No

If you circled *b,* you're in the right place. Read on.

One of our hopes with this book is that whether you have $500,000 to invest or $57, you'll learn enough to avoid using overpaid middlemen (brokers, financial advisors, mutual funds, you name it) and have more control, more satisfaction, more fun on the way to early retirement. But if, after finishing all 224 pages, you found you really learned only three things about investing, we hope that they are

Hey, I can do this.

It will require some perseverance.

I can reap substantial rewards if I'm patient.

Finally, learning to invest does require some work. But as it's quite fun, it's exactly the sort that we Fools enjoy. This workbook aims to demonstrate that you can enjoy investing. If by the end you find that you've not had fun, you are entitled to our Foolish guarantee:

The Motley Fool hereby guarantees you an e-mail response to any complaints about the opinions, the teaching methodology, the joking banter, the layout, or the design of this book (e-mail: FoolWorkbook@fool.com).

Let's begin.

TAKING STOCK: WHERE SOME PEOPLE ARE

The first step, taking stock of where you are, is the simplest but the most often overlooked of all the 593 steps we'll be covering. Too many people make their first investment without understanding what sort of disposition they have or what financial position they're in.

To get a little perspective on your own financial situation, it often helps to look at some other people's situations, to see how they're doing. So let's just take a trip to our local megabookstore and see whom we can find.

Bob and Carol Agee

As we pull into the parking lot in front, tunes blaring obnoxiously out of open windows, we see Bob and Carol Agee flipping through the books on sale out in front of the store. Who are the Agees? They're a married couple with two young rambunctious sons, Mike and John. The Agees moved into a renovated Victorian house on Amazon Lane about two years ago. Both have good jobs; Carol inherited a little money from a great-aunt she never knew; and the two of them have successfully budgeted their money. While they've taken out a mortgage on the house and have monthly car payments, they don't have any other debt.

Bob looks kind of bored as his wife pages through a book on the evolution of the English language. His eyes wander over to the cover of some personal finance book; boy, those things are everywhere these days. Bob hasn't thought a lot about investing. He thinks investing is something that really rich people do, and he certainly isn't rich. Carol reads the finance pages now and then but only just started investing some of her salary into mutual funds. They are both aware that in the future they'll need significant sums of money to send their boys to college (all that beer the first two years, then maybe a business class or two—something that'll get them a job, right?). And the Agees will need plenty of money left over, in the wake of all that schooling, to comfortably retire.

Bob and Carol haven't neglected their retirement planning. Both contribute 6 percent of their salaries to their employers' 401(k) plans (which allow employees to park a portion of their salaries in "tax-deferred" investments—more on that later). Their employers match those investments with 2 percent of salary.

Where is the money invested? Neither of the Agees is sure. When Bob's employer started the plan, there was a presentation by the company that handles the 401(k), and they offered a choice of three mutual funds. Bob has no idea how well these funds have actually done; all he vaguely remembers is that one was "high return, high risk," the other was "low risk, less return," and the last was something that promised "fixed income." What do those terms mean? He doesn't know. He just remembers that he chose the low-risk one, because he didn't want to take chances with his money.

Carol's plan includes a similar selection of funds. One is an "index fund" that invests in the five hundred companies that make up the Standard & Poor's 500—the largest companies in America. Another is a government bond fund. The last is a corporate bond fund. Carol wanted to put all of her contribution in the S&P 500 fund. However, Bob talked her out of that, because he thought it was much too risky. So she put her money in the government bond fund, which Bob feels is the best place.

Where does Bob get his approach to investing? Perhaps from his mother—who watched her godfather's fortune disintegrate during the Great Depression. Even though Bob is taking one of the safest routes possible—a fund comprising largely government-issued bonds—his mother still considers him a high roller. "Those corrupt politicians in Washington might be lining their pockets with your savings right now!" she says.

Money has definitely gotten in the way of familial relations in the Agee family. It's sad, but Carol has been ignoring her mother-in-law lately. She's still miffed that she can't put any of their money into an index fund. She sat down one day and calculated how much they need to retire. It's a lot of money, and with the performance of their investments to date, it doesn't look like they'll be able to save enough for their sons to get to college and for themselves to retire at sixty-five.

Carol insists that Bob sit down with her and just take a look at the numbers. She wants Bob to find out exactly what options are available in his 401(k) and to consider more seriously where he is putting his contribution. She wants to move her funds into the index fund in her plan and to contribute more. And Carol would love it if she could just get Bob to read one or two books about investing. But he won't. It's just easier for him to avoid the subject, since every time his mother hears of their plans, she starts talking about how the market will "crash any day now, and you'll be ruined, just like my godfather, Nim, was in '29. And if you do," she says, "I'm not going to bail you all out."

Let's leave Bob and Carol to enjoy their time *away from relatives,* and head into the store to see whom else we can find.

Jim Donatello

Over by the magazine rack, we find Jim—lanky, pensive, and sporting a goatee. He's looking at some music magazines. Jim plays a guitar, not well enough to quit his day job, not poorly enough to give up the thought of doing so. About two years ago, he graduated from college with a B.A. in medieval history. He's single and has a job driving a delivery van for UPS. It's not exactly what he wanted, but it's a start.

Jim grew up on a farm twenty minutes southwest of Bradford, Pennsylvania. His family raised horses and dairy cattle, and farmed oats. Growing up on a farm gave him a love of the outdoors, the ability to work hard, and an intense fear of the dreaded desk job. Jim now lives in an apartment in the metropolis of McKeesport, Pennsylvania, which is located at the confluence of the Monongahela and Youghiogheny Rivers. Enjoying an active social life, he dates a woman in the apartment across the hall, another who lives back at home in Bradford, and one who lives in Mine Hill, West Virginia. What a dog! When he is not working or dating, he can be found rolling over the hills of the state on a mountain bike.

Despite his active life, Jim is actually quite thrifty with his finances. His car is paid for, and he's almost paid off the loan he took out for the guitar. Other than his Dell Pentium computer, he doesn't have any other luxuries, nor does he see the need for them. This leaves him with a significant amount of extra money, which he has saved at the local savings and loan.

So far, Jim's investments have been twofold. On the advice of one of his girlfriends' brothers, he speculated in a penny stock—a gold mining company in Canada listed on the Vancouver Stock Exchange. The company was named Quick Pay Goldmines (VSE: QPGM), which used a new electromagnetic device to mine gold out of magnetic black sands in western Canada.

Jim was skeptical about this whole gold mining venture. But his girlfriend Alison reassured him; her brother Wade knew what he was talking about. Wade told Jim that the company was run by Trapshooter Reilly, a human fountain of liquid gold. Jim had heard of Reilly somewhere, but if he remembered correctly, the story wasn't good.

Still, at the urging of Alison, he invested $1,700. Besides, Wade said to him, "At 43 cents a share, how can you go wrong?"

Two weeks after he bought it, the thing was trading at 61 cents per share, and Jim began entertaining the idea of a biking tour of the Northeast. But a week later, CNBC ran a story that Quick Pay Goldmines was under investigation by the Royal Canadian Mounted Police. The gold mine turned out to be nothing more than a money-laundering operation. That evening, Jim brought up a picture of Trapshooter Reilly on the World Wide Web—with Reilly in handcuffs and leg irons, on his way to court. That was the first time Jim saw him, and all he could think was, "Holy cow, I invested my money in *that* guy?" The Vancouver Stock Exchange halted trading in the company overnight, and Jim's investment became worthless.

Jim's second investment was in a savings account down at the local bank. He still knows very well that the 3 percent interest he's getting on his account at the savings and loan in McKeesport isn't really adding to his wealth at all. In time, he'd like to move out of his apartment in McKeesport and into a house. That won't happen from promotions at UPS and a savings account. But Jim knows it's better to have money than to lose it in the market. He just doesn't have a clue about where to go next.

Ronald and Sandy Washington

Let's leave Jim at the magazine rack and step into the coffee shop. Sitting at one of the tables is a well-dressed couple. They don't look too happy. In fact, they're stressed out. Travel magazines are spread out all over the table, but something's ruining their dreams of a walking tour through the west of Ireland. This couple, Ronald and Sandy Washington, is doing very well professionally. They both earn high salaries, both drive new luxury cars, and both carry cellular phones. They have two children, but the live-in nanny, Rosy, does most of the work of raising them. Their house has the best furniture and a state-of-the-art home entertainment center. They belong to the local country club and a health club. And Ronald just bought a fifty-five-foot yacht. They're living large!

Everything must be fine, right?

Nope, doing all this comes with a price. Salary checks are racing out the door—for tuition and all the stuff that they believe their kids need, for insurance, hefty mortgage payments, those car payments, and for Ronald's "Syncho-Satellite Fish Tracker 2000," which his yacht dealer convinced him his boat would need. ("What are you going to do—just *float* out there?")

Commensurate with all that consumption, the bills are getting worse, and Ronald is afraid to look at them each month. Yet the debts aren't limited to those just mentioned. They have several credit cards and numerous store charge cards, which have exorbitant interest rates. Because they have overdraft protection on their checking accounts, every time they write a check for more than the balance of an account, money is kicked into the account by their bank, in $100 increments. This makes it impossible for them to keep track of their accounts.

There have been a number of warnings that the Washingtons were getting in trouble, but it really is becoming critical. When they bought their latest cars, the Schnauzer 900ZX and the Manatee Coupe, the dealer told them they owed more on the trade-ins than the trade-ins were worth. He said they were "upside down." So to get the loans on the new cars, they had to borrow more than the new cars were worth. Sandy had some doubts about whether they should buy those automobiles, but as a salesman, Ronald was worried about what business partners would think if they drove old cars.

Ronald does realize that a lot of the purchases he made on credit weren't necessary. He wonders if he needs all the different suits he has in his closet. Some he hasn't worn more than once. The home entertainment center is another thing they probably shouldn't have bought. The only one who seems to use it is Rosy (she enjoys it a lot, though). Also, why do they have three camcorders? No one watches the videos they shoot, anyway. The country club membership is nice, but Sandy never gets a chance to get over there. Same for the health club—they never use the membership.

We stumbled on this pair today just as they began confessing and reasoning their way through the giant knot of their financial state. The trip is certainly off. Sandy is now so worried about the payments that the thought of going away seems insane. The interest that is accumulating on the debt boggles the mind. After making payments each month, they have almost no cash left over.

To top it all off, Ronald's firm has seen business drop off recently, and he worries he may be reduced to consultant status. And Sandy's company is telling her that she is not a "team player," which raises concerns that they might ask her to leave. Both have been quietly on the lookout for other jobs, but they fear they may experience periods of unemployment. That could be a real disaster. Ronald just turned to Sandy and said, "We may look wealthy, but we're essentially broke." (Maybe he should get into the fishing business.)

Joanne Kurtz

Before we leave the bookstore, let's go downstairs. This store has a fireplace with comfortable furniture placed around it so that customers can relax while paging through one book after another. Sitting on the couch immediately in front of the fireplace is Joanne. She's in her mid-fifties and divorced. Several years ago, her husband left her. It was a devastating shock, but Joanne didn't waste any time feeling sorry for herself. She went out and got a job. She had been out of the workforce for many years raising children, which meant that getting a traditional job would be difficult. So she decided to sell real estate. She obtained her license, and after a few lean months, she started selling.

Joanne succeeded in the real estate business because she took the time with customers to determine what they really needed, and she knew her sales area thoroughly. She was careful to bring clients only to homes that fit their financial situations. Other agents habitually showed clients houses that sold $10,000 to $20,000 higher than what they'd requested, hoping to squeeze out some extra commission. Joanne knew better. If a client wanted a $100,000 house, she showed the client a $100,000 house. The consequence? She sold a lot of houses.

It wasn't long before Joanne accumulated a fair amount of cash from her sales. Plus, the divorce settlement had given her a lump sum. She set up an account with a full-service broker, tried that for a short while, but quickly became disillusioned. First, as a salesperson she knew her product; but her stockbroker didn't seem to know anything about the investments he sold. He offered only memorized responses to her questions. And he was extremely uncooperative. Once, she had wanted to buy stock in a company that performed relocation services. A number of her clients used them, and it seemed their business was booming. Her broker blew off her suggestion. He also never bothered speaking to her

about her specific investment needs relative to his ideas, which disturbed her even more.

Worse, he was constantly calling her with recommendations of what to buy or sell, talking down to her about unknown and unproven companies. She'd buy a stock that he insisted was hot, and two weeks later he'd urge her to sell it because "it isn't making earnings." One day he called her with his latest recommendation, and she had the nerve to ask him why. "It's on my company's recommended list," he answered.

"So?" she asked. "Is that the reason I should buy it? What if it misses earnings? Do I sell it in two weeks?"

Her broker steamed. "Look," he stammered at her, "if you want me to be your broker, you should go with what I say!" It didn't take Joanne more than a second to think about that. "I'm transferring my account." She's always been thankful that she said those words.

Where did she go with her money? Joanne set up an account with a discount broker, joined an investment club of friends, and began doing her own research. This worked for real estate— why shouldn't it work for the stock market? She went to the library and asked the librarian what books she should read on investing. The librarian suggested "any of the books by Peter Lynch," so Joanne borrowed a copy of *Beating the Street* and started to read it that night. Lynch's ideas were inspiring, and the guy actually seemed to be having fun with all this. And the idea that she might be smart enough to pick stocks fascinated her. On her next trip to the bookstore, she picked up *The Motley Fool Investment Workbook* and at this very moment is reading about herself. Hey there, Joanne!

Armed with knowledge and confidence, she started investing in stocks. How did she and the club choose which ones to buy? Just by focusing on companies she knew, checking out to make sure they were profitably run. For example, she enjoyed using Microsoft's Excel spreadsheets for her real estate dealings, and she realized every office she knew either had or was switching to Microsoft software. After calling the company for its financials, and after sorting through some basic financial work, she invested. Her stock rose from $79 to $140 per share in less than a year.

Overall, Joanne's investments have done quite well—some big winners, some average, others just plain dawgs. To her surprise, she has learned a lot of interesting things about how the business world works. Indeed, she's concluded that business is more full of stories and science and mystery and history and philosophy and the arts than common fools could ever have imagined.

OK, we've done our survey of a few bookstore patrons. Let's walk over to the lemonade stand, grab three cups of juice, ask the merchant how business is, and then sit down on the nearest bench and reflect on what we've learned.

Why Should These People Invest?

The people we've just met illustrate widely varied financial situations. Each has a different reason for investing, although, obviously, one couple needs to get its debt under control before even thinking about investing. Here are some reasons that our bookstore friends *should* be investing— perhaps one or more will strike a chord. Check any reasons that apply to you.

☐ To accumulate money for retirement because you have no retirement plan where you work
☐ To supplement retirement income from a pension fund

☐ To save enough money for a large expense you can foresee, such as sending children to college, buying a house, or starting a business
☐ To have resources for an unforeseen future emergency
☐ To make one hell of a lot of money and become Master of the Universe
☐ To learn more about the company at which you work
☐ To have something to talk to your dad about

If you checked at least one box, you're going to get your money's worth out of this Foolish tome—or we're going to die trying.

Now, let's debunk some commonly shared misconceptions.

1. *You* need *to be rich to invest.*
No, you don't. There are investment strategies appropriate for every financial situation.

2. *You* need *to put a lot of time into investing.*
No, you don't. You can put in as much or as little time as you want—anywhere from thirty minutes a month to as much of your day as you're willing to commit. Some people make a hobby of investing and regularly read about companies, financial news, and the latest fashion line from Sears. Others make a hobby of mountain biking or newts and *still* invest, by using strategies that require little effort and only periodic checks of their investment performance.

3. *You* need *to know a lot about stocks.*
Nope, you don't need this either. You just need to know about what you are investing in, or the strategy you are using. Some strategies, like index investing, require no knowledge at all. Others, like investing in small-cap growth stocks, require more

knowledge, and should usually be done after practicing for months (or years) without real money.

4. *Investing is* deadly *boring.*
No, it doesn't have to be—unless you're an MBA student assigned to follow the utilities industry by a mammoth investment firm. Otherwise, it's good, clean, educational fun. We still can't believe the subject isn't taught more to our children.

Make a hobby of investing and you learn what forces drive industry, the economy, and nations themselves. You learn how companies are run, how they treat their people, and how they continue to grow. Learning about investing gives you a useful new way to look at the world around you.

For some people, the word "learning" conjures up images of No. 2 pencils and filling out bubbles, or algebraic word problems, or ill-timed pop quizzes. Hey, that was then and this is now. At Fool Global HQ, we make it our business to ensure that you hardly notice how much you're learning.

Now, going back to the beginning of this chapter, remember what the talking head was saying on television? We'll quote him again:

"The market is entering a push-pull phase, as evidenced in the inverse parabolic formation that is occurring in the advance-decline line. The Dow will drop 342 points over the next two months, starting Monday."

Let's pull that apart word by word and analyze what he meant.

Naa, never mind.

You see, he said absolutely nothing useful. Sadly, the above quote is a compilation of actual statements made by "experts" on financial television. The business of Wall Street, and the Wise men and women who populate it, is to speak a language you don't understand, to convince you that you aren't smart enough. We already explained the reason for this: *Their livelihoods depend on being able to overcharge you for entrusting your money to them.* Fools that we are, we aim to convince you that you don't need the self-promoting and wily ways of the Wise. With a little education, you can make your own decisions, invest your own money, and significantly improve upon any results the Wise might ever offer you.

TAKING STOCK: WHERE YOU ARE

It's time to pull the Foolmobile over to the side of the road and ask: "Hey, who the heck *are* you?" In the pages just ahead we'll be pulling back briefly from the mechanics of investing—that's later—and instead we'll concentrate on your personality, your preferences. Get ready for a mix of Meyers-Briggs, Stuart Smalley, and our syndicated *Ask the Fool* column.

What Kind of Fool Am I?

Who am I?

If you know the answer to "Who am I?" you probably don't need this workbook. Having solved man's existential dilemma, you'll have already made millions and given it all away to those around you. Most of the rest of us are always trying to figure out what sort of person we are—and for the purposes of this book, what type of investor we are.

There are dozens of ways to successfully invest in stocks; we'll be identifying as many of them as we have space for here. But you're going to have to know thyself, because if you select a great approach that is wrong *for you*, you won't be pleased with the results. Even if you make money, your nerves may never get over it. And it's quite likely that you won't make any money. George Soros, a trader, and Warren Buffett, an investor, have entirely different ways of approaching the equity markets. Each has made billions, and each has profoundly affected the world around him. But force one into the other's shoes and you have the recipe for a small disaster, for failure and discontentment.

Figuring out who you are is critical to Foolish investing. Let's start by asking a few questions:

How much risk are you willing to take?

How much time can you really devote to investing?

Are you the sort of person who loves taking the dog for a walk in the evening or prefers buzzing around town to every cocktail party?

How do you feel about prosperity?

What has your family taught you about investing?

Do public companies inspire, frighten, bore, or disgust you?

And how about your personal finances—do you balance your checkbook, or does that little receipt from the ATM machine always surprise you with its contents?

Are you a saver, a spender, or both?

The above questions may help point your way toward how to invest successfully. Do you want to excel at it almost without effort? If so, you'll need a focused plan of what you want to achieve, the tools and skills to put your plan into motion, and for just a short period of time here, a

take-no-prisoners attitude to get through the initial research.

Begin to formulate your vision by filling in the list below. Heck, this stuff may seem sappy. But if you ponder it for a second, isn't it incredible that so many of us ramble through our lives without penciling down what it is we're hoping to gain out of all this? Perhaps Foolishness will ultimately help you focus on more global goals throughout your life—but you paid us only to teach you how to invest. So name a few of your financial goals, fellow Fool.

Ten Things I Would Like to Be, Do, or Have

1. _____

2. _____

3. _____

4. _____

5. _____

6. _____

7. _____

8. _____

9. _____

10. _____

Skim through the above list. Are there any dreams requiring some money that you don't have? You want to be a master magician? You'll need the tools and a marketing budget. You'd like to sail the Tyrrhenian Sea? The boat, the crew, the food, the cellular linkup to The Motley Fool Online—these aren't free. Oh, you want to open up local homes for struggling teenagers? Federal and state grants won't carry the full load of expenses. You'll need some of your own money.

Take a second and circle the items on your list that will require capital. Voilà! You know why you hold this book and why you're giving up an entire afternoon to the scrutiny of your finances. Refer back to this page often. We're working toward giving you the independent wealth to achieve them.

Now let's look to the root of some of your dreams: your family.

Family Background and Beliefs

Most of us are by now aware that messages from our parents or guardians early in life have a potent effect on the way we now see the world. The Kennedy children were required to summarize news highlights from the daily paper each night at dinner. It's not surprising that so many of them turned to politics: Politics is, after all, one of the few things as dismal as having to summarize news highlights. Anyway, if your family often sat around the dinner table discussing the need to stay out of debt, probably you took greater care to do just that. And some of you have mothers who loved to talk about stock market trends and ways to find undervalued companies; that gave you the confidence to know that such things were achievable (and you didn't even have to spend $40,000 per year on a business school degree!).

Conversely, if your parents lamented how much their forerunners had lost in market crashes or how brokers had ripped them off or how commercialism was killing the planet, you probably don't have too many positive associations with money. These beliefs can become so ingrained that fundamental logic or the experi-

ences of others hold no sway over you. Well, we're still going to try to make Foolishness work for you! In order to become a satisfied investor, you need to identify the negative beliefs you hold about money, reason them all the way through, discuss them with people outside your immediate family, and recognize that we all operate in a commercial world, we all consume to survive. You'll need to apply some of these basic commonsense and mathematical principles to ensure your prosperity.

How about writing down three negative thoughts about money from either family or friends in your past?

1. _____

2. _____

3. _____

Now take another two minutes and write down the best one-line refutation of each of those negative ideas.

1. _____

2. _____

3. _____

Reread all six. Now, the Fool Workbook isn't brought to you by one of those pseudoreligious self-help organizations interested in luring you into a mountain community and asking your parents for money. So we're not going to propose that you should be forever positive in your thinking about money. Instead, we're simply going to encourage you to look squarely at your three rebuttals and recognize them for what they are: your best shot at getting started on the right foot. Ebenezer Scrooge remade his own attitude toward money and radically changed his neighborhood and his life in the course of one night! Anyone can.

Now it's time to think about how much risk you can absorb en route to building a financial future that has you riding horses in Himalayan valleys or writing books about Ingmar Bergman or whatever you fancy. To get there without escalating blood pressure, you'll have to manage risk.

Risk Temperament

How do you feel about losing money? How much risk can you tolerate without upsetting your entire life? These questions need answering. You have to find the right risk level for yourself—the level where your investments excite you but don't cause any sleepless nights. Worrying about your money will not increase your success. In fact, worrying about anything won't much help. (It has, however, been statistically demonstrated that such worries *will* increase your internist's success.) You need to set yourself up for uninterrupted sleep and lazy Sunday mornings. So, let's determine whether you're Evel Knievel or Homebody Hank.

Risk-Tolerance Test

Respond to the questions below with the answer that most accurately reflects your point of view.

1. Which of these three cars would you prefer to drive?
   a. Ferrari
   b. Jeep Cherokee
   c. Volvo
2. You would rather eat
   a. At a new, exotic locale you've never been to before
   b. At your favorite restaurant
   c. Leftovers at home

3. You meet someone at a party who you've heard is a successful broker. He gives you a stock tip. Do you
   a. Call your broker immediately and buy 100 shares?
   b. Ask other people their opinion of this broker and this stock?
   c. Have another bite of scungilli salad?
4. If the speed limit is 65, do you
   a. Drive at a minimum of 75 and turn on your fuzzbuster?
   b. Drive between 65 and 74?
   c. Drive below 65?
5. Your cat gets stuck up a tree. Do you
   a. Climb the tree yourself and carry her down?
   b. Climb a ladder to carry her down?
   c. Call the Fire Department to carry her down?
6. You are given $1,000 from a rich aunt for your birthday. Do you
   a. Drive to Atlantic City, believing it is your duty to go forth and multiply?
   b. Put the cash in a money-market fund and research stocks to invest in?
   c. Put the cash in a lockbox in your basement?

Scoring: Give yourself 10 points for every *a*, 5 points for every *b*, and 0 points for every *c*.

Write your score here, followed by the appellation you've earned (listed below):

_____

If you scored over 40 points, you are *Captain Ahab*, willing to take risks to accomplish your goals. You *might* make a whale of a killing in the stock market.

If you scored 16–40, you are *Captain Kirk*, willing to take enterprising risks after scrutinizing the pros and cons and calculating which move is the most prudent.

And if you scored 0–15, you are *Captain Kangaroo,* preferring to tend the carrots in the garden while hobnobbing with Mr. Greenjeans. Protecting what you have is your utmost priority.

With the knowledge they will acquire from this workbook, Captain Kangaroos might feel empowered to venture forth and dabble in a little adventure. Captain Kirks will have all the necessary tools to support their methodology. And the Captain Ahabs out there might learn that saving some money and spending some quiet time at home won't cramp their style.

Now that you have some sense of how much risk you can bear, you'll need to figure how much time you have to dedicate to all this. If you have a couple of kids, it can be challenging enough just to remember your purse before vacationing. Many of us spend our waking hours on a tight schedule. Where the heck can we fit in the analysis and consistent operational management of our cash? Read on.

How Much Time Do I Have?

One of the great features of Foolish investing is that the amount of time you commit is strictly up to you. You can have successful investments by spending half an hour each year, month, or day. But you need to know, honestly, what's right for you. Start slowly—you can always devote more time when you begin to measure how much you enjoy this stuff. Set yourself up for success, not failure.

How Busy Am I?

Circle the response (true or false) that most applies to you.

1. I wouldn't consider visiting a deserted island without my personal planner.   T   F
2. I sometimes read the newspaper while meditating.   T   F
3. When things calm down, I only do two things at once.   T   F
4. Some weeks I'm too busy to sleep more than a few hours a night.   T   F
5. Someone else is in charge of my schedule, and I can't get an appointment with myself.   T   F
6. I haven't spoken to my parents or grandparents in six weeks.   T   F
7. I avoid air travel because on planes I can't use my cellular phone.   T   F
8. On occasion I have forgotten to feed my (pets) (children) (self).   T   F

If you answered *true* to any of these questions, you probably need a nap more than you need to be reading this book. Fold the top corner of this page, give yourself two hours with the shades drawn, and then come back. When you return, you'll be diving back into a book that proposes you need do no more than six hours of work per year to keep your budgets in order, your savings money flowing into investments, and your investments providing healthy long-term returns—and you won't ever have to meet with a trained salesman to do so. Sweet dreams!

How Much Am I Willing to Do?

So, how much time can you give over to your finances without compromising your already overloaded professional and personal life? The bottom rung on our Foolish ladder has you committing at least six hours per year to tracking your money. That's thirty minutes every month. From there, you can strengthen your financial position by adding extra hours. Of course, many people give hundreds of hours a month to saving and investing, but unless they're crushing the stock market's return by dozens of percentage points after all expenses are taken out, they may just be wasting a lot of time. First, let's see how much time you think you have for this stuff:

"I can reasonably commit _____ (number of seconds, minutes, hours) to investing each month."

OK, you put it in writing. We'll consider that a blood oath.

With time set aside, let's consider what financial tools you have at your disposal.

What Tools Do I Have at My Disposal?

Where would Delilah be without her scissors, Zorro without his sword, or Rocky without a side of beef? Nothing can be accomplished without the proper tools. The good news is that to excel at saving and investing, you already have much of the necessary equipment no more than an arm's length away.

While it is helpful to have a computer and access to The Fool Online, it isn't necessary. All the work in this book can be done with paper, pencil, and a calculator. And with a local library, TV, newspapers, and magazines, you can access all the information you need. Don't forget that you have some very valuable personal resources, as well. You have your brain, your experience, your instincts, and your sense of humor—all of which

(particularly the last!) are virtual necessities for surviving in the world of investing.

Since you're going to be learning a good deal about business here—the business of your personal finances and the businesses that you invest in—start by asking yourself about some of the shops in your local area. Wonder aloud with us for a second by naming what you consider to be the best and worst businesses in your vicinity.

The best business I know is _____.
The worst business I know is _____.

Now let's go one step further and ask you why you made those calls.

The three reasons that your chosen great business is great are:

1. _____

2. _____

3. _____

The three reasons that your chosen lame business is lame are:

1. _____

2. _____

3. _____

As we work together to improve your financial condition, concentrate your attention increasingly on the qualities of those businesses that you love. You're going to want to apply many of their principles to your own money management strategies, and heck, you may eventually want to aggregate enough wealth to be able to run a business just like theirs!

OK, perhaps you've realized some of the great tools and examples that lie minutes away from you. How about checking through the following list with us?

The Tools-and-Examples List

If you have the following, place a big phat *X* on the line next to the entry.

Brain	_____
Pad	_____
Pencil	_____
Sense of humor	_____
Investment workbook	__X__
Calculator	_____
Computer	_____
Telephone	_____
Common sense	_____
Curiosity	_____
Other people to talk to	_____
List of local businesses	_____
Champagne	_____
Kazoo	_____

OK, the tools are at your fingertips and you know what dreams you will invest for. It's time to take one large step backward before we plow ahead. Let's consider what experiences you've had as an investor already.

WHAT IS YOUR PAST EXPERIENCE?

Do you feel like the kind of person who never does *anything* right? Or does everything you touch turn to gold? Probably somewhere in between. Your past experiences are likely to color the way you approach investing.

The key is to take responsibility for your investments, to recognize your past mistakes or successes, and to move forward, knowing that the results you create are your own. It's a disservice to everyone involved—and an easy one at that—to blame your broker, your uncle Stuart, the chairman of the Federal Reserve, or Congress (OK, you can blame Congress). Everyone makes mistakes. Coca-Cola launched new Coke. Microsoft is managing what seems like its seventeenth incarnation of MSN Online. Bob Dylan has been booed off stages before. San Francisco used to have a horrible football team. Mistake and failure make us human; the key is to learn from your errors and to aim not to repeat them. If you're like us, you'll repeat at least a few (perhaps numerous times) just to keep from becoming perfect. (How boring.) Anyway, accepting that you'll have setbacks as an investor is a solid beginning.

My Dumbest Investment

I once heard a lot of fuss about a stock called Comparator Systems. There was some kind of exciting deal in the works, and the boat was leaving port. What was the deal? I had no idea. What did the company make? I had some vague notions, but never bothered to delve deeply. Yet, I bought it. Within days, the company had been found to have no new product at all. The story became a scandal as the company started getting hit with lawsuits, and investigations led to the halting of its trading. I lost everything I put into that one (fortunately, not too much!). My experience has shown me there is no such thing as "missing the boat." You always have plenty of time to learn about each investment, and good companies stay good for a long time. It took a bad approach in a bad company to discover this, but the resulting lesson was superb.

—Tony Miller

LESSON LEARNED: Don't invest in trains said to be leaving stations for good, or boats hurrying out of ports.

I drooled over Intel when the semiconductor industry was out of favor in 1996. Finally, I scooped some up at $68, planning to sell when it hit my price target of the low $100s. When the stock continued to drop, even though I knew the drop had nothing to do with the company's fundamentals, I panicked and sold. I was one of the only people, in the history of man, who ever *lost* money on Intel. If I had just held on to it, a year later I would have doubled my money.

—Barbara Eisner Bayer

LESSON LEARNED: **Don't let stock prices force you out of any holding if you believe the company behind that stock is still succeeding day after day.**

INVESTMENT OVER A 20-YEAR PERIOD

INVESTMENT VEHICLE	GROWTH RATE	$10,000 BECOMES
Treasury bills	3%	$18,061
Bonds	5%	$26,533
Stock market	10.5%	$73,662

Spending and Saving

We're assembling a nice profile of you now, dear Fool. (Whatever you do, don't let direct marketers get a hold of your workbook!) Now let's take a look at spending and saving habits. Actually, before we even think about how you're allocating funds, let's consider some of the numerical basics. Too many Americans think there's no reason to save money, claiming that it'll just sit there waiting to be spent, that their lives will just stand still waiting for some moola to jump-start them. Well, think for a second about what patience will do for you and consider what happens to $10,000 if you invest it in various ways.

As the growth rates continue to play out, one decade after another, the amount of money you have in common stock will absolutely blow away the cash you have sitting in a savings account at your local bank. Your initial challenge is just to save more money than you spend, to set aside as much as possible of those savings for long-term investments in stocks, and to repeat that strategy over and again. To paraphrase an old tune from the Golden Age of Disco—

> Save, save, save,
> Save, save, save,
> Save your booty,
> Save your boo-ooty!

And invest it.

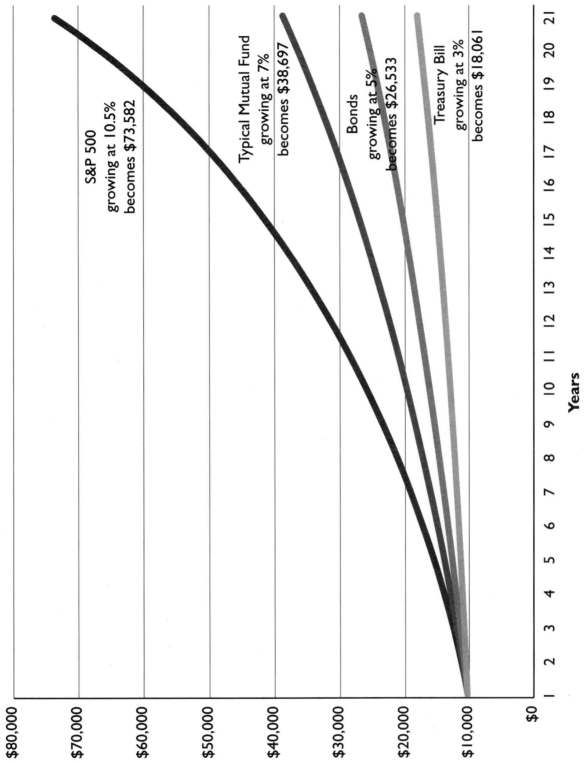

$10,000 COMPOUNDING OVER 20 YEARS

S&P 500
growing at 10.5%
becomes $73,582

Typical Mutual Fund
growing at 7%
becomes $38,697

Bonds
growing at 5%
becomes $26,533

Treasury Bill
growing at 3%
becomes $18,061

$80,000
$70,000
$60,000
$50,000
$40,000
$30,000
$20,000
$10,000
$0

1 2 3 4 5 6 7 8 9 10 11 12 13 14 15 16 17 18 19 20 21

Years

FIVE EXCUSES FOR NOT INVESTING

Given that the stock market has doled out such awesome returns over the past seven decades, it's a shame so many people aren't investing. Why not? Here are five reasons people sidestep stocks—and five short volleys.

COMMON EXCUSES NOT TO INVEST	WHY THEY'RE WRONG
I'll never know enough.	You don't have to be Einstein to be a successful investor.
I don't have enough money.	You can invest almost any amount of money.
I don't know where to start.	You've got this workbook, don't you?
It's for the boys' club on Wall Street.	You've come a long way, Fool.
I don't have enough time.	Half an hour a year? Sure you do.

So, Where Are You Now? The Big Picture!

Fill out this work sheet and see how far you've come already. You can draw many of your answers from previous exercises.

1. If I have many, many years to invest, I'm best off buying

   a. bonds
   b. stocks
   c. Treasury bills

2. My three investment goals are

   a. _____

   b. _____

   c. _____

3. My risk-tolerance type is Captain _____.

   _____

   _____

4. Three dreams I would like to make come true through investing are

   a. _____

   b. _____

   c. _____

5. One business I love is _____.

6. One business I can't stand is _____.

7. The amount of time I am willing to spend investing is _____ hours per month.

8. Tools I can use to implement my investing strategy are

   a. _____

   b. _____

   c. _____

   d. _____

9. One investing mistake I will never make is

   _____.

10. Just as Pete Sampras is consistently great in
    tennis, there are businesses that are consis-
    tently great in their industry.
    ☐ True   ☐ False

You are now ready to begin tackling financial information. Keep that pencil and mind sharp, and let's get ready to rummmmmbbbbbllllle!

CHAPTER 2

You and Your Money

HOW MUCH DO YOU HAVE TO INVEST?

Now that you've stopped and considered what kind of Fool you are—per financial perspectives and objectives—it's time to discuss the nuts and bolts of the issue. You may be sitting there thinking, "OK, so I know I am a low-risk, conservative Captain Kangaroo investor who needs to invest in something—now what?" (By the way, did you think you'd ever say anything as nutty as that?)

Whatever mental picture you have put together of what kind of investor you are, you're now ready to move on to the next and crucial point, what you should invest in. Let's get some stock picks out there. Let's start making some money. Right?

Wrong.

Those who are expecting an immediate detailing of different types of investments—like some sorry financial radio advertisement—picked up the wrong book. You'll want the one with that cover photo of a guy pointing at you

from inside a pinstriped suit and saddle shoes, promising you in the book's title—$1 million in five years! Good luck over there.

We're not even ready to think about specifics yet. Why not? Because we don't yet know how much you have to invest. Let's spend this chapter figuring that out, and we'll go from there. In fact, on the basis of what we learn, we may even discover that you shouldn't start investing in stocks for a couple of years. Patience will always win the day on Wall Street.

Your Foolish Financial Profile

Let's get started with a reminder that so few ever receive: *You* control *your* money. Even if you've given it over to someone else to manage, you're ultimately responsible for even that decision. We consider it both Foolish and necessary to take control of your financial destiny, instead of relying solely and blindly on other people for advice and guidance. We figure you probably agree, since you've purchased this book.

The quiz below is designed to help you figure out whether you're the sort who really does follow your money or whether you just let it run willy-nilly out of your wallet, into varying accounts, off to cover mortgage payments this month, off to cover minimum payments on three credit cards, helter-skelter, this way and that.

Show Us the Money!

Our list of answers is not exhaustive, so choose the one that most closely fits you.

1. What percentage of your take-home pay goes to pay for your house and/or rent payment?
   a. 95%
   b. I don't know, I just know it is too much.
   c. No more than 30%
2. How many credit cards do you use on a regular basis?
   a. So many that I have to leave some at home in the drawer.
   b. Ten.
   c. Two or fewer.
3. How many of those credit cards have balances on them that you do not fully pay off each month?
   a. All.
   b. Half.
   c. None.
4. Have you ever gone to pay with a credit card and had the merchant tell you that you are over your limit?
   a. This happens frequently. I just use another card.
   b. It happened frequently when I got out of college—but it hasn't happened in a long time.

c. Nah, they didn't tell me I was over the limit, they just made me cut up the card right there on the spot.
   d. Never.
5. Do you have a savings account?
   a. No.
   b. Yes, but there is very little money in it.
   c. Yes, and it has a decent amount of money in it.
6. Do you have an IRA account?
   a. No.
   b. Yes, but there is very little money in it.
   c. Yes, and it has a decent amount of money in it.
   d. I don't support radical political organizations.
7. Do you know what your percentage of debt is to your income? In other words, if you added up all your bills for a month, and compared that figure to your total income—what is your best guess as to what percentage it would be?
   a. 95%
   b. 50%
   c. 25%
   d. I have no idea.
   e. I don't want to know.
   f. Can we stop this now?
8. Do you eat out a lot? How much would you say you spend, as a percentage of your monthly income, on eating out every month?
   a. 40%
   b. 20%
   c. 5%
   d. I have no idea—I just know I hate to cook.

OK, dear Fool, you have your answers. Hey, possibly you're not running the tightest ship in the house and you believe that doing so would make for a lot of headaches and waste a lot of your vacation time. Not so. Nay, not so. Read on.

Creating Your Financial Profile

Your financial profile consists of two parts. One part, your *balance sheet*, looks at your overall financial situation at just one point in time. The other part, your *income statement*, takes a look at your average monthly income and expenses. Taken together, they give you a good indication of your financial health, as well as provide you a powerful tool that can help you gain more control of your money.

While some of the exercises below aren't the most fun way to spend a Saturday afternoon, if you have a rainy one, take advantage of it. Completing the following exercises is important, in order (perhaps for the first time) to see exactly what your financial situation really looks like. You don't have to do this every week or month. Let's just start with this one time. Maybe you'll find it sufficiently harmless to repeat every three or six months, or every year.

YOUR FINANCIAL PROFILE, PART I: YOUR BALANCE SHEET

The balance sheet is a snapshot of your financial position at any one point in time. We won't be following next week's salary payments or considering your financial position if one of your stocks grows by 30 percent. We're just going to pull the camera out and snap a picture of what things look like today.

How Much Am I Worth?

We grant you that figuring out how much you are worth may require a little field trip through those files and those drawers where lie discarded check stubs, loan information, and bank or brokerage statements for the last few years; it may even require a phone call or two. But if you're not going to play along with us, geez, why are we even trying? (Ah, the tug on the ol' guilt strings—works every time.)

Assets and Liabilities

Take out your pencil and your calculator. Imagine a sheet of paper with two columns on it. The left column will list your assets, and the right side will list your debts, or liabilities. We'll proceed item by item and have you figure each amount in turn.

To help you through this process, we have asked Ronald and Sandy (remember them from the bookstore?) if they would be so kind as to let us use their information as an example for you. As they need all the Foolish help they can get, they quickly agreed. (We'll also be sending them some nice prizes for participating.) As you calculate your net worth, we'll calculate their net worth. Let's start by listing your assets.

What is an asset?

Here's our Foolish definition of the word "asset": anything that you own that you plan to use to pay your expenses. In most cases, that's either cash or something that could be converted to cash. For our purposes, let's start with your "short-term" assets.

Short-Term Assets

What do these include? Actual cash on hand, any cash in your bank account, certificates of deposit (CDs), as well as any securities (a fancy word for stocks and bonds) that you own. Short-term assets are anything you plan to convert to cash to pay down expenses over the next twelve months.

In the case of Ronald and Sandy, they don't have much cash on hand. However, Sandy does admit she keeps a secret cash stash of around $200 under the mattress. So their cash on hand is $200. Time now for you to write down whatever amount of money you have on hand (maybe under the mattress, in the cookie jar, in your purse, your wallet, or in the glove compartment of the car). A rough estimate to the nearest $100 works fine—no need to count out those penny jars, unless you have a free hour, in which case go right ahead.

CASH ON HAND

YOU	RONALD AND SANDY
$_____	$200

Next, write down how much money you have in your bank accounts—both checking and savings. If you have accounts at several banks, include them all. (Of course, this assumes you have a balanced checkbook! If you do not have an accurate total of the money in your account, you may want to consider starting there before completing this part of the workbook—or take your best guess for this exercise.) Ronald and Sandy have $500 in their checking accounts. They don't

have money in any other type of bank account, nor do they have any CDs (certificates of deposit). If you do, make sure you include these as well. Our goal is to figure out how much you have in each account.

SHORT-TERM ASSETS

	YOU	RONALD AND SANDY
Checking accounts	_____	$500
Savings accounts	_____	$0
Certificates of deposit (CDs)	_____	$0

What about securities? If you own stocks, bonds, or mutual funds, get the latest copies of your various account statements and enter the amounts shown as the value of your holdings. As of their last brokerage statement, our happy couple had $3,000 in securities (all mutual funds).

SECURITIES

	YOU	RONALD AND SANDY
Stocks	_____	$0
Bonds	_____	$0
Mutual funds	_____	$3,000
TOTAL SECURITIES	_____	$3,000

What if you have an IRA, 401(k), 403(b), Keogh, or any other retirement account? Save that for the "long-term assets" list.

So, our short-term asset list for Ronald and Sandy looks like this:

SHORT-TERM ASSETS

Cash on hand	$200
Checking accounts	$500
Savings account	$0
Securities	$3,000
TOTAL SHORT-TERM ASSETS	$3,700

Long-Term Assets

The distinction between short-term and long-term assets is that the latter are not readily convertible into cash. Anything in long-term assets, you do not plan to convert to cash over the next twelve months.

Long-term assets are things like houses, automobiles, retirement accounts (such as IRAs, SEP accounts, Keoghs), valuable collectibles, and jewelry. When you list these items, you need to list them at "fair market value"—not what you paid for them. For example, your automobile is probably worth 30–60 percent less than you paid for it.

For our purposes, just make estimates. If you bought your house for $180,000 but you think it's now worth $190,000, list $190,000. Although you may have paid $4,000 for your fancy computer five years ago, you might find it's worth more like $850 today. How about cars, furniture, or CDs? You spent $4,000 on your stereo—and you think you could sell it for $3,000. You should just value it at $3,000, right? Nope. You have to

set a reasonable long-term value on all of your merchandise. Aha! so for all long-term assets, you must estimate their worth five years from now.

You probably already know that buying a sturdy house is much more important than buying a nice car or home entertainment center. Your house should hold or appreciate in value; the other stuff depreciates, in many cases down to zero. You'll want to list those depreciating long-term assets (you know what that means now, right?) at their reasonable value five years from today. In many cases, your depreciating assets are headed to that depressing ultimate value of $0. Here, make your best estimate of what they'll all be worth five years hence.

How Can You Determine What Your House Is Worth on the Open Market?

The best way to estimate the value of your house is via comparisons with similar houses in your neighborhood. Call a realtor who sells houses in your neighborhood and ask her for an opinion. She'll have access to all the recent sales in your area, along with details on each property. Be careful, of course. If she's a good agent, she'll not only have helped you pinpoint your price range—she might suddenly convince you to sell your house!

So now it's time to start a new section on our balance sheet, labeled "Long-Term Assets." Next to *House* enter the long-term asset value. If your house is worth $125,000, that's the long-term asset value of your house today. In our example, a quick call to a few different real estate brokers familiar with the Washingtons' house and their neighborhood gave us a reliable value estimate of $175,000. And they have other long-term assets (jewelry, partially owned cars, and a personal computer) that tote up to $12,000.

LONG-TERM ASSETS

	YOU	RONALD AND SANDY
House	_____	$175,000
Other	_____	$12,000

Let's now present the balance sheet for Ronald and Sandy thus far with all of our updated information.

BALANCE SHEET FOR RONALD AND SANDY

SHORT-TERM ASSETS

Cash on hand $200

Bank accounts $500

Savings account $0

Securities $3,000

TOTAL SHORT-TERM ASSETS $3,700

LONG-TERM ASSETS

House $175,000

Other $12,000

We will now close with an increasingly common (and good) form of long-term asset now shared by many Americans: *the retirement plan.* That includes individual retirement accounts (IRAs), 401(k) plans, and any number of similar devices with acronyms that scare people away. Below, add in the present value of all your retire-

ment plans. And that's exactly what we'd do for Ronald and Sandy, had they managed to maintain theirs. Alas, when they needed money to pay for that second car (the Manatee Coupe), they cashed in the two IRAs at a horrendous tax penalty. But they had to do it, they told themselves, as there was no credit left on their credit cards and they couldn't get a bank loan. Mercifully, though, Sandy has a 401(k) at work that she managed to fund, which is now worth $5,200.

Here then is our completed list of assets for Ronald and Sandy.

FINAL BALANCE SHEET FOR RONALD AND SANDY (ASSETS)

SHORT-TERM ASSETS

Cash on hand $200

Bank accounts $500

Savings account $0

Brokerage account $3,000

TOTAL SHORT-TERM ASSETS $3,700

LONG-TERM ASSETS

House $175,000

Other $12,000

IRA / 401(k) $5,200

TOTAL LONG-TERM ASSETS $_____

TOTAL ASSETS $_____

Now, activate that calculator of yours and add up all of Ronald and Sandy's numbers in the long-term and total columns. What did you get? Our Foolish calculator suggests $192,200 (long-term assets) and $195,900 (total assets). Jeepers! They're rich!

Right?

Ah, *to be* is very different from *to seem*.

Let's take some space out now to allow you to sum up in one place your own list of total assets. (And remember not to get too terribly excited until we've completed the liabilities section too.)

MY BALANCE SHEET (ASSETS)

Your name: _____

Date: _____

Your astrological sign: _____

(This is for our Fool Dating Service.)

SHORT-TERM ASSETS

Cash on hand	_____
Bank account	_____
Savings account	_____
Brokerage account	_____
TOTAL SHORT-TERM ASSETS	_____

LONG-TERM ASSETS

House	_____
Other	_____
Retirement plans	_____
TOTAL LONG-TERM ASSETS	_____
TOTAL ASSETS	_____

Fellow Fool, you are now done with the first part of the net worth exercise. We hereby declare a brief sabbatical so that you may take time to reward yourself. Be back here in fifteen minutes to start on the next part.

Liabilities

Your minisabbatical over, your pencil in hand, your mind once again a sharply honed razor, you are now ready to face down some accounting terminology.

The first thing to recognize is that if you're like most of us, you don't own outright all of your assets. Rather, you've borrowed money to pay for some of the things that belong to you. These debts are "liabilities," which will make up the second half of your balance sheet.

We will therefore begin unceremoniously and predictably with this first section . . .

Short-Term Liabilities

Given what has gone before, you may be able to predict some of what constitutes this category. Try, for instance, any bill that is paid on a monthly basis or is now current. Credit cards come to mind. If, like most people, you have at least one card with an unpaid balance on it, that counts as a short-term liability. It is thoroughly fitting to lead off our investigations of liabilities with America's Most Wanted: credit card debt. For most, this is the greatest portion of their short-term liabilities. Sadly, many are unable ever to rid themselves of these enervating financial burdens—or don't know that they should be trying to.

To begin throwing off the yoke, the first

thing you must do is to gather all your credit card statements. Add together the total owed on each into one grand figure, entering that on the first line, *Credit card debt.* For our example here, we went through the shoe box that Ronald brought to Fool HQ, and after digging around for the better part of an afternoon we determined that Ronald and Sandy owed the sum total of exactly $8,500 on all their credit cards. We hope it doesn't take half a day for you to do the same thing.

Our first line for Ronald and Sandy's short-term liabilities shows up like this:

BALANCE SHEET FOR RONALD AND SANDY (LIABILITIES)

SHORT-TERM LIABILITIES
Credit card debt $8,500

Are you paying any other debts off on a monthly basis? Dental bills, medical bills, student loans, personal loans, car loans? Perhaps even the IRS? We refer to these as "installment debts." For all of these, again, we need the total amount owed—not the amount of your monthly payment. For example, if you had a crown repaired and the total bill was $390 and you are paying your dentist $25 a month, we need to know how much you still owe the dentist in total. Make a call to the dental office if for some reason your bill does not reflect the total amount due. Almost all loans generate annual statements that tell you how much principal you still have left. If you haven't kept track of these, then go ahead and call your lender.

Whether it's nighttime there or not, it's time for you to put on your sunglasses because Ronald and Sandy have a glaring amount of installment debt. It is our Foolish hope that you'll have only a fraction of the amount they've saddled themselves with.

BALANCE SHEET FOR RONALD AND SANDY (LIABILITIES)

SHORT-TERM LIABILITIES

Credit card debt $8,500

INSTALLMENT DEBT

Dental $5,000	(Sandy's midlife orthodontics)	
Medical $12,300	(Sandy's tummy tuck and chin work)	
Home entertainment $8,000	(Ronald's big-screen TV with monster dish and surround sound)	
Car loans $38,400	(two 1996 cars)	
Graceland Travel $12,200	(balance from the last European trip)	
Cellular Nirvana $3,200	(balance from cell phone contracts)	
Ben's Bathrooms $11,290	(balance from Jacuzzi and tile work)	
TOTAL INSTALLMENT DEBT $_____		

Time to tot up all that installment debt. Our own computations suggest the figure is extremely close to $90,390. That figure is immense. Throw in Ronald and Sandy's credit card debt and one's admiration grows for their ability to even be here at the bookstore, eating crumpets and drinking large lattes.

Long-Term Liabilities

While large corporations often finance their growth through numerous complicated types of long-term debt, the average household's version typically consists of one major item—a mortgage. Thus, in this section of your balance sheet, you should list the total amount of all mortgages or home equity loans on any and all properties in your possession.

In many cases, this is easier said than done. How do you know how much you owe on your house? Well, if your mortgage didn't come with a payment booklet showing the balance after each payment is made, a quick call to your mortgage lender will get you your current balance. (Those guys are only ever too happy to answer, eh?) It really is that simple—even simpler if you track the information using a good financial software package, like Quicken.

Meanwhile, a quick call to Ronald's mortgage company told us they owe around $155,000 on their house. They had paid down the balance on their mortgage at one point, but then took out a home equity loan—Sandy told us it was for the second honeymoon, to Maui. Consequently, they once again have very little equity in their house.

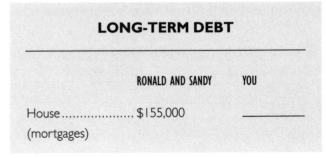

LONG-TERM DEBT

	RONALD AND SANDY	YOU
House.................... (mortgages)	$155,000	_____

Sound the foghorn! Why? You are *done* with your information gathering. Let's see how our balance sheet looks for Ronald and Sandy so we can calculate their net worth. In the meantime, you do the same with your information.

Net Worth

Okay, Foolish readers, flip back to the page where we calculated the couple's assets. What was the total?

BALANCE SHEET FOR RONALD AND SANDY

ASSETS
Short-Term Assets

Cash on hand $200

Bank accounts $500

Savings account $0

Brokerage account $3,000

Long-Term Assets

House $175,000

Other $12,000

IRA / 401(k) $5,200

TOTAL ASSETS $195,900

Now, what was the total of their liabilities?

LIABILITIES
Short-Term Liabilities

Credit card debt $8,500

Installment debt $90,390

Long-Term Liabilities

House (mortgage) $155,000

TOTAL LIABILITIES $253,890

OK, so what's the difference?

Total assets $195,900

Total liabilities $253,890

NET WORTH .... −$57,990

What does this mean? It means that Ronald and Sandy have a negative net worth of $57,990. You may very well have run across a couple like this in your life. On the exterior, they appear to be thriving. Behind the glitter doesn't lie gold. If they continue at this pace in this direction, look out below! Just as huge businesses like Macy's can declare bankruptcy while small local businesses inch forward profitably, so too can seemingly wealthy couples disintegrate while their frugal counterparts inch ahead.

Ronald and Sandy's owing more than they own isn't good, but it isn't hopeless either. If you find yourself in a similar boat (a yacht that you're no doubt still trying to pay off), don't panic. Let's look at *your* net worth now and then think a few of these assumptions through.

MY BALANCE SHEET

Name: _____

Date: _____

Worst blind date experience: _____

ASSETS

Short-Term Assets

    Cash on hand   _____

    Bank account   _____

    Savings account   _____

    Brokerage account   _____

Long-Term Assets

    Car   _____

    House   _____

    Furnishings, belongings   _____

    Retirement plans   _____

    TOTAL ASSETS   _____

LIABILITIES

Short-Term Liabilities

    Credit card debt   _____

    Installment debt   _____

Long-Term Liabilities

    House   _____

    TOTAL LIABILITIES   _____

    Total assets   _____

    Total liabilities   _____

    NET WORTH   _____

So now you know your net worth! But you may be left wondering what this all really means. Keep reading.

HOW TO USE THE FOOLISH BALANCE SHEET—THINGS TO LOOK FOR

Positivity Versus Negativity

Is your net worth positive or negative? If it's positive, we have little to say to you here, other than "Attaboy" and "Keep up the good work!" Our only suggestion would be that you continue to pay down your highest-rate debt as it comes. You shouldn't own mutual funds that might appreciate at 8 percent per year if you have outstanding credit card debt charging you interest of 17 percent per year. Start wiping out your highest-rate debt and you can be your own Microsoft—loads of cash assets, no long-term liabilities.

Now, if you fall into group two, with a negative net worth, you need to squint your eyes at the numbers and begin to figure out how you can improve the asset side of the ledger. You're going to have to simultaneously cut spending and attack the highest-rate debt. If you have credit cards charging you 18 percent per year, you need to consolidate all of those debts on lower-rate cards. A few phone calls to different card companies—and direct negotiation with your existing card company—should get you down a handful of percentage points. And every point enables you to pay off the debt that much faster. That can be critical to your success.

Let's take a closer look at Ronald and Sandy's debt.

Debts, Liabilities, and the Loss of Tranquillity

Take a look at the credit card and installment debt that Ronald and Sandy are trying to pay off. Sandy admits they are barely able to pay the monthly minimums anymore on all their bills. No wonder. Ronald was stunned when we pointed out to him that—if you take the total of their short-term debt and assume that the average interest rate is 18 percent—they'll have to pay approximately $17,800 per year in interest charges just to keep even. And all those payments without paying down any part of the underlying debt!

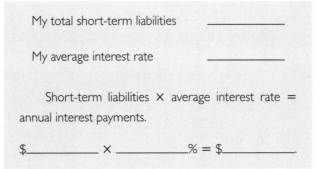

Short-term liabilities × average interest rate = annual interest payments.

THE WASHINGTONS' SHORT-TERM LIABILITIES

Credit card debt	$8,500
Installment debt	$90,390
TOTAL SHORT-TERM LIABILITIES	$98,890

$98,890 × 18% = $17,800

Paying Down Debt

Foolishly speaking, we think it is obvious that the Washingtons must reduce their debt levels immediately. If you are sitting there looking at your own level of short-term debt, what does it look like? Are you in the danger zone?

Paying Down Highest-Rate Debt First

If Ronald and Sandy had a great deal of equity in their house, we would recommend they pay down the more expensive short-term interest debt by taking out a second mortgage. The two advantages to taking out a second mortgage are

1. The interest rate is usually much lower than you might otherwise get.
2. The interest payments will be tax deductible.

Sadly, Ronald and Sandy have already taken out a second mortgage and spent the money. So this option is, unfortunately, not available to them.

Other Income Incoming

Even though his business has been facing hard times, Ronald mentioned to us that he expects to receive a substantial bonus for overtime work during the past year. He's expecting that bonus payment in the next sixty days and wondered what he should do with that cash:

- Put it in an IRA account and begin investing for the long term?
- Pay down existing long-term liabilities, like that house payment?

- Load up on fuel and try to outrun creditors to the Mexican border?
- Vegas, baby!?!
- Pay down existing short-term liabilities, like credit cards?
- Invest in real estate, since it holds or appreciates in value?
- A little bit of all of the above?

Fools, what do you think?

After much clacking of calculators, our laboratory mathematicians have determined that the single best decision the Washingtons can make is to *pay down the highest-interest short-term liabilities.* The short-term debt carries the highest interest rates, and in the case of the Washingtons is eating hundreds of dollars each year. Pay down the $8,500 in credit card debts, then when the next cash infusion comes, weigh the consequences of paying down the long-term debt (mortgages and car payments) versus investing the money in a retirement plan.

Jim's Balance Sheet

Let's leave the Washingtons be as they nibble through another round of raspberry crumpets, thinking through their financial standing, and let's visit with Jim, the UPS driver with a love for the guitar, several girlfriends, and that one horrendous experience investing in the Vancouver mining company. Let's take a look at Jim's balance sheet.

JIM'S PERSONAL BALANCE SHEET 5/12/97

ASSETS

Short-Term Assets

Cash	$1,200
Bank account	$3,200
Savings	$2,800
Securities	$0

Long-Term Assets

Car	$12,500
Personal things	$5,000
IRA/401(k)	$1,500
TOTAL ASSETS	$26,200

LIABILITIES

Short-Term Liabilities

Credit card	$670
Installment debt	$0
Tuition loan	$8,700
Car	$7,000
TOTAL LIABILITIES	$16,370

Total assets	$26,200
Total liabilities	$16,370
JIM'S NET WORTH	$9,830

OK, what can we learn from this balance sheet? First of all, hey, congratulations to you if this is your first time seeing and deciphering a balance sheet. To those of you for whom this is old hat, quit gloating and flip forward a couple of chapters. It's almost unthinkable, but most Americans have no clue what a balance sheet is, what information it presents, or what it even looks like. We hope that after 50 or 60 million people read this workbook, we'll lick that problem. So, again, if that's your first St. Pauli balance sheet, congratulations. Let's see what we can learn from it.

1. For starters, it's time to also congratulate Jim for maintaining positive net worth.

2. Jim has obviously been trying to sock some money away. He has more cash available for investing than do Ronald and Sandy. Funny, they make more than he does—quite a bit more—but his future is looking brighter.

3. However, as nice as it is for Jim to have some cash, he absolutely should not be carrying any credit card debt, racking up that 18 percent annual interest. Between his cash, bank account, and CDs, he has $7,200 stashed away. He should pay down his credit card debt of $670 in full this month.

4. Check out Jim's unpaid student loans of $8,700. Depending on what interest rate he is paying, he might be better off approaching the school and asking them if they'd accept a lump sum payment now—in lieu of extended payments. If the school accepted, and in many cases it will, there is a possibility that Jim might be able to pay off his loan completely for a reduced amount of money—sometimes as much as 50–60 percent of the amount that is owed. Instead of paying off the $8,700 in full with interest charges in the years ahead, he might be able to pay $4,500 today and be done with it.

5. Taking our advice to heart—and in just a couple of hours—Jim paid out $670 to clear up his credit card debt and $4,500 to close down his student loans. That's $5,170 going out the door. He now has $2,030 remaining from his cash position. Jim just successfully cleared his balance sheet of short-term liabilities. And because he bargained his way out of $4,200 in student loans, his net worth rose by as much. Huzzah! It's probably a good idea for him to buy a bottle of wine, have Alison or Tracy or Inga over for dinner, and celebrate a bit (or maybe all three—time to come clean, Jim!). On the liabilities side, only the car payments remain.

6. Jim now has to figure out how much of that $2,030 he'll need for living expenses over the next three months. He must sum up his salary checks, his other monthly bills, and his car payments and determine how much cash he'll need. Why? Because what he doesn't need should go either to prepay his car loan or into longer-term investments.

These are just some examples of what a balance sheet can tell you. The important thing is to study your own. How heavy are your short-term liabilities, and can they be immediately reduced? Are you carrying too much cash? Generally speaking, your personal balance sheet will help you see two main things:

1. If you are saddled with too much short-term debt, it'll be obvious. Remember—multiply that amount of short-term debt by the interest rate the lender is charging, and that will tell you how much you have to pay on a yearly basis just to keep the account current. Ooomph. Our advice is to pay that short-term debt down, period.

2. If you are sitting on cash in underperforming financial vehicles such as savings accounts and regular bank accounts, get it out of there and into an investment vehicle that provides a higher rate of return.

That was easy, eh?

YOUR FINANCIAL PROFILE, PART 2: YOUR INCOME STATEMENT

Where does my money come from and where does it go?

Now that you've created your personal balance sheet, know what your net worth is, and understand how you can use your stats to assess your financial health, it's time to get into the good stuff. It's time to figure how much money you make and where it all goes.

To adequately track whence your money has come and whither it is bound, the second part of the Foolish financial profile is your income statement. Unlike a balance sheet, which lists your assets and liabilities at one particular point in time, an income statement shows the flow of your money. Changes in your income statement will show up eventually in your balance sheet. And if you're thoroughly confused about the difference between the two, read on—we should be able to bewilder you even more.

What help is an income statement? It fires warning flares and triggers earsplitting alarms if your expenses are disproportionate to your income. It also shows us where you can slim down your spending and yield more money for investment.

Keep It Simple

To start out, we suggest you select one recent month for analysis. Here you'll need everything from checkbook stubs to credit card and brokerage statements to ATM receipts. If you're like us, there's a pretty good chance that at least a few ATM slips have skittered past each month and that you might have trouble locating a banking statement or two. If that's the case, then make your Foolish month in review an upcoming month.

As we study this month, please disregard all extraordinary one-time costs or gains—like buying a house, losing $420 during your last trip ever to Atlantic City, or collecting back wages from your brief stint as an elephant rider in the traveling circus. These are unusual benefits or costs that will only serve to skew what's really happening week in and week out with your money. In order to evaluate your *regular* income, let's set them aside.

What Information Will You Need to Have On Hand?

In order to determine your cash flow, you will need to gather together the following information. Get the pencil out and start putting check marks in there. If you've kept all records from a previous month, excellent; proceed! If not, wow, bummer; you're going to have to wait another few weeks before turning past this page. Hey, while you're out there, wear your seat belt (the automobile is the most dangerous tool in your life), don't forget to call home a few times, and drop by www.fool.com to talk turkey with fellow Fools.

OK, let's check the list:

All canceled checks and bank statements for the month   _____

Automatic teller machine deposit and withdrawal slips   _____

Your paycheck stubs   _____

Stubs for any other income that you received during the month   _____

Brokerage statements   _____

Your credit card statements for the month   _____

Receipts for all purchases—groceries, beer, movie tickets, bowling, books, magazines, etc.   _____

Monthly health insurance bill*   _____

Monthly life insurance bill*   _____

Monthly car payment*   _____

Monthly mortgage payment*   _____

Monthly rent payment*   _____

* Even if you pay for these on a quarterly or yearly basis, you'll need to calculate how much you pay out on a monthly basis. So, if your mortgage costs are $12,000 per year, that's $1,000 per month.

The Money You Make—Exactly How Much Are We Talking About Here?

Use the work sheet that follows to write down in one place all your sources of income.

If you work and are paid a salary, this one's simple. Just collect your paycheck stubs. If you are married, get your spouse's stubs too. (Yep, call us ol'-fashioned, but we believe in complete financial disclosure between spouses—particularly if you want to avoid the possibility of a few nasty, ugly, and downright awful surprises in the future.)

Now, what do you see when you look at your paycheck stub? The first line will be your total wages, followed by a list of deductions. For our purposes here, we want you to take the net amount, after all deductions, and put that amount at the top of the pad. For those of you who are self-employed or have additional sources of income, just enter the average amount you earn in a month, after you have taken into consideration your tax liabilities.

401(k) Money

A gold star to you if you already have money deducted automatically from your paycheck for a 401(k) plan, automatic share purchase, or other investment program. However, don't add that money back into your net income amount. Treat it just as if it is an obligation like a debt—it's a debt to yourself for the benefit of your future. You've chosen to "pay yourself" before your other debts. Since this money is out of sight, it should be out of mind.

MY INCOME

Net monthly income   _____

Other sources   _____

TOTAL   _____

Calculating Self-Employment Income

If you're self-employed, then you need to do a little extra work here. First you need to determine, after looking at your records, what an average month's income would be. Then, since there is no Social Security, state tax, city tax, unemployment tax, or federal withholding taken out of your gross income, you need to estimate these expenses as well. Hey, when you get to be your own boss, you have to do a little extra legwork!

It's almost impossible for us to guess what your tax rate will be, given differences by state and salary levels. If you haven't already done so, we suggest you talk to someone who is familiar with small-business accounting and tax requirements for your particular location.

Hey, all right, Jim just agreed to play guinea pig for us throughout our section on building an income statement. He was swayed by all that cheering back when he announced positive net worth.

We'll start by taking a look at Jim's paycheck stubs. He's netting $1,290 per paycheck and getting paid twice a month. So Jim is getting paid $2,580 per month.

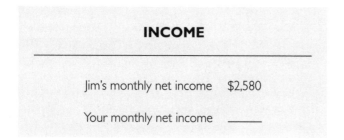

INCOME

Jim's monthly net income $2,580

Your monthly net income   _____

Now, do you get any other money each month? Do you receive stock dividends or income from other sources? If so, add that in. Jim tells us he receives a share of the monthly payments from the sale his family negotiated of some acreage in Bradford, Pennsylvania. This brings in up to $125 per month. Time to add another income line, which we'll simply call *Other income.* Add $2,580 and $125 and what do you get? $2,705.

CASH FLOW STATEMENT

	JIM	YOU
Monthly salary	$2,580	$_____
Other income	$125	$_____
TOTAL MONTHLY NET	$2,705	$_____

Voilà! Our income analysis for Jim is now complete. And so is yours. Hey, this stuff isn't too painful, is it?

The Money You Spend—Where the Heck's My Stuff?

And now we descend into the spending mire. We're not going to lament the amount of money Americans spend, consuming often needless stuff. That's not our thing. Plus, it is this very spending that is driving our corporations to greater heights. Would we be roving Mars without the money bursting out of the pockets of American consumers? Nope. So, we're not going to rail against all that spending—but we are going to suggest to you, the select group of Fools, that just a wee bit of trimming can do wonders.

OK, we need a nice clean worksheet to start on. So let's start a new one for "Monthly Expenses." We want you to list your expenses from most to least essential. Start with your basic necessities. Contrary to the modeling community in Manhattan, you do have to eat. Contrary to the technologists in Silicon Valley, you do have to sleep. Contrary to the Rolling Stones, you do need a stable home. Contrary to Howard Hughes's approach, you do need human contact and affection. And you also need some water, Fool. Let's cover the necessities first.

MONTHLY EXPENSES

Rent/house payment   ‾‾‾‾‾‾‾

Utilities   ‾‾‾‾‾‾‾

Groceries   ‾‾‾‾‾‾‾

Eating out   ‾‾‾‾‾‾‾

Car insurance   ‾‾‾‾‾‾‾

Health insurance   ‾‾‾‾‾‾‾

Renter's insurance   ‾‾‾‾‾‾‾

Car payment   ‾‾‾‾‾‾‾

Clothes   ‾‾‾‾‾‾‾

Other stuff   ‾‾‾‾‾‾‾

Installment debt   ‾‾‾‾‾‾‾

TOTAL MONTHLY EXPENSES   ‾‾‾‾‾‾‾

Now let's review Jim's expenses one by one.

Jim's Expenses

Rent. Jim is paying $550 a month in rent to live in that stylish one-room apartment overlooking McKeesport.

Utilities. How much do you spend on electricity? Gas? Water? For local and long-distance telephony? For cable or satellite TV? And for that cell phone or pager? When we asked Jim about this, he didn't know off the top of his head. Most people don't. So we went back and looked at his various canceled checks. It turns out that Jim is spending $95 per month on basic utilities and $70 per month on the telephone bill. He doesn't subscribe to cable and is given a cell phone by UPS for business purposes. So, all told, he's spending $165 per month for utilities.

Food. How much did Jim spend at the Piggly Wiggly last month? And how much at the 7-Eleven and McDonald's, and for that steak dinner at Lone Star Steakhouse, and for the dinner party he threw for Inga's family?

We're looking over some of Jim's bills now, and wow! The guy likes to eat. But clearly he hates to cook. In Jim's case, there are only two receipts from the grocery store for the entire month. As we spy his food receipts over the past week, it reads like a *Who's Who* of fast-food heaven. And, we might add, much more expensive than eating at home. Oddly enough, Jim's a pretty trim guy.

OK, so the total damage for food came to a whopping $686 for one month. Whew! As you're toting up your own numbers, if the thought of writing down all your food-related expenses for a whole month intimidates you, then simplify. Do what Jim did. Just keep track of the money you spend on food for one week, then multiply by four.

Food: How Much Do You Spend?

If you really have no idea how much you spend on food, then resolve right now to figure it out. Starting on the first day of this next month, write down every food-related expense that you incur for one week. Break the expenses up into two categories—eating out and groceries. People are usually aghast when they realize how much they spend on food. This is an area where Fools can cut back on spending without any great suffering. In fact, if there is any suffering, the cutting should stop. Food is a necessity. Eat like a horse if you need to. But any money saved can be used to knock out debts or find its way into the stock market.

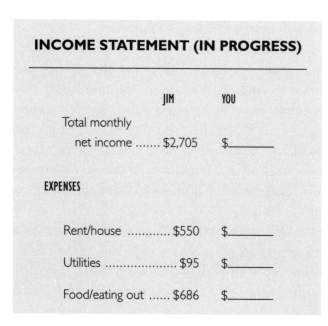

INCOME STATEMENT (IN PROGRESS)

	JIM	YOU
Total monthly net income	$2,705	$_____
EXPENSES		
Rent/house	$550	$_____
Utilities	$95	$_____
Food/eating out	$686	$_____

Insurance. OK, time to warm up those calculators. In our review of the cost of your car insurance, life insurance, home owner's or renter's insurance, and health insurance, we're going to need to reduce it down into monthly expenses.

Thus, if you pay quarterly, you're going to have to divide those payments by 3. If you pay twice a year, divide by 6. Hey, if you pay once a year, what must you divide by . . . ?

Yep, 12. Good job. Geez. Next we'll ask how many days are in a week.

Anyway, here is what Jim pays.

ITEM	EXPENSE PER MONTH
Car insurance	$200
	(speeding tickets, ouch!)
Health insurance	$50
Renter's insurance	$10

Enough with the monthly insurance expenses. Onward!

Transportation. Jim has about two more years before his car is paid off in full. He's paying about $180 per month in payments, on top of which he spends $50 each month on gas. All told, Jim's spending consistently about $230 a month between gas, regular maintenance, and car loan payments. A horse would be cheaper. Maybe.

Clothing. Jim likes to look good for Alison and the other women he dates. (By the way, in casual conversation with him, we're beginning to sense that Alison is the One. Only time will tell.) OK, so skimming through some of Jim's past month's receipts, it looks like he's spending anywhere from $150 to $200 a month on clothes. Swank.

Other expenses. Here we consider expenses that aren't necessary to survival. In Jim's case, these include beer, compact discs, computer software, and baseball tickets every once in a while. We averaged out these expenses and they came to around $300 a month.

Installment debt. Jim, as we noted by looking at his balance sheet, has been good about not racking up lots of credit card debt. He does have that heavy tuition loan, though, duly noted in this column.

How does Jim's income statement look now? While we're tallying his, get ready to tally yours.

JIM'S MONTHLY INCOME STATEMENT

Total monthly net income $2,705

NECESSITY EXPENSES

Rent $550

Utilities $95

Telephone $70

Food/eating out $686

Car insurance $200

Health insurance $50

Renter's insurance $10

Transportation $230

Clothes $200

Other stuff $300

INSTALLMENT DEBT

Tuition bill $235

Credit cards $50

TOTAL EXPENSES $2,676

TOTAL MONTHLY NET INCOME $2,705

MONTHLY OVER/UNDER .... +$29

Now it's your turn. Come on, jump in. This *is* a workbook.

MY PERSONAL INCOME STATEMENT

INCOME

Total net
    income per month $_____

EXPENSES

Rent/mortgage $_____

Utilities $_____

Telephone $_____

Food/eating out $_____

Car insurance $_____

Health insurance $_____

Renter's insurance $_____

Car payment $_____

Commuting expenses $_____

Clothes $_____

Other stuff $_____

More other stuff $_____

INSTALLMENT DEBT

Credit cards $_____

Other installment payments $_____

TOTAL EXPENSES $_____

Total monthly income $_____

Total monthly expenses $_____

MONTHLY OVER/UNDER $_____

WHAT DOES YOUR INCOME STATEMENT TELL YOU?

Just as when we looked at those balance sheets, let's study the monthly income statement and see what we can find. What better place to turn than Jim's statement?

1. Pay down the credit card balance in full. There's no reason to have that high-rate debt eating away anything.

2. As we suspected, that monthly tuition bill is steep. Negotiating a lower interest rate and lump sum payment would be a good thing. The $235 per month hurts. Ouch! Once it's gone Jim can push those monies into investing in the future. (Yes, he did this balance sheet before he did his negotiating magic.)

3. From here, the easiest way Jim can increase his cash flow is by cutting down a bit on his dining expenses. This year is as good a year as any to learn the basics of cooking. If Jim can save even $100 a month, his savings would mount up fast. And chances are he'd eat in a healthier way.

As we saw by looking at Jim's balance sheet, the man has money he could be investing. He has a lot of money in low-interest-bearing savings and checking accounts. He needs to sit down and figure what money he won't need for the next couple of years and start learning how to invest it in mutual funds or stocks.

OK, enough about Jim. What about you? Look at your monthly income and expense list. Now pencil in the three best places you could save money, without ruining your quality of life:

1. _____

2. _____

3. _____

If you can stick to those three suggestions, you're going to begin running up savings money and driving it into the stock market for enduring profit in no time. We kid you not—once you are "directionally" Foolish, the pace of growth into prosperity will bewilder you. Put your running shoes on and let's get going!

Five Warning Signs You're in the Doghouse

1. You have a negative net worth.
2. You struggle 'n' juggle to pay the minimum amount on your credit cards each month.
3. You have been asked to return or cut up a credit card.
4. You've forgotten what cash looks like.
5. You are now two to four months behind in most of your debt payments.

If you're nodding yes to two of these, it's time to call a halt on nonnecessity spending and to begin that emergency savings plan.

Short-Term Debt—The Biggest Financial Mistake You Can Make

We know, we know. We've said this about six different ways already. But it does bear repeating, since it doesn't look like our nation's high schools are about to teach their students this stuff anytime soon. Fellow Fool, do not let short-term liabilities get out of hand. Conquer your credit cards, first. The damage they have wrought on young professionals and newlyweds is verily great. They hit with the force of a tsunami—*splash!* (A lame sound effect, we know, but this is a low-budget production.) If you let short-term debt compound, it will grow so enormous and so hairy you might never get yourself out of the tangle. Pay it down now, and never let it rise again.

Recognize also that there are a lot of credit card issuers out there cheering *against* your ability to manage your money prudently. They're rooting like mad for you to cry, "What the hell!" a few more times each month. Then suddenly you realize that you're paying all your earnings out in interest payments, one month after another. And your creditors aren't rooting on the consumer in you anymore. They want those interest payments coming in *now*.

Remember what we said in the beginning of this section? Either you control your money or someone or something else will. When you let the credit card companies do this to you—when you spend, spend, spend without regard for how you'll eventually pay—you're letting the world's banking giants manage your money for you. And when they take over, things can get real scary.

So What Is a Fool to Do?

As you can see by looking at Ronald and Sandy and Jim, the biggest hurdle to starting a worthwhile investing program is excessive levels of short-term debt—credit cards and installment debt. If you find that you are saddled with way too much short-term, high-interest debt, here are some suggestions.

See if you can borrow money at a lower interest rate. Try consolidating many of your higher-interest debts onto a lower-rate card, and then just start paying them off.

Here's an example: Let's suppose that on all your credit cards you owe $10,000 at about 18 percent interest. Further, let's say that you can get a home equity loan that will let you pay off that entire amount, and the interest on the loan is only 10 percent. If you make the switch, the net effect translates to an increase of 8 percent on your bottom line. The interest on a home equity loan is also tax-deductible.

And if you don't own a home, you can apply for a debt-consolidation loan from many major lenders at a lower interest rate than credit card rates. In fact, you can also roll your student loans into that at a more favorable rate. As a last resort, sometimes you can negotiate low-interest loans with your parents or other relatives that will allow you to pay off your high-interest, short-term debts immediately.

It goes without saying that if you think you're in serious debt trouble, you shouldn't even consider an investment program. Get the debts taken care of first. That's free and predictable growth without any tax payments for it. Spend your money paying down the debt.

Now that you've completed your Foolish financial profile and have paid down your short-term debts, it's time to begin thinking about investing.

CHAPTER 3

Are You Ready to Start Investing?

You've defined some of your financial goals and assessed your financial situation, so let's make sure you're ready to do some investing. The single greatest mistake that would-be investors make is jumping into the market too quickly.

That's exactly what Jim did when he threw a couple of thousand dollars down on Trapshooter Reilly and the prospects for gold in Vancouver. Heck, how much does Jim—the farming guitarist who drives a UPS truck in Pennsylvania—know about mining operations in Canada? How much do *you* know? We don't know a darned thing about it. Remember this line because it will save you more money over your investment career than any other:

"I don't know a darned thing about it, so I'm not going to invest in it."

If you're like most Americans, that line means you shouldn't really be investing in anything yet. Why? Because the stock market seems huge, indecipherable, and more dangerous than Tommy Lee Jones in suede. And in some ways it is, until you know a few facts. Mishandled, the stock market can smush you, reducing your savings money to nothing and sending you back to the starting line. But learning to invest your money intelligently is less like learning to fly a 747 than learning how to ride a bicycle. Don't let the professionals make you think it's so tough that you need them to help you out at any expense. This ain't quantum physics. If you don't believe us, then let's start with a short quiz.

Are You Ready?

Have you

_____ eliminated your high-interest credit card debt?

_____ finished your MBA?

_____ stashed away at least $350,000 in your trading account?

_____ quit your job so you can trade stocks full time?

_____ selected a full-service broker who will tell you what to buy and sell?

_____ told your full-service broker just not to lose your money out there?

_____ learned about options, futures contracts, and day trading?

_____ learned about candlestick charting, the McClellan Oscillator, trend lines?

_____ paid $1,200 for expensive software and stock-quoting devices?

_____ smiled and emitted a mild chuckle just now?

We hope that you checked the first entry and the last, and left the remaining wholly unnecessary and largely satirical ones blank. It's unfortunate that so many people steer clear of both stocks and mutual funds because they figure they'll need a lot of money, a lot of expensive information, and a lot of graduate-level training when nothing could be further from the truth.

How well you invest will depend on many factors—and not one of them has anything to do with how much cash you start with or your ability to roll Wall Street jargon off your tongue at hoity-toity cocktail parties. Nope. Your success relies mostly on the degree to which you understand *your own* circumstances. If you've continued reading this far, you should have a pretty good idea of what your financial goals might be. To get to this page, you have some cash to invest, you have a regular stream of new money coming in, zero prepayable short-term debt, and you're fired up and ready for your money to start earning you more money. Onward to the castle then, Fool!

TIME HORIZON

One of the most important decisions about investing is also the most straightforward: What money should you invest in the stock market and what money shouldn't you invest?

One critical mistake that many greenhorn investors make is treating the stock market like a gambling machine; they invest money hoping to generate winnings over a short period of time. A simple rule of thumb is that any money you'll need over the next three years should not be in stocks or mutual funds. Let's say that again, and *louder* this time: If you need the money tomorrow or next year or anything short of 1,095 days from now, *stay out of the stock market*. The reality is that over that period of time, the stock market could get beaten about the head and neck like a rag doll. Stock values could disintegrate in just a few weeks, reducing what you "bet" on the market into half in no time.

Between 1972 and 1974, stock prices fell more than 40 percent. One of our nation's greatest companies, Coca-Cola, saw its stock fall by 65 percent. Had you invested money either into the market generally or into Coca-Cola specifically, and had you been forced to pull out at the darkest hour, you might have seen your house, car, job, dirt bike, golf clubs, parakeet, and/or scuba gear repossessed by your creditors. Make a short-term bet on stocks and you can bet that you'll get hammered eventually. So—what money shouldn't investors be putting in stocks? You tell us.

Money You Should *Not* Invest in Stocks

Below are ten investing scenarios. Number them from 1 (worst) to 10 (best) in terms of the attrac-

tiveness of the situation to Foolish investors. For the very worst, scratch in the number 1. Next worst is 2. Continue up to the very best, which you'll give a 10.

What do you think of investing money in the stock market for the following goals *or* from the following sources?

a. _____ for your retirement

b. _____ for your two-year-old's college tuition

c. _____ for a mortgage payment in three months

d. _____ for a down payment on a house in two years

e. _____ from an inheritance, once all short-term debts are paid down

f. _____ for tuition when you go back to school this fall

g. _____ from a 401(k) account at your last job

h. _____ from a cash advance you can get on your credit card

i. _____ for a top-of-the-line new sports car you plan to buy next year

j. _____ for medical procedures needed in the next eighteen months—which you can pay for in full if stocks do just average over the next year and a half

OK, let's go from worst to best.

First—*h*—is a disaster. Don't ever buy stocks on cash loans from your credit cards. The cost of those loans is, on average, far more substantial than the typical gains you can expect from stocks. As exciting as the stock market can get, hey, it's just a numerical beast. And the numbers don't justify buying stocks on credit.

Second—*c*—is nearly a disaster. Investing with a three-month time horizon just isn't *investing*. It's trading or gambling. Any gains you get over that short period will be taxed five times over—once by the IRS, twice by your broker in commissions, and twice by market makers who make money off the spread between what a stock can be bought for and what it can be sold for at any point in time. (Hey, if you don't know what "spreads" are, don't worry about that yet. If you figured out that you shouldn't buy stocks with money you'll need three months from now, that's plenty for now.)

Third—*f*—is potentially catastrophic as well. Why didn't we make it the second worst, given that "this fall" could be just a couple weeks away? Well, we figure if you blow your money in the stock market and have to miss college for a semester, that's a filly's nose better than losing your house! In fact, given that Bill Gates of Microsoft, Michael Dell of Dell Computer, and Larry Ellison of Oracle—three of our nation's greatest entrepreneurs—all dropped out of college, hey, maybe you *should* gamble that tuition money away! Nah, if you want to skip college, save the money for something other than "short-term" gaming on the stock market.

Fourth—*j*—is pretty darned bad in its own right. Eighteen months is a good deal longer than the other disasters, but in this case you're risking your health on the performance of the market. What if stocks fell by 40 percent over that eighteen-month period? You might have to skip the operation altogether. Again, the simplest concept here is just that you not invest in stock unless you have at least thirty-six months to spare.

Fifth—*i*—is only moderately less bad. In

this case, the investor has twelve months. That's a good deal better than the mere three months in scenario *c;* it's also not enough time. The only reason we don't consider this an out-and-out disaster is that, heck, losing a little money in stocks might save the buyer of a flashy sports car some money, all told. We don't think you should spend much on an automobile—given that its value depreciates the moment you drive it off the lot. But here as well, losing money on the stock market isn't the best way to reinforce a separate lesson. Don't fritter money away on unnecessarily snazzy new wheels—and don't gamble that money away over a short term on the stock market.

Sixth—*d.* OK, here you have two years, and what's at stake is a down payment on an unselected new house. There are enough fluid variables here that investment in stocks might not be a terrible thing. After all, if the market gets hammered, well then, you just rent for another year. Maybe you don't buy that new house for another five years, in a soft market. But if for some reason you *need* that money in two years, don't put it in mutual funds or stocks.

Seventh—*g.* Now we're finally getting into the good stuff. Transferring a 401(k) plan into, say, a self-directed IRA and then investing it for years or decades is an excellent strategy. Set to!

Eighth—*e*—makes for fine investment money. Wherever that money has come from, we suggest making a modest donation to an organization that champions your benefactor's ideals. Beyond that, with all your short-term debt paid down, we suggest plowing that money into the stock market; and, thus, we recommend continuing to read to the end of the workbook!

Ninth—*b.* Bravo! Your two-year-old will be eternally grateful at age eighteen, when he buys his first beer on your savings account. With each successive beer, the memory of whom to thank will grow dimmer, and you might start hearing from your dear son less than once a month! But, initially at least, he'll be thankful. Oh, and we strongly recommend that when the little guy reaches age seven or eight, you start him on his own investment portfolio—buying stocks like Nike, Disney, and Coca-Cola. But we'll speak of that in chapters ahead.

Tenth—*a.* Excellent! You'll be astonished at how much money you can earn via the stock market over one, two, three, and four decades. If you're twenty-two, without debt, and with savings to invest for the rest of your life, take a day off and celebrate. May we suggest bringing food over for all of us at Fool Global Headquarters, in Alexandria, Virginia? May we?

OK, now that we've walked through that, let's cut through some of Wall Street's jargon en route to readying you for a lifetime of investing.

THE JARGON DEMYSTIFIED—POOF!

Let's start with the three hyphenated terms that might simultaneously bewilder and bore you: *"tax-deferred," "pretax,"* and *"posttax."* These terms are important for a couple of reasons. But let's define them first.

Tax-deferred money is cash typically parked in longer-term savings vehicles like retirement accounts. You don't pay taxes on the earnings in these accounts until you withdraw the money. The government sets up these tax shelters in order to inspire you to save for your future and invest in American corporations. You know our government isn't *all* bad, Fools. Their incentives to invest for your future are on target. (Don't get us started on the Social Security debacle, though.)

Non-tax-deferred accounts are just what you'd expect them to be. They require you to pay taxes on money you earn from transactions, every year on April 15. If you buy $1,000 of stock at $10 per share and the stock rises to $15 per share and you sell your holding, you just made $500. Woohoo! Ah, but then the government swoops in and takes as much as 40 percent of those winnings—or $200 of your earnings. Youch. That's why we recommend putting as much money as you can afford not to touch for decades right into your retirement account, avoiding the annual tax bite and preserving it as permanent savings.

So what exactly is *pretax money*? It's simply the money that is deducted from your paycheck and dunked into an investment account. You haven't paid income taxes on this money. And if the money goes into your 401(k) or 403(b) retirement savings account, you won't pay taxes on this income until you withdraw money from the account, usually at age fifty-nine. We suggest that you max out the number of dollars that your employer will let you direct into your retirement plan—particularly if your employer is matching you dollar for dollar.

Posttax money is what most of us put into our savings and checking accounts on payday. You earn a salary, the company deducts for the IRS and other agencies, and what's left is your take-home pay. If you save part of this money each month (which we hope you do), the money goes into your investment or savings account "post tax." This kind of saving is not as favorable as the kind that doesn't meet up with the IRS until you turn fifty-nine, but then again, you have access to that cash today.

Hey, we later devote a whole section of this workbook to taxes and the tax implications of your investments. We just wanted to give you a little taste of the sugar here, first. Who said thinking about taxes couldn't be fun for the average Fool?

Uhh, we did.

But it's useful information, and you'll want to have tax considerations swimming somewhere in your head as you begin to invest. Now let's think about your retirement.

RETIREMENT SAVINGS

Take a second, close your eyes, and begin dreaming with us.

There you are. (Hey, how are you reading this . . . your eyes are supposed to be closed!) Yes, there you are. You're sixty-one years old. Your spouse is sitting right alongside you there. You're still in love. And there you are, on the deck of the *Fool-E-2*, sailing round the southern tip of Chile en route to Bouvet Island, then Cape Town, South Africa, then toward Malaysia, then Samoa, then Hawaii, then, finally, on to a three-game series between the San Francisco Giants and the Los Angeles Dodgers at 3Com Park.

Thank goodness you put that money into an IRA plan when you were twenty-four and working as a legal assistant at Procter & Gamble. Sometimes you wonder aloud what life would've been like if you'd started investing even earlier, when you were fifteen or ten. But then you click out of it. You don't want to beat yourself up. No, no. Life is pretty fine. The kids are through college. And you and Snookie (those nicknames are too much!) are just a few weeks into your gliding, year-long cruise around the globe. Aaaahhhhhhhhhhhhhhhh. OK, we hate to say this, but, "Hey, wake up, Fool!" Smack, smack. Ahh, there you are. Welcome back. We're sorry about that . . .

Your retirement accounts can take you nearly out of this world or right into the center of it, whatever your fancy. They are critical to the last few decades of your life. Social Security isn't going to be around a few decades from now—nor are the yo-yos who put it in place without thinking through some mathematical assumptions. Given that, you have to get your investments for retirement going as soon as possible. This can't happen until you've eliminated your short-term debt, but it can happen almost instantly after that. And it should.

Now, once you actually start thinking about investing, you probably remember just why you've avoided the whole matter. Fear, uncertainty, doubt, panic, confusion—pick your favorite word. How else are you supposed to react to critical financial issues, when our school system literally taught you nothing about your money? Add to that problem that people in the investment community make money by convincing you that they know *much* more about this than you! The whole world seems to be conspiring to keep you ignorant about your moola. And gigantic financial services corporations spend oodles of their research and development time trying to figure ways to confuse and abuse you.

If that sounds like the paranoid ramblings of a maniac, just look at the next unsolicited credit card mailer you receive. The fine print tells the whole costly, high-interest story—the marketing pitch obfuscates the financial horror show. Go figure. They don't want you to understand what you're doing with your money. Imagine that!

Wall Street is precisely the same; via mutual funds and brokerage firms it hits unsuspecting investors with a host of hidden fees. Hefty commissions and management fees pouring into Manhattan often earn investors little more than they'd get from a savings account, and often quite a bit less. It's because of nonsense like that and the fear Americans have about investing that we burn our Foolish candles late into the night here at Fool HQ, writing workbooks and answering questions online. After all, the best fear killer around is nothing more than learning and communication.

Your First Smart Investments Should Be in Retirement Plans

IRAs and 401(k) plans have one thing in common: they're both tax-deferred. Any money you earn on your investments in these accounts grows tax-deferred until you withdraw it. Sometimes even the money you put into the account to use for investments grows tax-deferred, if it is pretax money directly from a paycheck. Taking advantage of these accounts can be the difference between a slow sixty-first year on the *Fool-E-2* and a long sixty-first year pouring midnight coffee at a doughnut shop. Over time, your money will accumulate much faster if you aren't pulling taxes out each year, and that money will go right smack in the middle of your daily life when you retire.

There are many tax-deferred savings vehicles you can use for retirement, depending on your circumstances. These include Keogh plans and SEP IRAs for the self-employed. The first time you face investment decisions, you're likely to be deciding how to invest your IRA or choose from the options in your 401(k) or 403(b) plan. Most 401(k) and 403(b) plans have the choices limited to mutual funds, maybe some company stock, and a guaranteed-investment contract or money-market fund.

The money-market fund provides a set annual return, which, though secure, is generally poor. You're just putting money in the bank there and letting them invest it—at mostly higher rates than they're paying you—for their own profit. Given that you have a number of years ahead of you, this is a bad idea. If you have less than three years ahead of you before retirement, though, go for the money-market, yes.

Your next option is your company stock plan. This one is relatively easy to grasp because you already know a lot about the company. You know how strong or weak your company management is; you know how well your products are faring in the marketplace; you know how fierce your competition is; you can easily learn more about your company's financial standing; and you may even know what new products are being developed. We will cover stock valuation in more detail in a later section. You can start just by doing the qualitative work yourself. One way to think creatively about your investments is to consider whether you would invest in the people or organizations around you. Tell us whether you'd buy stock in the following and why or why not:

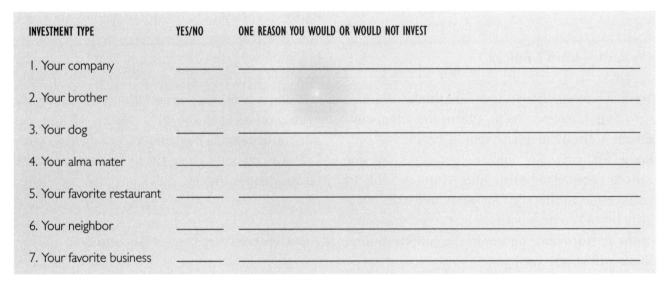

INVESTMENT TYPE	YES/NO	ONE REASON YOU WOULD OR WOULD NOT INVEST
1. Your company	_____	_____
2. Your brother	_____	_____
3. Your dog	_____	_____
4. Your alma mater	_____	_____
5. Your favorite restaurant	_____	_____
6. Your neighbor	_____	_____
7. Your favorite business	_____	_____

Your final option in retirement plans, and by far the most confusing one, is the chance to buy mutual funds. You'll hear of international funds, growth funds, index funds, bond funds, aggressive funds, emerging-market funds, technology funds, REIT funds. If you're not careful, you'll fall over backward thinking about all the choices.

Take a minute to jot down the investment options available to you in your 401(k) or 403(b) and what you understand about them. The list will serve as a handy reference later, when you want to make sure you've parked your money in the best spot.

My 401(k) or 403(b) Choices

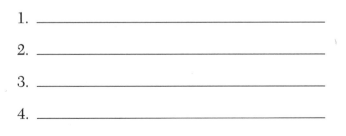

1. _____

2. _____

3. _____

4. _____

Living in America

One common 401(k) offering that makes very little sense to us is the international fund option. Mind you, there are many great foreign markets to invest in—but we also think that many American corporations give you the best way to be involved in those markets. General Electric, Microsoft, Gillette, Coca-Cola—these companies and many others have massive amounts of international business.

Don't be lured by the pressure to diversify out of the U.S. stock market. It's very hard for you and us to keep up with international investments.

Choices Within Choices

You have more choices than you think!

The choices you're given for company-driven retirement plans should be clearly outlined for you. Remember that investing for retirement is a long-term thing. If you're going to be invested in this stuff for years and years, do a little bit of research with us, first. We think some of the performance figures of the various mutual funds will startle you.

A useful fact that many people don't know about some retirement accounts and rollover IRAs—where money has been rolled out from a 401(k) or 403(b) plan and into an IRA account—is that the money invested via those vehicles is *not* limited to mutual funds. But you wouldn't know that from the sales strategies on Wall Street. In many cases an individual's first introduction to an IRA comes from a bank (a brochure that accompanies a bank statement) or from a mutual fund company flyer. Let's blow their cover right here. You can open an IRA account at a discount broker and invest in a wide variety of things—from individual stocks like Pepsi and Compaq Computer to mutual funds to whatever you want. The same is true if, when you leave a company, you roll your 401(k) or 403(b) money into a self-directed IRA in a brokerage account. Those kinds of choices afford you an enormous amount of flexibility. And again, when we take a look at the performance of managed mutual funds in the remainder of this book, you'll understand why that *flexibility* can improve your performance.

More good news. If you already have IRA accounts opened with mutual fund companies or banks and you get to the end of this book and realize you should be in stocks, you're not stuck. You can roll this money over, too. If you are unhappy with the returns and want to manage and invest the money yourself, you can do so by opening a brokerage account and asking for the forms you need to roll over existing IRA money into the account. The paperwork involved is painless. And no one's going to call you names or spit on your shoes. Really.

Tax-Deferred Brokerage Accounts

Oh, brother, that title looks pretty daunting, eh? Geez, we're talking about how to open a brokerage account before even teaching you how to invest! Well, it's not that tough. Let's race through it.

Opening a brokerage account is very much like opening a checking or savings account at a bank. You stumble down to a discount broker, fill out the paperwork, and deposit your money there. You can often take care of all the paperwork by mail, without going anywhere in person; if you're lazy and there's a good rerun of *Welcome Back, Kotter* on cable, this means you.

As for the cash you do not invest initially, or that gets doled out to you in dividend payments, you'll probably drop it into a *money-market savings account,* which will earn you small interest on that cash. And when you make investments—say, buying 10 shares of Apple Computer—the brokerage transfers money out of the interest-bearing savings account and into your investment. Remember, Fool, you won't be doing any of this with money you need in the next thirty-six months—right?!

OK, now let's review the sweet advantages that come from letting your money grow tax-deferred. (But first, a mild setback. There are annual limits to the amount of money that you can put into tax-deferred accounts. The guv'ment isn't going to let you grow *all* your money without a few licks!)

We recommend that you max out your IRAs and 401(k) plans, assuming your 401(k) plan contains at least one option. Why? Well, over the past seventy years, the stock market has grown at a rate of 11 percent per year. Just take a look at the chart on compounded growth in taxed and tax-deferred accounts.

COMPOUNDED GROWTH IN TAXED AND TAX-DEFERRED ACCOUNTS

	INVESTED CASH	GROWTH RATE	TAX RATE	40-YEAR RETURNS
Taxed	$15,000	11%	30% a year	$291,554
Tax-deferred	$15,000	11%	30% final	$682,509

It pays to delay your tax payments when the government encourages it! The same amount of money growing at the same rate as the stock market's average return in a tax-deferred account just blows away the taxed account. Use those IRA credits, dear Fool.

Getting Started, Looking for Magic

You don't need to be a master stock picker or even a portfolio-management guru to get started in the stock market. In fact, you don't have to be either one of these to forever excel at investing. Too many articles on investing have made it seem like the only way to beat the market is with magic, witchcraft, obscure calculation, expensive aca-demic training, or all of the above. Investing is as easy as looking around at the products and services you use and love, and just investing in the companies that offer them. There are one or two additional steps you'll want to toss in, but you can learn those in a few hours—the time it'll take you to get to the end of this book.

Chances are, if you're currently putting money into a retirement account, it's going straight into mutual funds. And there's a better than average chance that you don't know much at all about those funds—whether they're managed by superstars or duds, whether they beat the market or not, whether they're too expensive or not, whether an additional five minutes of re-search would improve your chances of spending your retirement aboard the *Fool-E-2.* Read on.

Be Ambitious: Meet or Beat the Market!

In the twentieth century, the U.S. stock market has grown at an average annual rate of 11 percent. That's a good place to start. Even though the market can collapse, its enduring returns not only have been positive—they've proved better than any other investment vehicle out there. Better than bonds, better than gold coins, better than your house, better than buying antique cars, better than betting on Spanky at the local dog track.

Stocks beat everything. And for good reason. When you buy shares of stock, you purchase an ownership position in a business that is fighting to grow bigger, more defensible, more rewarding to its management and employees, more profitable. You have hundreds or thousands of people working for you when you become part owner in a public company.

Now, why do you invest in stocks? To get better returns on your money than you can land at the local bank. But what's a good return when you're investing in stocks? Fools use the performance of the entire stock market as their measure. How is the performance of the whole mess of ten thousand stocks measured? By an index of companies listed on what's called the Standard & Poor's 500 Index, or the S&P 500. This index lists five hundred of the biggest names in business—from Coca-Cola to Microsoft to General Electric to Chrysler—and combines their individual performance into an entire group.

The S&P 500 has risen 11 percent per year since 1930. Our Foolish aim is to beat that. We'll talk more about this, but would it surprise you to hear that over the past five years, 80 percent of all mutual funds have *under*performed that average return from the S&P 500? Yep, it's true. Uh-oh, look out—it's time for a pop quiz!

Pop Quiz!

True or false?

There is no one perfect investment method. Different tools for different Fools. _____
You can invest in individual stocks through an IRA account. _____
Tax-deferred investments can save you lots of money over long periods. _____
Investing in multinational companies like Gillette or McDonald's can get you all the international diversification you need. _____
Professional investors want you to be confused so that they can charge you the big bucks to manage your money for you. _____
Garbanzo beans are sometimes called chickpeas.

_____
Your seven-year-old should be investing some of her allowance in companies she loves. _____
Buying shares of an unknown mining company that might hit it big is a bad idea. _____
Most mutual funds lose to the stock market's average return each year. _____

The answer to all of these is TRUE. Please pass your papers in to the front of the class. Have a great recess period, and we'll see you back here in fifteen minutes. Alex, if you push Sandra down on the playground again, you're going to lose your recess privileges for the week. Class dismissed.

HOW MUCH TIME YOU WANT TO SPEND

Welcome back, class. The first thing you have to learn is that time is on your side. No, the *buy-it-now* vacuum cleaner salesman doesn't want you to know this. And the insurance salesman doesn't want you patiently reading and rereading the contracts for that new policy, trying to figure out whether this is the best deal since the Louisiana Purchase. Nope. Salesmen want you to rush. Why do you think stockbrokers cold call you with a deal you have to take *now, now, now!* It's because every time you act hastily and buy, buy, buy, they get to take a slice of commissions. We're sorry, Wall Street; we apologize, Hartford, Connecticut (home of insurance in America); but with the Internet, Americans are getting a whole lot smarter. And much more patient.

Yes, dear Fool, once you realize that time is on your side, patience left, patience right, and patience off-tackle are the best plays in your financial playbook. The single most important decision you can make about your money (hey, we know we've listed, like, ten things under this heading now)—the single greatest thing you can do is just to take your time. You're investing for the long haul. You will end up making more money ten years from now than today, and more than that twenty years from now, and a slew more thirty years from now. So, start out slowly. Be methodical. And don't worry about how much you have to invest now—if you're starting with $35, hoo-hah! Let's get cracking.

Finally, don't even think about timing the market—trying to figure out whether now is the best time to buy or waiting in your rocker until the stock market crashes before buying. There are plenty of opportunities for folks with money

to invest for five years, ten, twenty, or more. The longer your time horizon, the less important is the timing of your entries and exits. And the amount of time you spend each year on investing needn't ever rise above fifteen hours. Perhaps, though, you'll come to view the market as a great learning adventure and want to spend more time thinking about it, learning from it. It is home to every business imaginable, making every product imaginable—from Windsurfers to Rollerblades, from gas exploration to wildlife preservation, from cheap red wine to the finest lobster on the planet. The stock market will teach you history, art, geography, biology, philosophy, mathematics, psychology; you'll learn about new technologies and new ideas; and you'll stumble across the same old miserable greed and deceit that has run through human history.

So, after that rousing appeal, you tell us how many hours you can spend learning more about saving, public business, and the stock market:

Fool, hey, I can comfortably commit _____ hours per month to learn more about all this.

Guess what? Even if you said you were willing to spend only *one* hour a month on studying the market, you committed to at least thirty more minutes than you need. You can still manage your money Foolishly even if you only put in *thirty minutes per month.* As long as you commit to the notion that time is on your side, that you're not going to let anyone rush you—not salesmen, not advisors, not brokers, not whatever they're calling those people who want to take care of your money for you these days—you can meet or beat the stock market's average return during your lifetime.

You will. Now stand up wherever you are and

shout, "I will! Yes, I will!" OK, now sit down and cover your face with your right hand. You shouldn't have done that. That was embarrassing! Cover this book up; we don't want to be associated with your antics.

OK, we now know for sure how much time you're going to put into this. Let's be absolutely sure we know how much money you have to invest.

How Much Money Do You Have to Invest?

Earlier in this workbook, you took a good long look at your current financial picture. Take a second and return to your *personal balance sheet* and write your net worth in here:

$_____

You've got a positive number there, right? Good.

Now let's go back to your *personal income statement.* What was your net income for that month? Write that amount here:

$_____

Another positive number? Good! Fool, you're on a roll.

So, how much of this money do you want to invest? We think you should be aiming to sock away at least 10 percent of your salary each year for reducing debt or investing in stocks. Hey, how much do you think you can afford to invest this upcoming month? Write that in here:

$_____

All right! That's just one month. Now multiply that by twelve and let's see how much moola you're planning to put away for your future over the next year. Write that in here:

$_____ × 12 = $_____

Outstanding. Your aim over the next twelve months is to meet or beat that amount. Our bet is that you can add fully another 5–10 percent to that amount, without cramping your style.

WHAT CAN YOU DO WITH WHAT YOU HAVE?

You have that money, but what the heck can you do with it? Say you wrote in $67.50 above. Or maybe it took you a minute or two to write that number down with loads of zeros after it. Either way, that money is going to open up unbelievable opportunities for you in the decades ahead. Let's figure some intelligent ways to get it invested.

If You've Got $3,000 or Less

If you have less than $3,000 saved, does that mean you can't buy stocks?

Well, no.

When you don't have much money to start with, consider buying stock directly from a company, bypassing all brokerage fees. Many large companies have programs for this that are known as DRiPs (dividend-reinvestment plans). Just call your favorite company directly and then methodically add new money to that investment every week, month, or quarter. You can add in as little as $10 into most DRiPs, so you can keep hiding savings away at every turn. Probably right now you're thinking, "Yeah, but it doesn't really add up." Oh, yeah? Let's say that your DRiP company grew at a rate of 13 percent per year for you over the next sixty years. Further, let's assume that you add $10 every week to that investment for the next sixty years. You tell us—how much pretax money will you have in sixty years?

a. $46,247	c. $246,453	e. $1.4 million
b. $124,170	d. $781,190	f. $5.6 million

You may be surprised to learn that the answer is *f.* Just adding $10 per week into the DRiP of a company growing a strong, but not outstanding, 13 percent per year will put $5.6 million in your pocket in six decades. If six decades sounds too far off for you, hey, consider that we were only talking about $520 of savings per year. Certainly you can do better than that, eh?

OK, so what if you invested $40 per week—equivalent to $2,080 in savings per year—into the same company for thirty years? You tell us, Fool. How much pretax dough do you have?

a. $159	c. $149,357	e. $3.1 million
b. $12,401	d. $610,322	f. $12.8 million

Aha, we caught you on this one, didn't we? The answer is *d.* And the astonishing lesson taken from these numbers is that what matters most is *how much time* you have to invest, not how much money you have. Certainly both are important, but the Fool saving 2,080 per year is going to end up making less after thirty years than the Fool saving $520 over sixty years. And so, the lesson here is, start early and invest often. If your chil-

dren aren't learning how to invest, they should be. It can be a game for them; it can be loads of fun; and it can lend them enormous opportunities in the decades ahead.

You Have $3,000–$5,000

If you have between $3,000 and $5,000, oh, the temptation is to get out there and buy mutual funds. The problem is that over 80 percent of those funds are managed by people who lose to the market each year.

Picture a well-dressed young man in a dark blue suit, peach yellow shirt, and red tie, with neatly cut hair, polished shoes, and bloodshot eyes. It's about 5 P.M. on Friday night and he's wandering through the streets of Manhattan's Upper East Side, looking for 1070 Park Avenue, apartment 3X. But he's having trouble finding Park, for heaven's sake. He has an open bottle of whiskey in his left hand, and whoa there! Holy cow, he's weaving through oncoming traffic. A bus driver is jeering at him now. Get up on the edge of your seat, dear reader. He's just tripped over a lamppost. Now there's an elderly woman helping him. He's up again. OK, there he goes. He's trailing slowly away, around the corner, and now he's out of sight.

If you buy mutual funds, there's a chance that a fellow like that is managing *your* money! We don't mean to mock revelry. We aren't suggesting that youths shouldn't spend some of their time bowing to Bacchus, the Roman god of wine. And we're certainly not going to suggest that young men and women who drink whiskey on occasion can't properly manage money. Hooey! Ahh, but what we do notice is that many mutual fund managers are living a rather high life these days, while *still* underperforming the market average! And how can this be possible? Because Americans are only just now learning how to measure investment performance after the deduction of all apparent and hidden fees.

We'll talk more about mutual funds in the next chapter, but fill in the blank with us here. What percentage of all mutual funds underperform the market's average returns?

_____ percent

Yep, you got it.

OK, so what should you do with more than $3,000 to invest? We have two suggestions, and their explanation is coming up in the chapter ahead. One of them is the *index fund,* a mutual fund that simply buys all five hundred stocks in the S&P 500, thus duplicating the market's return. And because of this, the index needn't pay a manager (it's mostly managed by computers), you needn't shell out much in fees, and you can expect to beat _____ percent of all the funds on the market.

Our second suggestion is that you move your money into *stocks.* Three thousand dollars is plenty of money to begin buying ownership slices of public companies. But here you're very much going to need to worry about commission costs.

What do commissions have to do with anything?

Well, it doesn't make much sense to buy $250 worth of stock and pay $25 to make the trade. You just paid 10 percent of your total investment right off the top—essentially eliminating the positive returns that an entire year would give you in stocks. And when you sell out, even if you've doubled your money, you'll pay another $25, or 5 percent, leaving. And then to finish it all

up, whoa there, you'll pay 20 to 40 percent taxes on your gains. So you tell us, fellow Fool, how much did you make when you put $250 into a stock that doubled—then sold in a year?

a. $415   *b.* $305   *c.* $144   *d.* $112

The answer is *c.* You paid $50 to your broker and $56 to the IRS. And while that may seem fine, on average you're going to double your money in stocks every six years. So that was six years of work for $144. Not worth it.

Nope, you'll want to keep entry commissions below 2 percent of your investment at all times. This means if your discount broker charges you $25 per trade, you should invest no less than $1,250 in any single transaction. How much money can you invest in a single transaction if your broker charges you the following? (We're really going after you with the numbers here. Good luck out there.) And we're not even going to help you figure how to calculate these. Yet!

FEE	MAXIMUM PERCENTAGE OF INVESTMENT	MINIMUM INVESTMENT
Discount broker A $10	2%	———
Discount broker B $35	2%	———
Full-service broker C $120	2%	———
Full-service broker D $225	2%	———

As usual, we're giving you the answers right here. We hope you're not sneaking a look there, buckwheat! Oh, by the way, all you had to do was to multiply each by 50, since 2% × 50 = 100%.

A: $500	C: $6,000
B: $1,750	D: $11,250

You see what happens when you take your money to an expensive, full-service broker, who justifies high commissions by impressing you with gold cuff links? That kind of appearance doesn't come cheap. To keep commissions under 2 percent, you'll have to have 12 times more money per transaction at full-service broker D than at deep-discount broker A. Whatever your fancy, you'll want to keep your transaction costs below 2 percent, always.

What If You Have More Than $5,000 to Invest?

Read on. We believe you should be investing this money directly into stocks, and aim to show you a handful of approaches that won't take much time, won't run up commission costs, and won't keep you up at night.

As you progress through this guide, keep considering how much time you want to spend managing your investments. The Foolish investment principles you'll learn—such as valuing a company's stock, evaluating a company's prospects, calculating returns, reading financial statements—are useful for helping you make decisions about your IRA and 401(k) and 403(b) plans, not just when you're buying individual stocks.

We've covered a lot of ground. Congratulations may possibly be in order for staying awake through this chapter. A lot of the hard work is behind you—more and more fun lies ahead. By now you have a good handle on where you are, what your goals are, and how to make some basic decisions about investments. You know to be patient, ask a lot of questions, keep the costs of investing to a minimum, and get as much moola into your tax-deferred retirement accounts as you can. If you don't start doing so now, you're going to be the only one on your block that doesn't spend the summer on Pluto in 2050. Don't fall behind!

Finally, before proceeding, hey, think how much you've learned already. Before your "impulse buy" of this book, due no doubt to its contagiously adorable cover, did you ever conceive in your wildest dreams that you'd learn how to read a balance sheet or income statement, let alone build your own? You're thriving, Fool. Now let's get back out there and nail a couple more gymnastic jumps, or sink a couple more fifty-foot putts, or blast through another 5k run. You're into the good stuff. We're going to start investing for profit in the decades ahead, starting on the *next* page.

CHAPTER 4

How Do I Start Investing?

Ahh, good, you're still reading. You've fought through all that budgeting, you've sucked the air out of your short-term-debt balloon, you've been saving money from your salary each month, and you're ready to make a go of investing (or at least you're pretending that you have so we can show you how and why you should). So, now you want to know, "Just how *do* I get started?" The answer has to be mutual funds, right? According to all your friends and all those ads you see on television and in the print media, mutual funds know the market inside and out. In fact, they're so big that it seems like they should be able to manipulate share prices by revving up and down their own holdings. Plus, isn't that where *everyone* has their money? Dear reader, you don't want to be the only one with a motley umbrella in a sea of jet black umbrellas, do you?

Yes   No

We're not going to *force* you to answer that question until the end of the chapter. But let's immerse ourselves in a few lessons about mutual funds, for starters. If you're investing right now, you probably have some, if not all, of your money in funds. How are they doing? Or more specifically, how are they doing compared to the S&P 500? Stumped? Then let's start with the basics and get back to this question.

MUTUAL FUNDS

Believe it or not, many Americans do spend less than a half hour each year thinking about their financial future. The money comes in, and *plink*, it goes out in heavy spending, or *plink*, it gets deposited into a savings account, or *plink*, it gets dropped into mutual funds.

Beginning to invest with mutual funds is like exploring the wide world by watching Discovery Channel documentaries and reading *National Geographic*. In other words, they're a great way to get started. You wouldn't want to end up alone in the Amazon jungle in blue jeans, a T-shirt, running shoes, and a Fool ball cap. Much better is watching professionals from the comfort of your bed, with a bag of chips on your stomach, as they navigate the Amazon River, taking all the right precautions. When you invest in mutual funds, you buy into the idea that the fund managers have a few decades more experience than you, know which strategy is safe and which fraught with peril, and are certain to grow your money consistently in the years ahead. And there's some truth in each of those beliefs. *Some* truth.

A mutual fund is a pool of money contributed by investors. The fund is managed by a bevy of researchers, mathematicians, marketers, and stock-picking gurus, and it buys stocks, bonds, gold, wheat, land, or lottery tickets, depending on the strategy outlined in the fund's prospectus. The most common sort of mutual fund is a *diversified* one, which is invested in dozens or hundreds of holdings with no single holding exceeding 5 percent of the fund's total assets. That ensures that if one investment takes a dive, the fund can't be hurt too badly. A diversified mutual fund with $500 million in total cash under management, with no single holding exceeding 5 percent of the total fund, has how much money maximally invested in one stock?

a. $10 million
b. $25 million
c. $50 million
d. $75 million

Nice job, just wanted to keep you on your toes. Five percent of $500 million is $25 million. OK, now that you have that straight, let's get confusing again. There are other kinds of mutual funds out there that can't just buy any good-lookin' stock that comes along. They're restricted by a rather different set of terms in their prospectus. This list includes things like sector funds, which shop only for, say, technology or restaurant stocks, or socially responsible funds, which shop only for ethically correct stocks, or international funds, which go overseas to find their investments. And then there are balanced funds, growth and income funds, bond funds, asset-allocation funds, money-market funds, hedge funds—funds, funds everywhere! Don't worry. The truth is, you don't have to know the lingo to succeed at investing. But with more than nine thousand mutual funds from which to choose, you'll have to be able to narrow the field considerably to have any sense of where to put your shekels.

What you need is a filter. And we're it, we few, we happy few, we Fools. Let's start by figuring out how the fund-sters get their money from you, and then we'll see what kind of money you can get from them. What's that mean? It means that we're going to take a look at mutual fund fees, and then we'll review mutual funds' performance—two things that they *hope* you never do.

Fees

Remember those pesky brokerage commissions we were considering in the last chapter? Remember how we proposed that you should keep them at 2 percent per trade or less? Well, managing costs when buying mutual funds is just as important. The investor can never be entirely free of transaction costs, whether she's buying or selling a mutual fund or buying or selling wares at an auction. Some of these fees are purposely hidden from sight—it's a nasty world out there—and some of them sit out like a babe in the noonday sun. Let's review the most common fees: *loads, expense fees,* and *12b-1 fees.*

Loads

In the mutual fund industry, the word "loads" is simply a euphemism for the word "charges." A loaded fund is one that compensates the salesman (er, broker) who sold you that fund; he and his company get your "load." A typical load fee is between 2 and 4 percent, though they can vary substantially.

Many firms charge you "front-end" loads, taking a percentage of the money you initially invest. Perhaps you've invested in a mutual fund that carries a front-end load of 3 percent. That means that for every $1,000 you invest, you pay $30. If you put in $100,000, you just paid a sales fee of $3,000. Does that feel good? Hey, how about if you invest $3,554,134 in that fund. What would be your front-end sales commission there, huh?

> *a.* $10,135
> *b.* $4,845
> *c.* $106,624
> *d.* $182,549

The answer is *c.* You'd pay over $106,000. For the richest Fools out there, look out: Percentage fees are your bane.

So, there's the front-end load; they hit you up-side the head when you enter the fund. Appropriately, there are also "back-end loads," where they give you a swift kick in the arse for leaving the fund. The back-end loads are a little sneakier, designed as they are to keep you in the fund, even if the going ain't good. Conceptually, though, a backend load of 2 percent and a front-end load of 2 percent amount to the same thing, the same total payment coming and going. *Except,* hopes are that your initial investment has grown since you plunked it in the fund, and if so, a back-end load essentially "penalizes" you for that growth— slurping off a larger percentage of your initial investment than would a front-end fee. For each year that you hold *some* mutual funds, though, the back-end load that you would be charged upon selling automatically decreases, sometimes all the way to zero. This is meant to deter you from selling, even if the fund is a howling dog of a performer.

OK, there's only one more of these beasts left.

Less favorable than either front- or back-end-loaded funds are those with "annual loads." Rather than a one-time charge against your assets at the start or end, the annual-loaded fund levies a fee once each year. Let's imagine that you're going to invest $5,000 into a mutual fund and hold it for five years. And let's assume the fund will grow at 10 percent per year. Which fee structure ought most appeal to you? (This one's tough. Our recommendation is that you either take some time before answering or cheat and read ahead. *Jeopardy* music please, Alex.)

> *a.* Front- or back-end load of 4 percent
> *b.* Annual load of 1 percent

We can hear those calculators. Tap, tap, tap. Tap, tap, tap, tap. Times that. Click, click, click.

Times that. Tap, tap, tap. (Hey, we're actually doing the work here!) Tap, click, punch! Bing!

It turns out the front- or back-loaded fee, though apparently higher, is more favorable. These loads are one-time charges against your assets. The annual load, though 75 percent lower, is hitting you each of those five years. The difference over very long periods of time will prove substantial. (As if you really want to invest in *any* of these things—but we're getting ahead of ourselves.) You do see, dear reader, that five 1 percent loads add up to more than one 4 percent load, eh?

All those charges. Well, rest easy. A bunch of people realized pretty early on that loaded funds were getting too much money without offering comparable value. So what did they do? They created "no-load" mutual funds, funds that come with no sales fees attached. This is not to say there are no *fees* attached, however!

Expense Fees

Every mutual fund out there—even the ones with loads—charges an annual administrative fee called an "expense fee." This money is used to run the fund, paying for salaries, advertising, trading costs, advertising, research materials, and advertising. These fees average between 0.5 and 2.5 percent of the fund's total assets (or money invested) per year. When the fees are expressed this way, they're referred to as the "expense ratio." Unfortunately—though it's entirely to be expected—the differences between the expense ratios of no-load funds and the already high sales loads of loaded funds are blurring.

When buying a no-load, you should pay particular attention to the expense ratio. Sometimes a fund with a load and a low expense ratio can cost less over time than a no-load fund with high expense fees. What you'll need is a silly little calculator at every turn, and the willingness to spend a few minutes a year applying basic grade-school mathematics. *Or* you can keep reading and learn why you should avoid most mutual funds.

12b-1 Fees

Oops, we have one fee left, and it's a fee that the Securities and Exchange Commission (SEC), which regulates the stock market, should've exxed out from the start. It's the dreaded 12b-1 fee. You'd usually have to read the seventy-eight-page legalistic fund prospectus in order to find mention of this additional 0.50 percent annual expense. To our thinking, mutual funds should not be allowed to run a prospectus longer than five pages, and on the very first page all fund expenses should be clearly represented in bold type. Pipe dream?

Why the expense ratio at all? Well, fund managers *are* entitled to salaries, for one thing. But these fees are used to support advertisements and marketing campaigns for your mutual fund, as well. They put your management team on financial television, or nestle them between beer ads during the Super Bowl, or lay them down between the pages of your favorite magazine. Yep, you've probably seen a lot of ads for mutual funds in magazines. Those are typically paid for by the mutual fund's shareholders, via 12b-1 fees. A typical 12b-1 fee costs 0.5 percent per year, though some of them can ride as high as 1 percent. The comical thing about 12b-1 fees is that they eat into shareholder monies without providing any direct benefit to the shareholders. Interesting concept, that one.

POP QUIZ!

CIRCLE WHICH IS BETTER IN EACH CASE.

1. Front-end load:	1.25 percent	or	3.75 percent
2. Back-end load:	5.75 percent	or	0 percent
3. Expense ratio:	0.5 percent	or	1.5 percent
4. 12b-1 fee:	0.21 percent	or	0.66 percent
5. Sugar water:	Coke	or	Pepsi
6. The obvious:	paying undeserved exorbitant fees	or	not paying undeserved high fees

Answers: 1. 1.25 percent   2. 0 percent   3. 0.5 percent   4. 0.21 percent   5. Coke?   6. Don't give 'em a farthing!

The Turnover Rate

One final important statistic that speaks to the cost of your mutual fund is its turnover rate. The word "turnover" here refers to the fund's trading activity. The more a fund is buying and selling positions, the more it will be paying in brokerage costs. And the higher will be your tax payments at year end because of all those cashed-in profits! So, you want a low turnover rate. A turnover rate of 0 percent means that nothing was bought or sold. A rate of 100 percent means that, on average, every share of stock in the fund was sold during the year. The turnover rate for some mutual funds exceeds 200 percent!

Performance and Management

So we've slogged through all the various fees, and your head is hanging a bit. All this stuff about Foolish investing ain't what your next-door neighbor said it would be. Here we are dealing with petty mathematics and walking through charges as if we were price shopping down at Kmart. This may surprise you, but we hate this stuff as much as you do. Writing about mutual fund fees is about as much fun—inside, on this lovely summer day—as volunteering to spar with an Olympics-bound boxer. But it must be endured before we can get to our main dish, common stocks. Why? Because so many Americans are wasting substantial amounts of their time and hard-earned money buying mutual funds that we want you to understand enough about them to walk away with your head high and your conscience clear.

But what if we could find a fund with reasonable fees?

As we've mentioned a few times by now, over the past five years more than 80 percent of all managed funds and all equity funds have underperformed the stock market's average return. We have to keep writing this because we just can't figure out why trillions of dollars keep getting poured into a mold that is cracked! Why are so many Americans so easily persuaded that these fund managers are worth paying, when they're underperforming the market?

The reasons so much money is going into

mutual funds are, of course, that they're extremely easy to invest in, that they give at least some sense of diversity, stability, expertise, and that everyone else is doing it. Never mind that, over the past five and ten years, they would have finished behind the Chicago Cubs *each year*! Never mind that betting on them to beat the market is like betting on the ten-to-one horse every day and every race at Pimlico. Today, mutual funds are popular mostly because they're *popular*.

We have a feeling all that is going to change, sooner than we think. In fact, it already is changing. The change started two years ago. Read on and you'll see.

Making Sense of Returns

Let's take a look at a somewhat fictional mutual fund, the Well-Dressed Wise Man Fund. You've probably seen these guys advertising everywhere you look. They ran that promotional spot during the Sunday night Movie of the Week, proposing that you let trained pilots drive your financial airplane. They've run similar ads in financial magazines and the *Wall Street Journal*, and they always proudly feature their performance report in these broadsides.

The tag line goes something like this: "If you want strong growth and security, get wise with the Wise Man." Then, *ka-chung*, their numbers appear on the screen:

THE WELL-DRESSED WISE MAN FUND

(Annual Rate of Return)	
1-year rate of return	+29.5%
3-year rate of return	+19.2%
5-year rate of return	+13.5%

Ka-chung! The screen goes black, then you get the next set of numbers from the Wise Man, focused on total performance over the one-, three-, and five-year periods.

THE WELL-DRESSED WISE MAN FUND

(Total Return)	
1-year total return	+29.5%
3-year total return	+69.4%
5-year total return	+88.4%

Geez, what do all those numbers mean? Take a look at the first set of numbers; these are simply the average growth per year of the mutual fund's investments. Had you put $1,000 in one year ago, it would have climbed 29.5 percent, to become $1,295. Had you invested that money three years ago, it would have grown 19.2 percent per year, or a total for all three years of 69.4 percent. And had you invested your thousand bucks with them five years ago, it would have grown 13.5 percent per annum, for total growth of 88.4 percent. Your $1,000 investment would tote up (untaxed) to $1,884 after five years. Was that clear? If not, just read back over the paragraph; there are a bunch of numbers, but the underlying concept is simple.

OK, so the money invested with them has grown a total of 88.4 percent over the past five years, and now the Wise Man Fund is running all over the nation telling people about it. With them, they say reassuringly, you steadily make great money. Be Wise, dress expensively, invest with them.

Because so many mutual funds do and say things just like this, the world must suffer Fools a little longer. What's flawed in their presentation? The numbers are plain enough; the mistake is in the promotion. You see, even though that mutual fund gained ground, consider with us now the performance of the overall stock market during that period.

THE S&P 500 INDEX		THE WELL-DRESSED WISE MAN FUND	
(Annual Rate of Return)		(Annual Rate of Return)	
1-year rate of return	+41%	1-year rate of return	+29.5%
3-year rate of return	+24.8%	3-year rate of return	+19.2%
5-year rate of return	+17.5%	5-year rate of return	+13.5%

Holy cow, look at those numbers. The performance of the total stock market, as reflected by the S&P 500 Index, has sped right past the Well-Dressed Wise Man Fund over the last year, the last three years, and the last five years. Blammo. Let's take a look at the total-return comparisons and then work up some Foolish conclusions.

THE S&P 500 INDEX		THE WELL-DRESSED WISE MAN FUND	
(Total Return)		(Total Return)	
1-year total return	+41%	1-year total return	+29.5%
3-year total return	+94.4%	3-year total return	+69.4%
5-year total return	+124%	5-year total return	+88.4%

Some significant differences, eh? Your $10,000 invested in the Wise Man Fund over five years would grow to $18,840. In the meantime, the same money invested in an S&P 500 Index fund would grow to $22,400. And if those rates play out over the next fifty years, the differences between the two funds will run into the hundreds and hundreds of thousands of dollars. Not a believer yet? Then let's actually run some numbers. The difference between the five-year per-formance of the Wise Man Fund and the S&P 500 is 30 percent per year (17.5 ÷ 13.5 = 1.3, or 130%). Let's apply this 30 percent difference to the *market's historical rate of return*, which is 11 percent per year. Since 30 percent beneath the market's 11 percent average is roughly 8.5 percent, let's use that as an average yearly return for the Well-Dressed Wise Man Fund. Now, invest your $10,000 in both for fifty years, and here are the differences:

	MONEY INVESTED	ANNUAL RATE OF RETURN	NUMBER OF YEARS	ENDING PORTFOLIO VALUE
Wise Man Fund	$10,000	8.5%	50	$590,863
S&P 500	$10,000	11%	50	$1,845,648

What's the difference between the closing values? $1,845,648 − $590,863 = _____?

You got it. The difference is $1,254,785. The market underperformance of the Wise Man Fund essentially "cost" its investors over $1.25 million during the five-decade period. Can you believe they *celebrated* that very same performance on every media platform?! Well, you should believe it, because it's happening all over the place every day. When you consider that more than 80 percent of the managed funds out there today underperform the market every single year, and when you further consider that most Americans don't know how to measure fund fees and performance, then you'll know that the great majority of mutual fund advertisements can get away with celebrating market underperformance! Incredible.

Right about now, you're probably asking yourself if there's a way to just buy the whole darned stock market—to buy all those five hundred stocks on the S&P Index and avoid all the hassles of investing in submediocre mutual funds. Aha! Cast your eyes on the next two words of this Foolish tome.

INDEX FUNDS

An index fund is a mutual fund that buys and holds the same stocks—all of 'em—that are in a particular index. The most common one is an S&P 500 Index fund, which holds all five hundred stocks in the Standard & Poor's 500 Index in the same proportion. Its performance essentially mirrors that of the S&P 500—the index that outperforms 80 percent of all mutual funds each year. The most prominent S&P Index fund is the Vanguard Index Trust 500 Portfolio. It's a fund that The Fool has championed for four years

now; it's been the fastest-growing large mutual fund on the market; and it presents investors with no loads and no hidden fees.

You are right to now ask, "OK, Fools, what are the five hundred stocks on the S&P Index?" We won't bore you with all five hundred, but here's a brief sampling.

What Companies Are in the S&P 500 Index?

Read the clues below to identify some of the companies that can be found on the S&P 500 Index.

_____ Atlanta-based giant soft-drink business.

_____ They brought Snap Crackle Pop to the cereal business.

_____ They make more razors than anyone, and also own Duracell batteries.

_____ Cliff Robertson was this phone company's spokesperson in the 1980s.

_____ This car company makes the ever-popular Jeep Cherokee.

_____ Featuring 55-cent meals and a big guy in a clown suit.

_____ The conglomerate that brings you *Seinfeld.*

OK, this time we're going to wait a paragraph before listing the answers.

Let's chat a little more about the S&P 500 Index while we're waiting for those answers to come through. The purpose of this list of five hundred companies is to provide a benchmark or measuring stick for the performance of the entire group of ten-thousand-odd public companies in America. The index is considerably more popular in the investing community than is the Dow Jones industrial average, since the latter factors in the stock prices of only thirty giant corporations. Increasingly, money managers, financial publications, and private investors are using the S&P 500 to measure performance. Although the exact number changes each year, in 1996 more than 90 percent of all equity mutual funds failed to match the return of the S&P 500. Over the past ten years, 80 percent of mutual funds got clobbered by the index.

OK, so what companies are on the S&P?

The answers to the clues above are Coca-Cola, Kellogg, Gillette, AT&T, Chrysler, McDonald's, and (if you said NBC, we gotcha!) General Electric. (General Electric owns NBC.) The index also includes technology companies like Microsoft, Intel, Dell, Compaq, and Oracle. For the most part, the five hundred companies are cash-rich massive American companies with experienced management, long operating histories, and business around the globe. Basically, this is the list of the A students in the class of American business. And much like A students, these folks tend to rack up good grades over and again.

By investing in an index fund, you virtually guarantee yourself the market's average performance. (Because index funds do require some money to operate, their low expense ratios do cause them to underperform *very slightly*.) If only the rest of the mutual fund industry could do the same.

What's So Great About Index Funds?

Let's list a bunch of things you get when you buy index funds:

1. Participation in America's robust corporate growth.
2. Ownership of five hundred of the best companies in the world.
3. Investment returns that will mirror the S&P 500's growth rate.
4. No load fees and no sneakily hidden expenses.
5. A very low turnover rate and, thus, minimal tax consequences.
6. Instant diversification into hundreds of companies operating around the globe.
7. Zero research costs and none of your time wasted.
8. Long-term growth on your savings while you learn more about investing.
9. They help you laugh at other mutual fund ads when you see them.

Managed Funds Versus Index Funds

Right about now you may be scratching your bell-capped head and saying, "Hey, well, I know how capitalism works. Why don't index funds cost more than the managed funds?"

Fools, is that good thinking? _____
    Or bad thinking? _____

Hey, it's good thinking. That logic should work. After all, in an open-air free market, quality should rise to the top. The best stuff should cost more than the good stuff, and both of them should cost more than the OK stuff, which itself should be priced higher than the bad stuff, which, even though bad, should still cost more than *the pits*. And that continuum should play out from one industry to the next in a capitalist system. Right? Yah?

Well, actually, no. When freedom of speech is protected—as it should be—marketing becomes an essential component. Managed mutual funds have every right to be as promotional as Don King, as aggressive as used-car salesmen, as glitzy as a Hollywood flop. They are *not* duty bound to represent their performance clearly, in such a way that everyone can see how bad it is. Nope. They can market as aggressively and misleadingly as the credit card company that hasn't stopped knocking down trees across the planet for its unsolicited promotional mailings. Mathematics isn't their trade—pure sales is.

So, nope, the index fund is not more expensive than managed funds. Ironically, the absolute reverse is true. Because index funds don't much *need* managers—they just use their computers to methodically buy and hold the five hundred stocks—they don't charge loads. Because Vanguard (the biggest of the index funds) keeps its marketing effort down to a dull, barely audible roar, there are no 12b-1 fees. And finally, because their staff is relatively small, Vanguard's expense ratios are minimal. The total expense for buying the Vanguard index fund is 0.2 percent. Compare that to the 2–5 percent charges in front-end-, back-end-, or annual-load funds. Compare it also to the 12b-1 fees that many no-load fund investors pay in order for these mutual funds to promote themselves to new investors. Finally, compare that 0.2 percent to the expense ratios of all other load and no-load mutual funds and you'll find that it's dramatically lower. To beat 80 percent of the mutual funds on the market and to charge a mere 0.2 percent, considering the much higher fees of the competition, the Vanguard fund is the mutual fund industry's _____. (Fill in the blank.) (We selected "worst nightmare.")

Why Do Managed Funds Lose?

Why *do* managed funds perform so poorly? Are they really managed by blockheads? Or are there factors beyond managerial control that are hurting their returns?

Truth be told, the funds' problems aren't all their fault. Diversification is their blessing and their curse. Most mutual funds cannot, by federal regulatory charter, let one holding make up more than 5 percent of their money. Right there, funds have to diversify into at least twenty different companies. Then, because so much money has been pouring into mutual funds, they must diversify into dozens of new holdings on a regular basis. This diversification forces the portfolios into an almost-index-fund appearance. Ah, but then you add the various expenses, and their performance sours. Beyond that, the pressures from the marketing department, from the legal department, and from stodgy management teams has most equity funds spinning their diversification out of control. They buy huge numbers of companies in an attempt just to stay close to the market's returns, and recognize that through positive promotions they can convince nonnumerical American investors to buy, buy, buy! In essence, they rake in as much money as possible, power up the marketing, and collect fees all the way to the bank.

Although many funds stress a long-term outlook, the marketplace of major shareholders (banks, pension funds, and the like) holds them rigorously to short-term standards. For this reason, mutual funds often trade positions wildly in an attempt to keep up with the market this quarter, this month, next week, tomorrow, this afternoon, right now! That short-term mentality makes bettors out of folks who should be investing money; it drives up management expenses, since brokerage fees and large trading staffs cost money; and it jacks up the end taxes that shareholders must pay come April 15.

It ain't _____. (Fill in the blank . . . Here, we'll recommend "pretty.")

Concluding Points on Mutual Funds

Fools, we highly recommend that you drop by our Fool School on the World Wide Web (www.fool.com/funds) and check out our ongoing, updated coverage of the mutual fund industry. The results, no doubt, will continue to astonish. From high fees to hidden fees, from heavy promotions to marked underperformance, the mutual fund industry in its present incarnation ain't going to survive much longer, 'cause the biggest profits are going in the wrong pockets.

We close this chapter with two short notes.

One, if you're being sold mutual funds by bankers, brokers, insurance salesmen, best friends, or brothers, always ask questions about the funds' performance relative to the S&P 500 over the past five years—after all fees have been extracted.

Two, hey, it was painful for us to spend so much time on an investing vehicle that consistently underperforms. But due to funds' popularity, we had to. The saving grace is, of course, the index fund. The index fund is a great starting point for curious investors and a great ending point for those of you with no interest in learning more about business or with no more time than half an hour a year to invest.

We started the chapter asking you how you felt about taking the road less traveled and not buying the mutual funds that the rest of America is. We framed it this way:

Dear reader, you don't want to be the only one with a motley umbrella in a sea of jet black umbrellas, do you?

Yes   No

Your answer actually should be formed as a circle somewhere just to the right of "Yes." There's nothing wrong with joining the crowd in an investment vehicle that makes sense. Over the past four years, Vanguard's Index Trust 500 Portfolio has been attracting all the black umbrellas its way. If you want to ride that wave as well, we Fools think that makes plenty of sense.

But don't swear off the motley, the patchwork umbrella. Common stock is just around the corner, and our belief is that you can do much better than the "just average" that the index fund offers. In the next chapter, we'll be teaching you an investment approach that has on average doubled the market's return every year for the past twenty-five years. *And it takes only thirty minutes a year to do it!* So, fellow Fools, *onward!*

Your Retirement Plan

Remember that index funds are a great choice for tax-deferred retirement accounts like 401(k) and 403(b) plans and IRAs. If your employer doesn't offer index funds in its plan, do just as Dan Dalton did at his company, Universal Press Syndicate, in Kansas City. He asked the retirement-plan manager there to include index funds. Now, guess which of that plan's investment choices outperformed all others in 1997?

CHAPTER 5
The Foolish Four Approach

Ahh, young Jedi, you're still reading.

So you are interested in learning about common stocks—what our high schools, colleges, and business schools often neglected to teach us. You will, with time, come to recognize that the greatest wisdom about the stock market comes from where you least expect it: from yourself, from your family and close friends, from the world immediately around you. The world of business ownership is not about jargonized English. To understand it, you do not need an interpreter. To succeed at it, you don't need to live in Manhattan, bound to a supercomputer, with a trading team waiting for your next peep or stammer or shout. One thousand times more valuable than any of these are common sense, common interests, and even commonplace thinking. These are the qualities that will help you master *common stocks*.

By the end of this book, do you think you'll be relying on celebrity investors to tell you what stocks to buy?

Yes   No

If you circled "Yes," well then, we hope you're a celebrity investor yourself. Because perhaps even by the end of this chapter, we'll have you buying stocks with your savings, outperforming the index fund—which clobbers 80 percent of all professionals in America—and singing your own praises from one picnic table to the next at the company barbecue. And we think you can put yourself in that position by working less than an hour a year on your investments.

What we're talking about here is nearly heretical. We're proposing that by spending a few idle moments every eighteen months you can outperform the wizards on Wall Street, who spend ten hours a day hustling through financial statements, poring over research reports, flipping through a dozen trades, and kerplunking on their bed each night anxious enough about how the market will open the next morning that they can't doze off without a good *Geraldo* rerun. We're proposing that you have much more cash and opportunity than you think and that you don't need expensive professional help to supervise your money. And by the end of this chapter, we believe you'll agree.

Do you think we can pull that off?

Yes   No

THE DOW DIVIDEND APPROACH

So, Fools, for you to get started, all we ask is that you step right up and shake hands with the Dow Dividend Approach. Over the past twenty-five years, this approach has returned over 20 percent per annum—23 percent annually, in fact. Since you've already learned that any gain should be measured against the S&P 500, let us point out that this was during a period that saw the S&P 500 rise at a rate of 12 percent per year. An 11-percentage-point gap between the two may not seem substantial up close, but you've also learned the magic of compounding and how to do it. So, if you want the Big Picture, take a few steps back and run the numbers to see what that outperformance over a twenty-year, thirty-year, forty-year, or even fifty-year period means to your pocketbook. Take $1,000 and grow it at 11 percent annually, and you can determine how much more money you would have made in The Fool Four over the index fund.

The Dow Dividend Approach—we'll be hanging our belled caps on the principles that undergird it and the performance that it hath wrought, so we might as well define it for you here and now. Put in simple terms, this approach often has you buying very large U.S. companies that have fallen on considerably hard times. You will possibly be buying these stocks near to their darkest hour in the last five years, possibly the last ten, possibly the last thirty. Your expectation will

be that these companies, by virtue of their size and strength and former reputation, will right their ship and steam forward into glorious new adventures once again.

In fact, let's turn up that *Rocky* sound track and ask you to please name five notable people or organizations that were considered sunk, but rose again to new glory.

1. _____
2. _____
3. _____
4. _____
5. _____

You didn't have any trouble with that, did you? With glittering phoenixes like boxer George Foreman, Chrysler Corporation, Coca-Cola, Intel (oh, yes, these all had their bad years), and so many others out there, how can anyone doubt the ability of great businesses to overcome momentary problems? But this is a concept largely ignored on Wall Street, where professionals are so tied to short-term performance that they often spend their entire careers chasing those stocks that have recently risen the most. These professionals may consider the Dow Dividend Approach to be contrary, may scoff at this belief that occasional failure is necessary to success, but the reason for their disbelief is simple.

If your performance is graded for getting close to market performance every quarter—*every three months*—and you have a lot of money to manage, chances are you're going to hip and hop between short-term-momentum stocks. So, since the quarterly reports pretty much rule Wall Street, it has to love a pretty face. Fools, what do you have more of than any Wall Street money maven? Time.

That's why we're asking you to look a little deeper than that, into the mind, heart, and soul of the companies in which you invest, to look past the flavor of the day and see some beauty in, well, vanilla perhaps.

How Does the Dow Dividend Approach Work?

Get ready for a sentence that you might not understand.

The Dow Dividend Approach proposes that, in equal dollar amounts, you buy the five highest-yielding companies among the thirty that compose the Dow Jones industrial average.

OK, to interpret that, let's pull the meat from that bone, piece by piece. First, *equal dollar amounts*. What we'll be suggesting here is that you take a portion of your savings—anywhere up to 75 percent of your savings money—and split it out into five equal amounts. If you have $20,000 saved and you ultimately plan to invest $10,000 of it into the Dow Approach, you'll break that up into five equal parts of $2,000.

Second, what does *highest-yielding companies* mean? This one is a little complicated, so take your time. The yield we're referring to here is the "dividends" that companies pay in cash directly to their shareholders. "The what?" you say. Many of the larger companies in America methodically pull out some of the money that they earn each year and distribute it directly to their shareholders. If, for example, Marcuppio's, a fictional U.S. women's fashion conglomerate, makes $500 million in profits next year, it may

well pay as much as 15 percent of those profits directly out to its shareholders in the form of dividends.

Why? Because the company believes it can better reward its owners by paying that cash directly to them than by trying to invest back into its own growth. It's made a typical business decision that reflects its huge size. Marcuppio's doesn't believe that its prospects are sufficiently rewarding to plow back every dollar of profit into operations. So it pays back some money directly to its owners, its shareholders—to you, if you own some of its stock. Typically, smaller and more rapidly growing companies don't offer dividends. Why? Because they need to invest every dollar of extra cash into new factories, more employees, additional advertising, and the like. Older companies, like many Dow stocks, are generating more cash than they need, so they distribute some to shareholders.

For example, let's say Marcuppio's has 100 million shares of ownership. Now, dividend payments are represented as a dollar amount per share of common stock. In the case of Marcuppio's, the company is paying out an annual dividend of 75 cents per share. Given that, let's see if you can answer this one.

> IF Marcuppio's is paying a $0.75 per share dividend each year, given the information above, how much money is it paying out in dividends over the next twelve months?

Bing!

The company is paying out $75 million per year in dividends. It has 100 million shares existing and pays an annual dividend of 75 cents per share. The math is then simply 100,000,000 × $0.75 = $75,000,000. So, Marcuppio's is paying its shareholders back $75 million of its profits each year, in *quarterly payments* of . . . ?

You tell us. What are the per share payments every three months, and what is the total dollar amount paid by the company every three months?

Tick, tock, tick. Tock tick. Tick tock. Tick tick tock tick tock.

Bing!

The company will pay 18.75 cents per share each quarter, or $18.75 million per quarter in total dollar payments. Hey, we've thrown a lot of numbers at you, and some more are on the way. Are you comfortable with what's just happened here? The concepts and the mathematics are pretty simple . . . but if it's the first time, you may be swimming a bit. Just reread the last few pages over once or twice more, and you'll be able to start out-talking your financial advisor! (If you *still* can't figure that math out, e-mail us for help at Fool-Workbook@Fool.com.)

(Intermission . . . a number of readers go back to the beginning of the chapter. Others wait. Now we're ready to go.)

We have one more mathematical ratio to teach you, then blammo! You're ready to travel to Manhattan, walk down Wall Street, and grin broadly as you tell your family and friends, "I own this place." So, here's the ratio.

It's called the "dividend yield." It simply relates the payment per share to the company's stock price. Let's do the math first and then consider the rationale. In the case of Marcuppio's, the stock is trading at $50 per share, and management is making that annual dividend payment of 75 cents per share. To determine the dividend yield, simply divide the dividend by the share price: $0.75 ÷ $50 = .015, or 1.5%. Marcuppio's dividend yield is 1.5 percent.

Calculate Some Dividend Yields

COMPANY NAME	DIVIDEND PER SHARE	STOCK PRICE	DIVIDEND YIELD
1. Ask Max Inc.	$1	$100	____
2. Opie Data Inc.	$2	$30	____
3. ZZR	$4.50	$192	____
4. Westloafer Smokes	$2.50	____	2%
5. Jefe Airlines	____	$60	5%
6. Unger's Hungries	$1.71	$72	____

Answers: 1. 1%   2. 6.7%   3. 2.3%   4. $125   5. $3.00   6. 2.4%

OK, so you know how to calculate dividend yields, but what's their significance? Well, obviously the dividend yield tells investors how much money per share they can expect in cash payments in the year ahead. With Ask Max trading at $100 per share and offering a $1 dividend, investors can expect 1 percent of their total investment to be paid back to them in dividends alone. If you have $5,000 invested in Ask Max, you'll receive $50 in dividend payments over the next twelve months.

The dividend as a percentage of the share price is affected by two factors—the amount of the dividend and the price of the stock. You should know that companies that pay dividends are loath to ever reduce that payment—for fear of communicating that they're in financial trouble. So, the more critical of the two factors is the share price.

Consider Opie Data Inc. When the stock is at $30 per share and the dividend is at $2 per share, the dividend yield is 6.7 percent. What happens when the stock rises $5—does the dividend yield rise or fall? Get your calculators out.

COMPANY NAME	DIVIDEND PER SHARE	STOCK PRICE	DIVIDEND YIELD
1. Opie Data	$2	$30	_____
2. Opie Data	$2	$35	_____
3. Opie Data	$2	$57	_____
4. Opie Data	$2	$89	_____
5. Opie Data	$2	$22	_____

Answers: 1. 6.7%   2. 5.7%   3. 3.5%   4. 2.2%   5. 9.1%

You have your answer. As the stock price rises, the dividend yield falls, and vice versa.

You now have all the underlying mathematical concepts you'll need to manage the Dow Approach, a strategy that has smushed the stock market's returns—which have smushed the professional investment community—for decades running. How do you match high dividend yields with the beaten-down large companies that we mentioned before? Read on.

Putting the Dow Approach into Play

We have two concepts here, one qualitative and one quantitative. The mathematical one reveals that *as share prices drop, dividend yields rise.* Read that again. Flip back one page if you need to. Do you understand that idea? Good.

The nonmathematical concept, introduced at the start of this chapter, proposed that *our nation's largest and most veteran businesses don't often file for bankruptcy.* In the darkest hours, they bring in new management, adjust the business model, take a new game plan out to the world, and correct the problem. Meantime, Wall Street is fixated on the prettiest face, on the busi-

ness that doesn't need restructuring, on the stock that has just risen six consecutive months. Using the Dow Approach you often buy the company whose stock has been falling, expecting that the company will turn things around. Perfect examples of this are: Merck during the national health-care debate; Sears a few years ago, when their stores were thought dismal; American Express when it seemed credit cards were a commodity; Exxon after the awful oil spill in Alaska; and International Paper in 1997, when technologists forgot that paper was still useful. And when those prices are falling, that's when you'll be buying. And that's when you'll start beating the market.

The timing of your purchase will simply rely on the size of the stock's dividend yield. Remember that as the yield rises, the stock price typically is falling, and the company has dropped out of favor; then (snap!) you make your purchase. Given all that information, we expect you now understand what we meant when we suggested you'd be buying equal dollar amounts of the highest-yielding stocks. But where do you find the companies to buy *among the thirty that compose the Dow Jones industrial average?* Where's that?

The Dow is an index, much like the S&P 500 Index, but different in that it lists fewer companies and concentrates exclusively on the giants of American enterprise. You won't find a small start-up company sitting on the Dow. Even though these companies are popular, you won't find Starbucks or America Online on the Dow; these two are still medium-sized, more volatile businesses. On the Dow you'll find monsters like Disney, which, of course, owns amusement parks as well as ABC Television, ESPN, Miramax Films, Hyperion Publishing, the Mighty Ducks hockey team, Snow White, and Mickey Mouse—streams of revenues and profits coming from every direction. You'll also find monsters like General

Electric—which owns NBC, GE Capital (the largest financial services company on the planet), and a massive home appliances business; which manufactures locomotive and airplane engines, has an enormous aerospace program, and is also among the largest businesses on the planet. Also on the Dow are Exxon, General Motors, Hewlett-Packard, Eastman Kodak, J. P. Morgan, Coca-Cola, AT&T, IBM, and McDonald's, and nineteen other *giant* companies.

We're talkin' BIG business. The Dow Jones index comprises these companies and tracks them; our challenge is to find Dow companies prepped for a turnaround. In fact, let's return once more to that earlier line in this chapter, which you may not have understood: *The Dow Dividend Approach proposes that, in equal dollar amounts, you buy the five highest-yielding companies among the thirty that compose the Dow Jones industrial average.*

You understand all that now, right? Well, embedded in that sentence are investment returns that have dramatically outperformed the market and rattled Wall Street in its cage. Now all we have to look for is those five stocks. But first we're going to insert a little complexity. We'll actually be reducing the five high-yielding stocks to four Foolish ones for your portfolio. More on that in a bit. There are a few special steps to take to create your own Foolish Four portfolio. We'll explain those steps in a bit, but for now, take a look at the performance of the Foolish Four stocks relative to the S&P 500 Index over more than the last quarter century.

FOOLISH FOUR AND MARKET-AVERAGE RETURNS COMPARED

	(26 Years)		
	ANNUAL RETURNS	CAPITAL INVESTED	26 YEARS LATER
Foolish Four	22.9%	$10,000	$2,129,850
S&P 500	13.3%	$10,000	$257,000

The market turned $10,000 into more than $250,000. The Foolish Four turned it into more than $2 million. And 80 percent of the mutual funds out there *lost* to the market.

FINDING THE HIGHEST YIELDERS

OK, let's go out in search of our five-stock universe of monster winners, and then we'll neaten up the strategy for buying, holding, then eventually selling and profiting off the Foolish Four. We've packaged it all into seven steps to Folly.

Step 1: Buy a financial newspaper.

Pick up a single copy of the *Wall Street Journal*. Every day it publishes the list of individual stocks that constitute the Dow Jones industrial average. If you have access to the online world, travel over to www.fool.com on your Web browser or keyword: FOOL on America Online. At the Fool sites, you'll find the list of Dow industrials as well as daily coverage of all thirty companies—for free, along with the rest of the site. Whether you come online or pick it up in the pages of your financial paper, you need the list of thirty Dow industrials to get started building your own Foolish Four portfolio.

Step 2: List the thirty companies that make up the Dow Jones industrial average.

Your financial paper publishes this list daily as an inset into a graph showing the most recent performance of the industrial average. Just for your edification, here's the list of thirty Dow companies as of this writing. This list doesn't change more than a few times every decade. The chances of changes 'twixt today and the publishing of this tome are slim. But you should check anyway. Here's the current list.

THE DOW 30 STOCKS: AUTUMN 1997

COMPANY	TICKER SYMBOL
Alcoa	AA
Allied Signal	ALD
American Express	AXP
AT&T	T
Boeing	BA
Caterpillar	CAT
Chevron	CHV
Coca-Cola	KO
Disney	DIS
Du Pont	DD
Eastman Kodak	EK
Exxon	XON
General Electric	GE
General Motors	GM
Goodyear	GT
Hewlett-Packard	HWP
International Business Machines	IBM
International Paper	IP
Johnson & Johnson	JNJ
McDonald's	MCD
Merck & Co.	MRK
Minnesota Mining & Manufacturing (3M)	MMM
Morgan, J. P.	JPM
Philip Morris	MO
Procter & Gamble	PG
Sears Roebuck	S
Travelers Group	TRV
Union Carbide	UK
United Technologies	UTX
Wal-Mart	WMT

Unfortunately, if you're not hanging in Fooldom, you'll now have to leave this list of companies and venture out into the individual stock listings of the paper. But, no biggie there. All those columns and numbers are not as bad as you might think. And we suggest you now begin using index cards for each entry.

In the *Wall Street Journal* you can navigate the stock tables by knowing the name of the company. They are listed alphabetically by exchange. And here, you'll need to look only at the New York Stock Exchange listings, since all thirty of the Dow stocks trade on that exchange. What you'll need to look for first is the *dividend yield* of the stock; lookie there, all the calculation has already been done for you.

The Dow Jones Industrials and the New York Stock Exchange

So far, the Dow Jones industrials have always been chosen from stocks that trade on the New York Stock Exchange, but that may not always be the case. For example, one day Dow Jones might add a company like Microsoft to the list of the thirty Dow industrials. Shares of Microsoft trade on the Nasdaq.

Below is the list of thirty Dow companies with prices and yields, just as you might obtain them from the paper.

THE DOW 30: PRICE AND DIVIDEND YIELD

COMPANY	PRICE	DIVIDEND YIELD
Alcoa	84.75	1.2%
Allied Signal	93.38	1.1%
American Express	79.25	1.1%
AT&T	36.00	3.7%
Boeing	59.63	0.9%
Caterpillar	55.63	1.7%
Chevron	77.00	2.9%
Coca-Cola	70.00	0.8%
Disney	78.00	0.6%
Du Pont	68.00	1.9%
Eastman Kodak	69.00	2.6%
Exxon	61.00	2.6%
General Electric	72.75	1.4%
General Motors	59.00	3.6%
Goodyear	63.38	1.7%
Hewlett-Packard	66.00	0.8%
IBM	105.50	0.8%
International Paper	59.50	1.6%
Johnson & Johnson	63.50	1.4%
McDonald's	51.75	0.6%
Merck & Co.	105.00	1.5%
3M	99.00	2.1%
Morgan, J. P.	107.50	3.2%
Philip Morris	42.75	3.8%
Procter & Gamble	153.50	1.3%
Sears Roebuck	60.00	1.5%
Travelers Group	68.25	0.8%
Union Carbide	53.00	1.4%
United Technologies	86.00	1.4%
Wal-Mart	37.00	0.7%

The figures above are from the close of trading July 1997. The share prices have been converted from fractions to decimals.

We hate to put you to work, but just to make yourself familiar with this process, how about picking up that financial newspaper of yours and entering in the thirty companies' names, followed by ticker symbol, price, and dividend yield in the following list? How 'bout it, Fool?

Date: _____

	COMPANY	TICKER SYMBOL	SHARE PRICE	DIVIDEND YIELD
1.				
2.				
3.				
4.				
5.				
6.				
7.				
8.				
9.				
10.				
11.				
12.				
13.				
14.				
15.				
16.				
17.				
18.				
19.				
20.				
21.				
22.				

COMPANY	TICKER SYMBOL	SHARE PRICE	DIVIDEND YIELD
23. _____	_____	_____	_____
24. _____	_____	_____	_____
25. _____	_____	_____	_____
26. _____	_____	_____	_____
27. _____	_____	_____	_____
28. _____	_____	_____	_____
29. _____	_____	_____	_____
30. _____	_____	_____	_____

Step 3: Arrange the list of thirty companies from highest to lowest yield.

Right about now you begin wishing you had a spreadsheet managing all of this for you, plus a link into the online world. They speed the plow. But for the many still not yet on computer, now you'll have to sort these companies by dividend yield. A bit of a pain, but only a couple of minutes of work. Just place those companies with the highest dividend yield at the top of your list. Here's what it would've looked like back in July 1997. Remember, put each individual company with its price and yield on an index card. It will make sorting and listing easier going forward.

DOW STOCKS ORDERED BY DIVIDEND YIELD, JULY 1997

COMPANY	PRICE	DIVIDEND YIELD
Philip Morris	42.75	3.8%
AT&T	36.00	3.7%
General Motors	59.00	3.6%
Morgan, J. P.	107.50	3.2%
Chevron	77.00	2.9%
Eastman Kodak	69.00	2.6%
Exxon	61.00	2.6%
3M	99.00	2.1%
Du Pont	68.00	1.9%
Caterpillar	55.63	1.7%
Goodyear	63.38	1.7%
International Paper	59.50	1.6%
Merck & Co.	105.00	1.5%
Sears Roebuck	60.00	1.5%
Union Carbide	53.00	1.4%
United Technologies	86.00	1.4%
General Electric	72.75	1.4%
Johnson & Johnson	63.50	1.4%
Procter & Gamble	153.50	1.3%
Alcoa	84.75	1.2%
Allied Signal	93.38	1.1%
American Express	79.25	1.1%
Boeing	59.63	0.9%
Coca-Cola	70.00	0.8%
Hewlett-Packard	66.00	0.8%
IBM	105.50	0.8%

COMPANY	PRICE	DIVIDEND YIELD
Travelers Group	68.25	0.8%
Wal-Mart	37.00	0.7%
Disney	78.00	0.6%
McDonald's	51.75	0.6%

You guessed it: Now it's time for you to sort *your* list for the updated prices and yields. Our list dates back to July 1997. You may well be reading this book for the first time in 2014. Hello, over there! (How are things then? Good?) Fellow Fool, you'll have to create your own list.

DOW COMPANIES ORDERED BY DIVIDEND YIELD

Date: _____

	COMPANY	PRICE	DIVIDEND YIELD
1.			
2.			
3.			
4.			
5.			
6.			
7.			
8.			
9.			
10.			
11.			
12.			
13.			
14.			
15.			
16.			
17.			
18.			
19.			

	COMPANY	PRICE	DIVIDEND YIELD
20.			
21.			
22.			
23.			
24.			
25.			
26.			
27.			
28.			
29.			
30.			

Step 4: Exclude all but the ten highest yielders. Exclude the highest-yielding stock if that company also has the lowest share price.

Now we'll need to select the ten Dow companies with the highest dividend yields. Our ten are to the right. There is one special exception to this step: *If the top-yielding stock also has the lowest share price, we ignore it too.* Historically, this has been a deeply troubled company and has underperformed. This way we don't have to invest in it. You'll notice in our July example that the highest yield (Philip Morris) is *not* the lowest priced (AT&T is nearly seven bucks cheaper), so we keep it. If, on your worksheet below, the top yield *does* belong to the company with the lowest share price, eliminate it and keep only the top nine yielders. Simple as that. (One other exception: If you have a tie for the tenth-highest yield, select the stock with the lower share price.)

TOP TEN YIELDERS, JULY 1997

	COMPANY	PRICE	DIVIDEND YIELD
1.	Philip Morris	42.75	3.8%
2.	AT&T	36.00	3.7%
3.	General Motors	59.00	3.6%
4.	Morgan, J. P.	107.50	3.2%
5.	Chevron	77.00	2.9%
6.	Eastman Kodak	69.00	2.6%
7.	Exxon	61.00	2.6%
8.	3M	99.00	2.1%
9.	Du Pont	68.00	1.9%
10.	Caterpillar	55.63	1.7%

Now what about your top ten yielders?

YOUR TOP TEN YIELDERS

	COMPANY	PRICE	DIVIDEND YIELD
1.	_____	_____	_____
2.	_____	_____	_____
3.	_____	_____	_____
4.	_____	_____	_____
5.	_____	_____	_____
6.	_____	_____	_____
7.	_____	_____	_____
8.	_____	_____	_____
9.	_____	_____	_____
10.	_____	_____	_____

Voilà! If you put the Foolish Four approach into play, you'll be selecting them from this group. Ahh, but which ones?

Step 5: Order the remaining nine or ten stocks by share price, lowest to highest.

We must now order the nine or ten stocks above by share price, low to high. Here were ours.

HIGH YIELDERS ORDERED BY PRICE, JULY 1997

	COMPANY	PRICE	DIVIDEND YIELD
1.	AT&T	36.00	3.7%
2.	Philip Morris	42.75	3.8%
3.	Caterpillar	55.63	1.7%
4.	General Motors	59.00	3.6%
5.	Exxon	61.00	2.6%
6.	Du Pont	68.00	1.9%
7.	Eastman Kodak	69.00	2.6%
8.	Chevron	77.00	2.9%
9.	3M	99.00	2.1%
10.	Morgan, J. P.	107.50	3.2%

YOUR HIGH YIELDERS ORDERED BY PRICE

	COMPANY	PRICE	DIVIDEND YIELD
1.			
2.			
3.			
4.			
5.			
6.			
7.			
8.			
9.			
10.			

OUR FOOLISH FOUR STOCKS, JULY 1997

	COMPANY	PRICE	DIVIDEND YIELD
1.	Philip Morris	42.75	3.8%
2.	Caterpillar	55.63	1.7%
3.	General Motors	59.00	3.6%
4.	Exxon	61.00	2.6%

YOUR FOOLISH FOUR STOCKS

	COMPANY	PRICE	DIVIDEND YIELD
1.			
2.			
3.			
4.			

By focusing on lower-priced stocks in this group, what you're doing is banking on a little bit greater volatility. Lower-priced stocks tend to move more than higher-priced stocks. Thus, you're shooting for more pronounced upswings during the turnaround. And now, only two simple steps remain.

Step 6: Starting from the top of this list, buy in equal dollar amounts the first four stocks, the Foolish Four.

OK, we've narrowed the list of ten thousand public companies down to the thirty Dow stocks. We then pruned that list down to the ten highest yielders. From there, we've narrowed it to the four lowest-priced stocks in the group, the Foolish Four. And now, drumroll, please: We're going to create the final portfolio.

We believe you should invest no less than $1,000 into each in order to keep commissions from eating away too great a percentage of your capital. If you do not have $4,000 to buy all four, buy fewer than all four, starting from the top of the list.

Let's pretend you have $5,000 to invest in the group. What would your Foolish Four portfolio look like in July 1997?

FOOLISH FOUR PORTFOLIO, JULY 1997

COMPANY	PRICE	COST	TOTAL SHARES
1. Philip Morris	$42.75	$1,197	28
2. Caterpillar	$55.63	$1,224	22
3. General Motors	$59.00	$1,180	20
4. Exxon	$61.00	$1,220	20
		TOTAL	$4,821
Commissions	$25/trade	$100	

Voilà, you'd now be ready to make your trades. Note that we reserved $100 of your $5,000 to pay commissions. Thus we were buying as close to the $1,225 of each stock as we could, leaving $75 left over due to imperfect rounding. Now, if you don't want to have to run the numbers yourself for your own Foolish Four again, just drop by our online site at www.fool.com—all the numbers and daily reports sit there.

Some years will be good, some fair, some poor, but if the next twenty-six years are as good as the last, our $5,000 in a tax-deferred account will be valued at over $1.1 million in 2024. We highly recommend using this approach in IRAs and other tax-deferred accounts, otherwise you'll have to dole out the annual capital gains taxes. If our money did go into a taxed account, then the portfolio would grow to $286,063 by 2024. (That's assuming one stock per year carries over to a second year, which is what happens on average. That's still an after-tax return of 16.8 percent, beating the market and crushing mutual funds. And that doesn't account for any additional savings you'd add to the market. Keep adding more savings every week, month, and

year, and you'll do even better than that!) So, now it's time for you to build your own Foolish Four portfolio.

YOUR FOOLISH FOUR PORTFOLIO

COMPANY	PRICE	COST	TOTAL SHARES
1. _____	_____	____	___
2. _____	_____	____	___
3. _____	_____	____	___
4. _____	_____	____	___
	TOTAL INVESTED	____	
Commissions	$_____/trade		

Now, remember that you're really ready to buy these stocks only if

- You've paid down all short-term debt.
- You have enough money so that commissions won't hurt.
- You understand the principles that underlie this approach.
- You plan to stick to this discipline.
- You can find thirty minutes every eighteen months to invest.
- You are entirely comfortable making this leap.

That last point is critical. Investing by the Dow Approach isn't for everyone—no matter how much we believe it should be. Some people simply won't be able to stomach a year in which the group falls fully 15 percent, as it did in 1990. Others just don't like the idea of investing any money through what are called "mechanical" investment approaches. Still others will alter the strategy because, for instance, they feel uncomfortable buying stock in Philip Morris or another conglomerate whose activities they don't support.

Know this, Fool: You can tinker with this approach and still find ways to handily outperform the market. You can throw out a stock that you don't like, invest in the remaining three, and expect to do quite fine over the long term. The mechanical model we've presented here has been tightened by diligent research from Randy Befumo, Robert Sheard, Ann Coleman, Bob Price, and others at Fool Global HQ. What they have found is that this four-stock variation has proven superior over the past twenty-six years. (You'll be happy to know that even they debate these theories daily in our online area and, when necessary, revise them.)

You are now ready for the final step.

Step 7: Eighteen months and a day later, go through steps 1 to 6 again. Having generated your list of the new Foolish Four, make any transfers necessary.

After eighteen months and one day in the Foolish Four, you'll need to take about twenty minutes to repeat the steps above. It'll be time to adjust your portfolio, selling any company that no longer makes your list, and adding new ones that do. While you should try to be precise, don't worry about doing your switch on that exact day (but definitely hold for a bit more than eighteen months, to minimize your capital gains taxes) and don't worry too much about having exactly equal dollar amounts.

Typically, one or more of your old Foolish Four will carry over into the new set. That's fine. Move money out of the old ones into the new ones and leave the existing ones alone. If there's a sizable discrepancy in the amount you're holding in carryover stocks compared to new holdings, you could rebalance the amounts by doing any necessary buying and selling. Just don't waste too much on commissions. Here, as always, use your Foolish common sense.

And that's it! Yep. In a single chapter, you put yourself in position to outperform both the stock market and the thousands of funds that lose to the market each year. There's no guarantee that this approach will work like a charm for the next hundred years. But we Fools believe far more in the underlying logic of this approach—buying huge companies that are temporarily out of favor—enough that we're pretty confident that in the year 2041 we'll all be gobbling up raspberries from the bottoms of our champagne cups on space station *Joaquin* orbiting Jupiter, having used the Foolish Four to beat up on the market. Time, only time, will tell.

One of the beauties of the Dow Approach is that it takes less than an hour to administer every eighteen months. Another of the beauties is that investors buy into four of the largest, most secure companies on the planet. Still another one of the beauties is that the commonsensical approach has smushed the stock market's returns like a plum under a fruit truck. Still one more beauty is that you needn't but smile at mutual fund advertisers, can largely ignore the sales pitches from financial advisors, and need not suffer through cold called brokerage tips at dinner. (Oops, that was three.) And then one final attractive quality is that you can roam around the Italian countryside fifteen years from now—on the vacation the Dow

Approach paid for—and you can tell all who will hear you: "I am a Fool."

As we look ahead to the rest of this book, the possibility exists that you'll want to immerse yourself in the study of business and aim to outperform the returns that the Foolish Four might reward you. Exploring these worlds might teach you more about your place of work, more about the world around you—from the environment and population control to football helmets and water skis to multinational banks and your state government. Whatever your fancy, the stock market houses it all.

Read on for what we believe will prove monetarily and intellectually rewarding. And your spirit might get a charge, too. (Please note, though, that if you wanted a place to park your savings without having to do more than an hour of work every eighteen months, you have it now. You may close this book, dear Fool, and seek your fortune.)

CHAPTER 6

How Do I Start Looking for Individual Stocks?

You have your Foolish Four portfolio all allocated, and maybe you're asking yourself, "Why should I do any more work than that? I've got my four stocks. I'm done with all this." And if you are thinking that, that's outstanding. Go get 'em. Mix in an index fund with some heavies from the Dow Approach, keep adding more savings every month, and immerse yourself in other things. Strangely enough, though, no matter where you spend your time, once you've discovered the power of ownership, you won't be able to stop noticing the public companies that swarm around you. Are you a mountain climber? A high school Spanish teacher? An army lieutenant? A squash player? A medieval historian? A book reader?

Public companies are all around you, and understanding them—whether or not you choose to invest in them—is essential to understanding the world around you. And if you give them even just a few hours of your attention each year as an investor, you can wend into a world where your savings money grows and into a life where you have better control of your destiny. But, you say, you don't know a thing about public companies and picking stocks? You're no expert? Well, surprise! You, dear Fool, have an inside track on stocks in a way that the so-called experts don't and never can.

> Stop listening to professionals! Twenty years in this business convinces me that any normal person using the customary three percent of the brain can pick stocks just as well, if not better, than the average Wall Street expert.
>
> —former Fidelity Magellan fund manager
> Peter Lynch, *One Up on Wall Street*

Looking for great individual stocks to research and invest in is no more difficult than studying the companies that provide great products or services in your life. Wall Street professionals trapped forty stories up in Manhattan may get overpaid to do just this, using a variety of tools, but then in contests against a chimpanzee armed with a finger (and some stock symbols to point at), the pros often lose. *The Wall Street Journal* runs a regular contest that demonstrates this, pitting expert stock pickers against stocks chosen randomly via the dart and a board, and the dartboard often wins. Nor will these experts at big investment firms win in competition with you, Fool.

We're going to start—and pretty much end—by simply opening your eyes to the businesses in your immediate vicinity. Have you stumbled across a store with long lines? A bank with better checking deals? A manufacturer placing lots of "Help Wanted" ads? Each of these points to a company worthy of investigation. Before we get right down to company analysis, though, for a moment consider with us some of the past century's great individual investors.

Some Great Investors

Who's gone before you into the wide world of investing? Match these investors with their descriptions below:

a. Henry Taub
b. Cornelius Vanderbilt
c. Anne Scheiber
d. Peter Lynch
e. Sir John Templeton
f. Warren Buffett
g. George Soros

1. _____ Cities Service Inc. was his first investment, at age eleven. By thirty-eight, he would have investment holdings worth more than $100 million. He's now Coca-Cola's largest shareholder and provides the ultimate example of the advantages to long-term investing.

2. _____ At twenty-two, this man started a payroll-processing company that would merge and acquire dozens of companies. His business, ADP, is now the largest payroll processor in America, worth over $1 billion when he retired, in the mid-eighties.

3. _____ As a child he worked on ferries around New York City, then gained control of the ferry lines, got into shipping, and wound up a railroad magnate with fortune enough to found a university and create an American dynasty.

4. _____ Hungarian-born immigrant and billionaire financier, his mathematical mastery of the world's currency markets built his wealth. In 1993, he made $1 billion in one day, by shorting the British pound. He now donates hundreds of millions of dollars annually to charity.

5. _____ Flying Tiger Airlines put this investor through grad school. Since then he's been preaching that investors *buy only companies that they know* and suggesting that the boys' club on Wall Street is overrated. He's largely considered the greatest mutual fund manager that ever lived.

6. _____ This former IRS employee invested an initial $5,000 in stocks in the 1940s. When she died fifty-one years later, her portfolio had grown to $22 million.

7. _____ This financier managed the world's most successful international fund by looking for neglected, undervalued stocks. His inter-

est in religion led him to establish sizable grants for advances in religious thought.

Answers: 1. Warren Buffett (*f*) started investing when he was eleven years old.   2. Henry Taub (*a*), at 22, started a payroll-processing company.   3. Cornelius Vanderbilt (*b*) wound up a railroad magnate after riding ferries as a child.   4. George Soros (*g*) donates hundreds of millions of dollars annually to charity.   5. Peter Lynch (*d*) flew Tiger Airlines to get through grad school.   6. Anne Scheiber (*c*) grew savings from an average salary into $22 million in fifty-one years.   7. Sir John Templeton (*e*) provides huge prizes for advances in religious thought.

What these people achieved is remarkable, but not inimitable. Their successes were not made of magic, but of method. The first challenge you'll have as an investor is simply to keep your eyes open to what's going on around you.

WHY BOTHER WITH INDIVIDUAL STOCKS?

You're still reading, so we have to ask you why you're interested in following individual public companies and directly investing in them. Just by reading on, you're making a commitment to learning more—and we're curious as to why, Fool.

Your Reasons for Following Individual Companies and Possibly Investing in Them

_____ I want to earn even better returns than the Foolish Four can give me.

_____ I love the game of investing—using logic to build the best portfolio I can.

_____ I enjoy working with numbers.

_____ I want to learn more about my company's stock.

_____ My financial advisor said I'm not smart enough to understand the market. Hoooey!

_____ I know that I'm a Fool.

_____ Because I have many years to invest, I'm willing to add some short-term volatility.

_____ I want to retire early from my job at the plant/office/school/store/farm.

_____ I'd like to learn more about how corporations work.

_____ I paid for this book and, darn it, I'm going to read it through to the end.

_____ This will build common ground between me and my father/mother/sister/brother.

_____ I'm eleven years old, and Buffett's got nothing on me.

_____ I'm an environmentalist who wants to understand how business affects the planet.

_____ I can see a dozen ways the world can be improved, but I'll need cash to fund them.

_____ I've already raised nine children, written a best-selling book (sold the movie rights, too), and learned cooking from the master chefs in Europe. I'm bored and ready for something new to master.

Scoring:

0–1 points: Turn back. Don't pass Go. Don't collect $2,000 (was once $200, before inflation).

2–5 points: Very good. Read on.

6–10 points: Excellent. The future is yours.

11–14 points: Fool.

15 points: Holy cow, you raised nine children!?

Keep in mind that identifying the stocks you're interested in doesn't mean you have to buy them now, if ever. Identify them, research them, and then watch them for a while—maybe even for a few years—to see how your ideas play out. During that time, you can easily learn how to read financial statements and value entire companies. Once you get it down, you'll be able to glide through company reports in short order and speedily nail down a fair value for the entire business. And you'll actually enjoy the process.

Don't be impatient. There will always be great new businesses around the bend. Even if you miss a few great opportunities while learning—and you will—you're going to win in the end.

SO, WHERE DO I FIND STOCKS?

Stocks are everywhere around you, but where should you begin? Well, in the middle, of course. You're sitting smack dab in the center of a portfolio right now. You are wearing stocks. You brushed your teeth with stocks this morning (you did brush your teeth, right?). Your house is built with stocks. And the gooey junk food that you're craving this very moment is, most likely, a stock. The simple fact of the matter is that every American consumer is doing stock analysis every time he or she buys *anything*, uses *anything*, or goes *anywhere*. Whenever you make a consumer choice, you're making a value judgment about some company somewhere.

If you don't believe us, let's all go get a snack.

Fridge Picks

Since you want proof, hop up off the sofa and head over to the fridge with your workbook in hand. Read this sentence: Close your eyes, open the fridge door, and grab the first item in front of you. OK, now do it! Really. Close your eyes and grab the first item you can in the fridge.

Open your eyes now. Are you there?

What did you get (or spill)? A carton of milk? A tub of butter? A jar of juice? A box of strawberries? (You know you should keep those in the crisper.) If your product has a label, write the company's name right here: _____. If you picked up leftovers, you'll have to default to Rubbermaid Inc. or try again. And if you picked up something furry and blue and you don't know how long it's been in your refrigerator, the industry of waste disposal is interesting, very possibly rewarding to investors, and a necessity for your daily life.

OK, let's look at your specific pick.

Your Fridge Pick: What You Already Know

That company name you wrote on the line above is very probably a stock, too. Now, what do you know about the company? Let's find out.

So, why did that product find its way to your refrigerator?

_____

What do you like about it?

_____

Is it more or less expensive than other brands?

_____

What else does the company make?

_____

Who else do you think would buy things made by this company?

_____

Do you remember reading or hearing any news about the company?

_____

Where is this company located?

_____

Let's say, for example, that you picked out a jar of pickles—Heinz pickles. While you were chomping away or wishing you'd opened the freezer and grabbed at that Sara Lee ice cream pie, you might have noted the following:

Why did that product wind up in your refrigerator?

They're the only kind of pickle I can stand.

What do you like about it?

Seems fresher than the generic, store-brand pickle.

Is it more or less expensive than other brands?

About the same price as other major brands.

What else does the company make?

Heinz, they're the ketchup people. They probably make a lot of stuff.

Who else do you think would buy things made by this company?

Probably almost everyone. I don't know people who wouldn't, unless they stick to the generics.

Do you remember reading or hearing any news about the company?

I read something about them in the Sunday business section last month.

Where is this company located?

Lookie there on the label, they're located in Pittsburgh. I'm just a couple of hours north of them.

Fool, already you're well on your way to researching a great company. You don't think so? Well, H. J. Heinz Company has seen its stock rise from $12 per share to $47 per share over the past ten years, for an annual growth rate of 15 percent. Had you invested $6,000 in Heinz in 1987, you would have suffered the market crash, but now your investment would be worth $23,500.

We'll revisit the fridge pick momentarily, but right now let's keep hunting for stocks in your vicinity.

Not on Wall Street—on Your Street

When you walk or drive around your neighborhood, what companies do you notice? None? OK, next time keep your eyes open.

Has a big bank taken over the little bank on the corner? Has some clothing chain opened a popular store near you? Is there a gas station that somehow compels you to go to it? Do you dash down to the same ice cream shop every hot summer day? Is there a new conglomerate in the area, hiring in your neighborhood? Do you live near a McDonald's or Wendy's?

Once you've located a few interesting local businesses, you can gather a good deal of information just by asking the salespeople one question: "How's business?" Or just stand there and watch things for a few minutes. You can learn a lot from ten minutes of observation. How many people are going in and out of the building? Are they buying stuff? Do you feel like buying stuff? Does this whole thing look like a fad, or like the future?

Noticing these things and just very casually researching them is a great way to discover potentially excellent investments. Had you asked your computer salesperson a couple of years ago whether his toughest competition was the guy down the street or that computer mail order outfit Dell Computers, blammo, you might have made one of the great investments of the 1990s. Had you asked the same question of the cashier at shopping mall furniture dealer Bombay Company in 1996, whoa, you'd have learned that business was not at all good. Your initial casual research will turn up winners *and* losers. Taking what you've found in your fridge and around your neighborhood and preparing to do more research on it—*very* Foolish of you.

Let's not end things with just one or two, though . . .

Field Trip!

Go get your coat, sweater, umbrella, or your tube of sunscreen, and hold on to your workbook. It's time for a tour of your neighborhood or a trip downtown for an hour or two. Those of you living on Panther Pond in Raymond, Maine, a good distance from any businesses, you'll have to buzz over to town in your Humvee. While you're there, jot down any companies that arouse your interest. In the remaining pages of this Foolbook, we'll be digging in for a more thorough researching of these companies. Let's find ten businesses.

Ten Companies in My Neighborhood

1. _____
2. _____
3. _____
4. _____
5. _____
6. _____
7. _____
8. _____
9. _____
10. _____

Hey, we're just getting started. We still have two *more* spots where you can look for potential investments. And some of you thought you knew nothing about companies to invest in!

In the Papers and on Television

Newspapers and television programs are other great places to get investment ideas. Just pay attention to the trends or developments that surface. Follow the advertisements as well. And think about the effect they'll have on consumers in America.

Perhaps a *Seattle Times* news story says that scientists have discovered the gene for blindness. If that interests you, you might want to e-mail or call the business editor and ask the name of the company that funded that research. Investing in medical research can be a huge boon for you, if you know the industry well.

Flip your television set on and, whoa there, the screen fills up with buff guys and gals in red bathing suits, playing volleyball after a long day of lifeguarding. If you can stand it, tune in to the rest of the show and just casually keep your eyes open for any products that roll through. Television shows like *Baywatch*, for better or worse, drive public opinion among their demographic reach. There are investment possibilities there. You just have to use your imagination a bit to figure what the show communicates to people.

One more channel flip and the grinning game show host Wink Martindale is pitching prizes at America. Home entertainment centers, automobiles, vacation packages, even a meat smoker! And all of those products are from companies that you could partially own. You could also invest in the company that syndicates Wink's program.

Finally, occasionally resist channel surfing and keep your eyes on the advertisements. When Intel began its enormously successful "Intel Inside" advertising campaign, the ads showcased one of the nation's premier businesses. When Nike embarrassed exclusive country clubs with its world-beating Tiger Woods campaign, there lay one of the great investments of the 1990s. And when Coca-Cola and Pepsi dueled it out in a taste test in the 1980s, there were another two extraordinary companies in which you could become a part owner.

Finally, the owners and distributors of all those programs and stories often make for great invest-

ments as well. Newspaper companies like Times Mirror, film and television companies like Disney, and radio syndicators like Westwood One—these have made for phenomenal investments as well. And you run across them week after week.

Let's name a few, then, shall we?

Being Your Own Media Mogul

Five companies whose products are on, or are, the tube:

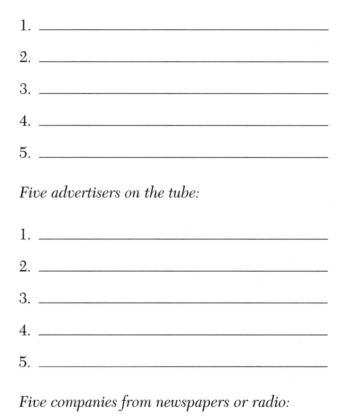

1. _____

2. _____

3. _____

4. _____

5. _____

Five advertisers on the tube:

1. _____

2. _____

3. _____

4. _____

5. _____

Five companies from newspapers or radio:

1. _____

2. _____

3. _____

4. _____

5. _____

Credit Card Purchases

The final place we'll look for potential investments is among credit card purchases. By consuming, you're already investing in dozens of companies every week. You're just trading your present or future savings for a product. When you buy a piece of the company instead of just the product, you'll be trading your cash for the possibility of monetary reward in the years ahead. It makes sense when investing to always consider first the companies you buy from directly. Let's do so. Grab your credit card bill from the last month or months and list ten companies that you bought stuff from.

Ten Companies You Bought Stuff From on Your Credit Card

1. _____
2. _____
3. _____
4. _____
5. _____
6. _____
7. _____
8. _____
9. _____
10. _____

Bonus company! The bank that issued your credit card: _____

YOU HAVE GREAT IDEAS, BUT WHAT DO YOU DO WITH THEM?

Gathering Basic Information

You've named about forty companies in this chapter, everything from Campbell Soup Company to the *Oprah Winfrey Show* (distributed by a public company, King World Productions). All forty of these companies may be excellent investments. Or maybe only twenty are. Or maybe only five. To winnow them down to a group of potential investments, though, you must first find out which of those companies are publicly traded. Let's work through this second step.

Wait! Second step? Well, what was the first step? It was so painless that you didn't even notice. Remember when you closed your eyes, opened the refrigerator door, and grabbed something? You wrote down a few notes about it. Right there, what you did—in industry parlance—is a bit of "fundamental research." For a few minutes, you studied the goodness and purpose (or lack thereof) of a product. Often it doesn't take much longer than that to determine whether something is successful or flawed, a potentially great investment or a dud.

But you'll need to know which of these companies you've noted are publicly traded, "ownable" by average Fools like all of us. Because we don't know what you grabbed out of the refrigerator, we've picked Heinz as an example. What if you had picked Thelma's Rutabaga Tarts, a slightly less global enterprise than Heinz? How do you know if Thelma's is a stock you can buy? How do you find out?

The easiest way is simply to call the company and ask. Read the label of the item you picked. If the label doesn't have the phone number or a Web site listed, it most surely will have an address, which'll lead you to an area code. Call information to get the phone number. Heinz, our label says, is in Pittsburgh. That's area code 412. Guess what we just did? *We just called Heinz on the phone* and asked:

1. Are you guys a public company? (They are.)
2. What is your stock symbol? (HNZ.)
3. Which exchange does your stock trade on? (The New York Stock Exchange.)
4. What's your address? (H. J. Heinz Company, 600 Grant Street, Pittsburgh, PA 15219 / 412-456-5700.)
5. Hey, so how's business? (As they should, they said it was great.)

At the end of your call, say, "Cool, thanks." Just like that. It's critical that you say, "Cool, thanks," at the end just so that you are, in fact, cool yourself. Also, you might tell them you decided to ring them because you're a Fool, a Motley Fool.

Finding Out If a Company Is Publicly Traded

Step 1: Get the company's address and phone number off its product label.

Company: _____

Address: _____

Phone Number: _____

Step 2: Call the company and get a few answers.

Call the company and ask if it is a public company: ☐Yes ☐No

Then, if yes, find out what the stock symbol is:

_____

Then find out what exchange it trades on:

_____

Finally, if the company you've called is publicly traded, ask them to send you some investment information. In a few weeks, you'll receive an investor's packet. In the chapters ahead, we'll be helping you dig through it all.

Get a Sense of the Big Picture

Our next step is to figure out the size of the companies you selected. As you can imagine, the larger the company that you invest in, often the lower the risk. General Electric's business, valued at over $200 billion, is so fundamental to the world's economy, the likelihood of its crumbling is slim. Conversely, Checkers Drive-In Restaurants, Inc., whose business is valued at $60 million, could go under in the years ahead. Its stock has fallen from $16 per share to $1 per share. Big companies are more secure in their position and usually make for safer investments. Of course, smaller companies—though more volatile (more likely to have significant swings in their business and their stock price)—can provide superior investment returns, since they can have much more room to grow. Whichever you fancy, we suggest that you consider investing in a selection of both. You'll want to know how big or small your companies are.

Let's consider a few examples.

Checkers Drive-In Restaurants has 60 million shares of ownership and its stock is trading at $1 per share. You guessed it: The number of shares multiplied by the price per share gives you the total value of the company. In this case, that's 60 million shares times $1 per share, for a $60 million company. Or, as experienced investors are wont to say, Checkers has a "market capitalization" of $60 million.

How about *H. J. Heinz Company?* Heinz has 367 million shares of ownership outstanding, and its stock is trading at $47 per share. Whoa, brother, time to get the calculator out: 367 million shares times $47 per share equals a total company value of $17.2 billion. Just for the heck of it, consider how much larger Heinz is than Checkers Drive-In Restaurants. Divide $17.2 billion by $60 million and you'll see that the ketchup maker is 287 times larger than the restaurateur.

Now let's look at the *Coca-Cola Company.* Coke has 2.5 billion shares of ownership outstanding, and its stock as of this writing is trading at $70 per share. That values the company at $175 billion, which makes its market capitalization a little more than 10 times bigger than H. J. Heinz and some 2,870 times bigger than Checkers Drive-In Restaurants.

Market Capitalization

Try calculating the total value of the following public companies. Each share of stock is trading at a particular price, and each public company has a set number of shares outstanding.

COMPANY	SHARES OUTSTANDING	PRICE PER SHARE	MARKET CAPITALIZATION
Sears Roebuck	391 million	$53	_____
Rainforest Cafe	17 million	$27	_____
Microsoft	1.2 billion	$137	_____
Polo Ralph Lauren	100 million	$25	_____
Johnson & Johnson	1.3 billion	$62	_____
America Online	100 million	$66	_____
Gap	270 million	$42	_____
Filene's Basement	21 million	$6	_____
Lone Star Steakhouse	41 million	$24	_____

Answers (arranged from smallest to largest market value):

Filene's Basement	$126 million
Rainforest Cafe	$459 million
Lone Star Steakhouse	$984 million
Polo Ralph Lauren	$2.5 billion
America Online	$6.6 billion
Gap	$11.3 billion
Sears Roebuck	$20.7 billion
Johnson & Johnson	$80.6 billion
Microsoft	$164.4 billion

Stock Markets and Size

The three major markets that American stocks trade on (from largest to smallest) are the New York Stock Exchange, the Nasdaq Stock Market, and the American Stock Exchange. These three differ in the minimum requirements they impose on the companies they list.

For example, under one requirement, the minimum market capitalization for a stock to start to trade on the Nasdaq National Market is $75 million. If the market capitalization dips below $50 million, the stock may be "delisted." Or, under a second option, companies may have no required minimum capitalization as long as they have $6 million in assets and $1 million in pretax income. For the New York Stock Exchange, the minimum market capitalization is $40 million. For the American Stock Exchange, it is $3 million. Here are the exchanges of the companies mentioned just above:

Rainforest Cafe	Nasdaq
Filene's Basement	Nasdaq
Lone Star Steakhouse	Nasdaq
Polo Ralph Lauren	New York Stock Exchange
America Online	New York Stock Exchange
Gap	New York Stock Exchange
Sears Roebuck	New York Stock Exchange
Johnson & Johnson	New York Stock Exchange
Microsoft	Nasdaq

Capitalization Taxonomy

In addition to the precise dollar capitalization (or "cap"), investors use a basic taxonomy for classifying companies by size. Here are the classifications:

Micro-cap	below $150 million
Small-cap	$150 million to $500 million
Mid-cap	$500 million to $5 billion
Large-cap	over $5 billion

Based on these criteria, which of the companies whose values you calculated are

Micro-caps: _____

_____

Small-caps: _____

_____

Mid-caps: _____

_____

Large-caps: _____

_____

Now, let's talk a little about the general qualities of each category of capitalization.

Large-Cap Stocks

Large-cap stocks, also known as "blue-chips," are well-known, huge companies that typically have business in many different corners of the world. As we noted, these are considered safer investments than smaller companies. They pose less risk of company failure—but little chance of enormous intermediate-term gain as well.

It's not that large-cap stocks can't beat the market. The best companies certainly do—and of course the Foolish Four is based on large-caps. It's just that given their size and reach, these necessarily have less potential for fast growth than do smaller companies. In exchange for that reduced growth potential, you'll usually get a regular dividend from a large-cap stock. All told, great money can be made investing in large-cap companies.

Large Caps That Are (Probably) a Part of Your Daily Life

The company that made the oldest, most reliable major appliance in your house:

_____

The company that refined and sold the gasoline you put in your car:

_____

The company that made your car:

_____

The company that sells you long-distance phone service:

_____

The company that refined and boxed your breakfast cereal:

_____

Mid-Cap Stocks

We don't have to go into much detail here. Mid-caps fall right between large and small. You'll often get speedier growth than with a giant, but usually without the dividend. And you'll typically get slower growth than with the small-cap company, but without the heartburn.

Small-Cap Stocks

These are companies that don't have oodles of money invested in them yet, and often ones still in an embryonic business phase. In two years, they could be wiped out. In ten years, they

could be a large-cap with operations around the world and a brand name that your entire family knows.

With small-caps, investors are hoping to find good growth potential. Such companies might be small, established firms with a long record of success, or they could be newborns that just started selling their stock to the public and have only been in business for three years. Investors are also looking for companies whose stock prices don't tell the whole story. One of the tenets of the Foolish philosophy is that the smaller the company, the less likely it is that major investment firms are following it yet. And the fewer the number of firms that are following it, the more likely the company might be dramatically over- or undervalued.

The market on which you'll find most small-caps, and most high-growth companies, is the Nasdaq. Most of these companies need to pump profits back into their business and rely on a mathematical and enterprising management team to not miss a beat. You won't find but a few small-caps that pay dividends to shareholders, and you won't find many that let you rest easy at night. But find the right one or two or three and they can fuel your entire portfolio.

Micro-Cap Stocks

Beware to any investor who travels into this universe. These very small companies too often have short operating histories, fragile business models, and glorious stories about how they plan to conquer the world. The odds against publicly traded micro-cap companies are huge. Historically, too many of them have collapsed under poor management or have been blown out of the water by competition—or both—for us to recommend that you spend much time or money here. This isn't to say that people haven't made money investing in the mites, just that you'd better know an awful lot about the business and probably ought to know management personally before putting your hard-earned money into one of these companies.

Three Reasons to Invest in Small-Caps

Small-cap stocks can be risky, but being able to identify, research, and evaluate them successfully is Foolishly delightful. Why? There are a number of reasons, but the biggest one is that doing so lets you beat the Wise to the punch. If you get in before they do, and if you've bought a great company, when they start investing their gazillions of dollars in it, blammo, your holdings can increase dramatically. Let's walk through three specific reasons to consider some small-cap investing in your portfolio.

1. Due to the size of most mutual funds, the way they are set up, and some federal regulations, fund managers have a hard time establishing any kind of meaningful position in small-caps.

The first hurdle is their size—most funds are just too darn big to be able to take advantage of small-caps. They can't start investing in these companies until they've grown larger. Why?

In order to buy a position large enough to make a difference to their fund's overall performance, they'd have to pick up sometimes 10 or 20 percent of the entire small-cap company's stock. Before they can do that, though, they have to file with the SEC. By doing so, they tip their hand to

the market; buyers swarm and begin buying at a greatly inflated price.

Another factor that handcuffs many mutual fund managers when it comes to small-caps is their own prospectus. One of the things a fund has to put in its mission statement is its investment approach. And in an attempt to sell their funds as "safe" vehicles, they insert clauses about minimum market capitalization of stocks in the portfolio. If they were to buy a stock that didn't fit their stated investment objectives, they could be held liable, even if the stock rises!

That the big boys can't play these small-cap reindeer games is a great asset to the individual investor, who has the ability to spot promising companies and get in before the institutions do. That institutions cannot compete with individuals for smaller companies creates numerous opportunities. Individuals are in the enviable position of being able to sell to large institutions at significantly higher prices, once the company has grown. Of course, not all small-cap companies grow!

2. Another reason to buy small-caps is management. Lots of small-caps are owned by their managers—men and women who wake up every morning and worry about the overall value of the enterprise. Since most of their potential for wealth is tied to their own shares, you can bet that they'll be working very hard to increase the value of the stock.

3. Probably the best reason to buy small-cap growth companies is that they grow—sometimes very quickly. America, more than any country on the planet, embraces start-up entrepreneurialism, recognizing that more jobs are created by small companies than any other group. And a small company's rapidly multiplying earnings often translate into quick growth in share price.

This isn't any great revelation of ours. Investors like Peter Lynch have encouraged small investors to scour the nation for small companies, buy them if their prospects look good and their management is sound, and hold them for profit. We'll be learning how to value these and other companies later in the book.

And Now, Four Reasons Not to Invest in Small-Caps

Small-caps certainly aren't for everyone. In a single day, you might see your stock rise or fall 15 percent without a lick of news, with no explanation for the move.

1. Small-caps aren't for the novice investor. To buy intelligently from this group, you have to know your way around an income statement and a balance sheet, as well as be thoroughly familiar with the industry that the company is a part of. Cut your teeth on some large- and mid-cap issues first. Follow some of your small-cap ideas on paper for a year or two before plunging in with your rupees.

2. Small-caps should only be part of a larger whole, part of a well-balanced diet. Just like sugared cereals, they can be fun, they can give you a little extra kick, but too much of either is not a good thing. Eat from this bowl of Fruity Pebbles in moderation. Indeed, moderation in all things, dear Fool.

3. Time is another dissuading factor—or rather, the lack of it is. Finding good small-caps can involve a lot of work and takes even more attention after you've made your purchase. If you don't have the time, energy, or inclination to keep

up with the news on your portfolio, you're better off with the Dow Dividend Approach or in an index fund.

4. The last reason to stay away from small-cap growth stocks may be your natural aversion to risk. How did you rate yourself back in "What Kind of Fool Am I?" Remember that Risk-Tolerance Test? Go back to it now and remind yourself—were you a Captain Kangaroo? Captain Kirk? Captain Ahab? If the mere thought of a single-day 5 percent drop for your entire savings account gives you an ulcer, save your stomach! Small-caps aren't critical to beating the market, as we noted in our Foolish Four section.

Everyone has his or her own risk tolerance, and you should never make any investment that makes you feel uncomfortable. Money in an index fund and the Foolish Four will get you respectable returns and keep you off the acid blockers that advertise during the nightly news. Those approaches also give you time to learn how to invest without leaving your money just sitting in a cash account at the bank.

All of those warnings noted, once you have some experience under your belt (even if it's only on paper), and if you aren't averse to volatility and know thoroughly the companies you plan to invest in, small-cap growth stocks can make a wonderful addition to your portfolio.

It's time for recess, students! We suggest the following exercise to keep you out of trouble during the break, and in the future.

The Motley Small-Cap Fool Lib

TITLE: _____'S SMALL-CAP ADVENTURE
         (your name)

_____ _____ decided one day to invest in _____ small-cap stocks. With-
(your name)   *(adverb)*   *(adjective)*

out reading or _____ing much about them, he/she just plunked all his/her _____
               (verb)   *(adjective)*

money into three companies: Allied _____ Conglomerators, _____
                                    (noun)   *(adjective)*

_____ Corporation, and International _____ Transmogrifier. _____
(noun)   *(noun)*   *(your name)*

didn't keep track of these _____ investments, though, and didn't notice when
                            (adjective)

_____ of the companies fell on _____ times and plummeted.
(number between 1 and 3)   *(adjective)*

_____ learned some _____ lessons with this experience. Now, _____
(your name)   *(adjective)*   *(your name)*

has become a lot more Foolish, researching and _____ing any stocks before buying, and
                                                (verb)

following them afterward. This has paid off in a _____ way, as _____'s invest-
                                                  (adjective)   *(your name)*

ments are now doing well and the whole portfolio is something to _____ at.
                                                                 (verb)

Beyond Fundamentals: Thoughts on Industries

As you begin to move out into individual stocks and away from mechanical approaches like the index fund and Foolish Four, you're going to have to learn more and more about entire industries. It won't be enough to buy a company without knowing who its competition is, what its business plan is, and the strength of its management team. Understanding the company's entire surroundings will be critical.

Why?

Companies don't exist in a vacuum. The performance of competitors matters greatly and leads to distinct changes in the way the market values the shares of their stock. Factors that may affect the price of one stock will likely affect the price of the stock of related companies. You see, companies are in many ways like teenagers—they tend to hang out in packs and act a lot like one another. In the case of companies, this is because investors often treat one like another, even if sometimes they have to stretch a little to find similarities.

One excellent example of this is the so-called "technology industry," a motley collection of mostly computer-related businesses. Although computer games and semiconductor components as true industries face largely different challenges, big-money little-research investors like to lump them together as "technology stocks" when they are considering their prospects.

Understanding individual companies in their larger industry context is an important step in making sense of the numbers and figuring out why the price of the stock is changing. And with that, let's push on into the next chapter and—you guessed it—a look at some of the numbers.

Don't fret, don't pout. It's painless, we tell you, painless.

CHAPTER 7

How Do I Read All Those Numbers?

Where did our love for numbers go? As kids, we thrived on hopscotch. We raced through "One potato, two potato." We fanatically followed baseball statistics. We were at one with digits as we kept score on sandlots and sang travel songs about beer on the wall and ways to leave your lover. Yet, older now, we somehow believe that math is for accountants and engineers and toll-booth operators and all those high school baseball coaches who also teach math. We dread balancing our checkbooks; we snarl at budgets. We've become financial lightweights; Julia Child could box us around the ring and gnaw on our ears, with her quarter cups of egg whites and her four teaspoons of vanilla extract. Beyond the numerical elements of time and date, many of us consider ourselves numerically challenged.

Enough!

It's time to learn again the love of numbers, to rediscover the joys of the simple art of calculation. Today we have more counting devices to assist us than ever before. Let us show you how to dig into a company's balance sheet with pencil, calculator, and, yes, your ego. This stuff is simple. The business concepts and the mathematics are a piece of cake.

So, dispatch your dreads. Let's crack open a company's annual financial report with zeal. Let's go beyond the glossy pictures, where we often learn no more than how wide the CEO's smile and her mahogany desk are. Instead, we'll embrace the colorless and drab financial tables. Yes, bring your childhood zest, pack a light snack if you must, put on your high school football or ice hockey helmet, keep your chin up and a wide stance. We're going in.

THE BALANCE SHEET

Do you remember the personal balance sheet you created for yourself a while back? We used the balance sheet to assess how your financial situation is looking right now, reviewing your short-term debts, your cash position, how much of your savings you had invested, and so on. Flip back to Chapter 2 and spend two minutes looking through your notes.

Pretty straightforward, right? Well, a very similar company balance sheet and all the other financial statements that we'll soon cover are exactly what American public companies are required to compile for the public every three months. This means that every thirteen weeks, any U.S. public company must tell the world about the state of its finances. Financial reporting requirements are stricter in the United States than anywhere else—and the level of accountability driven by those requirements has resulted in greater efficiency and superior performance in America.

The balance sheets that companies present, much the same as the one you did, show assets (reflecting what the business *owns*) and liabilities (representing what it *owes*). Think of them as a snapshot of a company's underlying financial situation, with everything reflected, from cash to heavy equipment, from office desks to business travel costs.

What Exactly Are Assets and Liabilities?

Let's quickly review the balance-sheet categories. Assets can be everything from cash in the bank to unsold products to that three-legged desk propped up by a pair of phone books. Assets cast such a wide net that, on the balance sheet, they are broken out into two groups: "current assets" and "fixed assets."

Current assets are those that can be turned into cash quickly, like money in a savings account. Businesses that list items under current assets

expect to translate all of that "stuff" into cash over the next twelve months. What could that "stuff" be?

1. Cash itself, and investments in Treasury bills, bonds, and stocks.
2. Bills that a business expects to collect in the next twelve months, called "accounts receivable."
3. Inventory in all stages, from raw materials to finished products waiting to be delivered to stores for sale.
4. Company-owned office buildings slated for sale in the next ten years.
5. Interest payments on that cash sitting in the bank.

Whoa there! Number 4 is bogus. Office buildings are *not* current assets. Take your pencil and draw a line right through the middle of number 4, and give yourself three blue stars if you were paying attention.

Among long-term assets, called *fixed assets,* sit the bulkier items, like machinery, land, and equipment. Since these items can't be quickly translated into cash, they ain't "current." As you'll see in the latter chapters of the workbook, we particularly like companies with few heavy assets, since they usually represent large investments that had to be made to run the business. Our preference is toward lighter, more agile businesses, for which smaller up-front investments had to be made. But we'll get to all that in due time. It's important here only that you understand the distinction between current assets (oncoming cash) and fixed assets (stuff that you can't lift with two hands that probably isn't getting turned into dollar bills anytime soon).

Then what are liabilities?

Just flip-flop everything, Fool. Like assets, they can be either current or fixed—though, in name, they are classified as either "short-term" or "long-term" liabilities. *Short-term liabilities* are debts that the company must pay within the year. If they license products from other companies, they have to pay those suppliers, and all outstanding short-term bills are listed under accounts payable. Do you remember the current-asset equivalent of "accounts payable"?

Current Assets   *Short-Term Liabilities*

Accounts _____ able   Accounts _____ able

Routine, yep. On the liability side, you have bills that have to be paid over the next year (payables). On the asset side, you have payments outstanding to you that will be collected over the next year (receivables).

Elsewhere in the short-term-liability category, you have regular lease payments and short-term bank loans. And over in the long-term-debt group, the heavy stuff, you have all the money that the company has borrowed and must pay down in the years ahead. Nothing listed under long-term debt is due in the next twelve months.

So, to sew up the introduction to the balance sheet, you have assets, current and fixed, listed on the left side of the page. And you have liabilities, short- and long-term, listed on the right side of the page. Anyone with questions, raise your hand. Any questions? No? Good. Now, let's see how good you are.

Balance-Sheet Taxonomy

Circle each item's asset or liability class.

1. Cash
   a. current assets   *b.* current liabilities
   c. fixed assets   *d.* long-term liabilities

2. Accounts payable
   a. current assets   *b.* current liabilities
   c. fixed assets   *d.* long-term liabilities

3. Finished products
   a. current assets   *b.* current liabilities
   c. fixed assets   *d.* long-term liabilities

4. A big orange crane
   a. current assets   *b.* current liabilities
   c. fixed assets   *d.* long-term liabilities

5. Outstanding bills to be collected by guys with tire irons in the next three months
   a. current assets   *b.* current liabilities
   c. fixed assets   *d.* long-term liabilities

6. $15 million owed to Bank of New York over ten years
   a. current assets   *b.* current liabilities
   c. fixed assets   *d.* long-term liabilities

7. Credit card bills that the company owes
   a. current assets   *b.* current liabilities
   c. fixed assets   *d.* long-term liabilities

Answers: 1. *a*   2. *b*   3. *a*   4. *c*   5. *a*   6. *d*   7. *b*

You nailed them all, right? This stuff is so cotton-pickin' easy. And to think, not that long ago you may never have thought you could read financial statements!

Scrutinizing the Balance Sheet

We are going to concentrate on two ways to analyze balance sheets:

1. comparing the entries from this year against those from last year
2. studying the relationship between assets and liabilities

We're betting that you already know exactly why we'd do both. But here's a brief explanation.

First, we'll compare this year to last year in order to draw conclusions about how the company is changing. Is it borrowing a lot more money this year than last? If so, is this because it's in trouble, or because it sees oncoming opportunities that will demand some cash? Are finished-product inventories going through the roof this year, indicating trouble in the sales department? How much more (or less) cash does the company have today than twelve months back? Comparing the financials from one year to the next is critical to understanding the present state of business.

Second, we'll consider the relationship between assets and liabilities in order to grasp how well the company is managing its money. Is it collecting its bills promptly? Is it holding more cash than long-term debt? How "heavy" is the overall business—meaning, when you compare fixed assets and long-term debt to current assets, does the company have to spend heavily on assets to keep itself going, perhaps even taking on more debt and draining current assets, namely cash?

To show how fundamental this is to investing and how simple it is to grasp, let's take the balance sheet from our now legendary, still mythical company Messages Incorporated—the tasty little manufacturer of edible messages slipped into fortune cookies and the like, featured in *The Motley Fool Investment Guide*. On the following balance sheet, you'll notice that next to each class of asset and liability we offer three columns. The first represents operations in 1999; the second, operations in 1998; and the third, the growth between the two, represented as a percentage. We'll first consider the "assets" half of the balance sheet, and then the "liabilities." Check it out.

(*Note:* When dollar amounts are given "in thousands," just add three zeros to ascertain the proper figure. For example, "24,000" stands for "24,000,000"—because 24,000 × 1,000 = 24,000,000.)

MESSAGES INCORPORATED BALANCE SHEET
YEAR 1999 COMPARED TO 1998

(In Thousands)

ASSETS	1999	1998	CHANGE
Current Assets			
Cash and equivalents	24,000	20,000	20%
Accounts receivable	34,000	14,000	143%
Inventory	20,000	10,000	100%
Prepaid expenses	1,500	1,000	50%
TOTAL CURRENT ASSETS	79,500	45,000	77%

Fixed Assets			
Property and equipment subtotal	12,000	6,000	100%
Less depreciation	1,200	800	50%
TOTAL FIXED ASSETS	10,800	5,200	108%
TOTAL ASSETS	90,300	50,200	80%

Let's break in right here and review a couple of interesting points.

1. Cash and equivalents (those being largely money-market funds) have increased by 20 percent over the past year. So, the company has added bucks from more sales, or more borrowing, or another sale of stock to the public. Cash is up; we consider that a plus.

2. Accounts receivable has risen 143 percent since 1998. One phrase fits here, "Uh-ohhh!" When companies have dramatically rising receivables, it *may* mean that they are announcing significant amounts of revenues before getting any money for them. This is generally not a good thing. Investors prefer receivables to be held in check; they want buyers of the company's products to hunger so much for them that they're willing to pay up front. Consider the accounts receivable in terms of total assets. Divide the $34 million in receivables by the $90.3 million in total assets, and you'll see that over 37 percent of the company's assets are bills they've yet to collect. Maybe, in order to sell their product, they had to promise to collect only six months after its delivery, and only if the customer was keenly satisfied. This is a weak position. If accounts receivable are rising faster than sales, this may be a disaster in the making. That said, receivables generally track

sales growth, so if the percentage growth rates of the two are comparable, that's probably OK. Ideally, though, receivables fall or remain flat as sales rise.

3. Inventory is up 100 percent, from $10 million to $20 million. Whoa there! We're going to have to dig deeper into Messages' strategy here. If those are finished products that have been sitting around for a while, Messages might well be in big trouble. If, however, the growth reflects the company's investment in the development of important new products that they expect consumers to greet with great demand, then we weight its importance differently. As with accounts receivable, these are either neutral or very bad signs. We'll keep our eyes open. Also, like accounts receivable, inventory growth should be compared to sales growth.

You'll see later on that Messages' sales growth is 94 percent, so all in all, the assets side of the balance sheet doesn't sparkle and it doesn't stink. You'll notice that, with the exception of cash, we generally do not want the things that our company owns—its assets—to rise dramatically. A ton of inventory may very well be a bad thing. But let's maintain a "wait and see" attitude and continue over to the statement of liabilities.

MESSAGES INCORPORATED BALANCE SHEET
YEAR 1999 COMPARED TO 1998

(In Thousands)

LIABILITIES	1999	1998	CHANGE
Current Liabilities			
Accounts payable	6,500	3,200	103%
Accrued expenses	18,000	10,000	80%
TOTAL CURRENT LIABILITIES	24,500	13,200	86%
Long-term debt	0	0	0%
TOTAL LIABILITIES	24,500	13,200	86%

What have we found here?

1. Accounts payable have risen by 103 percent, to $6.5 million. The company owes its business partners over $6.5 million now. At first blush, this looks like a bad thing. Ah, but there is a twist here. Payables carry low interest charges. In other words, holding off these payments allows the company to use that money for its own gain before paying it to creditors. For this reason, we treat the rise in payables as a good thing and the rise in receivables as a bad thing. Please stop for a few moments to ponder this. Put the pencil and book down and think about the relationship between payables and receivables. One last reminder—if there are low interest charges on both, then for aggressive cash management, wouldn't you want to be getting paid up front for all your receivables and be delaying payment of all your payables as long as possible? It makes sense.

2. Whoa! Accrued expenses, up 80 percent! We dropped a note to Dale Wettlaufer, one of our top staffers at Global HQ in Virginia, and asked him for a definition of accrued expenses that might explain this change in the fortunes of Messages Incorporated. Here's what he came up with:

Accrued expenses are expenses that the company has racked up (on the income statement) but has not yet paid out in cash. Here are two examples of what may be going on with your company: One, the balance sheet is released to the public on June 30, reflecting all costs, but the salary checks don't actually go out until July 1. Because the payments haven't been made yet, they are listed as "accrued expenses." Another possibility: Messages Incorporated knows that insurance bills are coming down the pike in mid-July for costs of coverage during the June period. The costs have been incurred, but the payments haven't been made yet. Given this, they're listed as accrued expenses.

Hey, guys, do I get to go on *Oprah*?

Thanks, Dale. So, knowing that there may be an innocuous explanation for this 80 percent rise in accrued expenses, how should we interpret it? We'll call it a neutral. It may indicate just that the company has added a bunch of new employees; it may tell us they're toying around with payment periods; it may suggest nothing more than the date of the report.

Concluding Thoughts on Annual Comparisons

When you compare the assets and liabilities entries in 1999 to those in 1998, what do you think about Messages' situation? You tell us.

_____

_____

_____

_____

_____

Very interesting. You're showing us something there. If ever one of your high school or college instructors gave you grief for not grasping things quickly, patooey to them. You did a nice job. Right? If you stalled here, please reread this section. This is important stuff!

Here's our take. No final judgment can be made on how sound a company is simply by looking at its balance sheet. That said, with inventories and receivables climbing, there are some warning lights and sirens firing off. In the quarter ahead, we would hope to see Messages Incorporated collecting its receivables, demanding more receipts up front, and more aggressively managing its inventories. In the end, none of these may be possible—the company may just have products that don't much sell anymore. If that's the case and we own the stock, we'll sell it. We'll have to keep our eyes on Messages Incorporated.

Let's take a look at three more items on the balance sheet, and then be done with it for now.

Working Capital

The first new item is working capital, which is an expression of what liquid assets the company has to build its business, fund its growth, and produce shareholder value. "Liquid assets"? That's simply another phrase for "current assets," those which will be converted into cash over the next twelve months. If a company has ample positive working capital, it is considered to be in good shape, with cash enough to pay for growth. So let's take a gander at Messages Incorporated's working capital in the year 1999. You can do the math. Just turn back a few pages and look on the balance sheet for total current assets and total current liabilities.

WORKING CAPITAL FOR MESSAGES INCORPORATED, 1999

NOTE:

Working capital = current assets less current liabilities

Current assets _____

Current liabilities _____

WORKING CAPITAL _____

No peeking. OK, now take a look at the answer.

WORKING CAPITAL FOR MESSAGES INCORPORATED, 1999

Current assets	$79,500,000
Current liabilities	$24,500,000
WORKING CAPITAL	$55,000,000

The company has ample working capital of $55 million, which includes cash on hand of $24 million. As of this moment, Messages Incorporated could pay off nearly all but $500,000 of its current liabilities with existing cash. In other words, the company is in fine financial shape for the upcoming year.

But, Fool, in studying *working capital,* don't blind yourself to the rise of receivables and inventories. Those assets may not be as liquid as you think. What if the inventory cannot be sold for cash? And what if the receivables cannot be collected for cash? Even though the company appears to be strong for the year ahead, the best of all current assets by a long shot is simply *cash.* For example, on the balance sheet of Microsoft, perhaps the greatest business of the twentieth century (if not of all time), you will find that *cash* makes up over 80 percent of the current assets. For Messages, cash makes up only 30 percent of current assets. Not everyone is Microsoft! But Messages Incorporated's assets line isn't as definitively liquid as we'd like.

The Foolish Flow Ratio

The Foolish Flow Ratio is the latest introduction by Fool scientists. It is designed to stack the noncash current assets against current liabilities, in order to measure how well a company is managing the dollar bills that flow through its business. Allow us to introduce the ratio first and then provide a more comprehensible explanation.

To calculate the Foolish Flow Ratio, simply (*a*) subtract the cash from current assets, then (*b*) divide that figure by current liabilities. In the case of Messages Incorporated, you'll get something that looks like this:

$$(\text{current assets} - \text{cash}) \div \text{current liabilities}$$
$$(\$79.5 \text{ million} - \$24 \text{ million}) \div \$24.5 \text{ million}$$
$$\$55.5 \text{ million} \div \$24.5 \text{ million} = 2.27$$

So, Messages Incorporated's flow ratio is 2.27. Now, fellow Fool, pause for a second and tell us whether you'd ideally like your company to have a high or low flow ratio relative to its competitors. Tick tock tick. Tick tock tick. Fill in your answer and explanation here:

_____

_____

_____

Interesting! Here's our answer: Ideally, a company's flow ratio is low. Once cash is removed from current assets, we're dealing almost exclusively with accounts receivable and inventories. In the very best businesses, these items are held in check: Inventories should never run high; they should be constantly rolling out the door. And receivables should be kept low; the company should require up-front payments for its products and services.

So we certainly want the numerator of the equation to be held low.

What about the denominator, current liabilities? Rising payables indicate one of two things: Either the company cannot meet its short-term bills and is headed for bankruptcy—or the company is so strong that its suppliers are willing to give it time before requiring payment. You can be sure that companies in the latter category use their advantageous position to hang on to every dollar they can. Again, think of every unpaid bill as a short-term interest-free or low-rate loan! If a company has plenty of cash to pay down current liabilities but doesn't, it's probably managing its money *very* well. Those are the companies that we're looking for.

To close out the Foolish Flow Ratio, then, ideally we like to see this baby sit low. The very best companies have:

1. Plenty of cash
2. Noncash current assets that are dropping (inventories and receivables kept low)
3. Rising current liabilities (unpaid bills for which cash is on hand)

PRACTICE FLOW RATIOS

	CASH	CURRENT ASSETS	CURRENT ASSETS LESS CASH	CURRENT LIABILITIES	FLOW RATIO
Microsoft	$9.1 billion	$10.2 billion	$1.1 billion	$3.5 billion	0.31
Coca-Cola	$2.2 billion	$6.3 billion	$4.1 billion	$7.3 billion	0.56
Bombay Company	$2 million	$123 million	$121 million	$24 million	5.04
Starbucks	$213 million	$328 million	$115 million	$111 million	1.04
Hershey Fools (er, we mean Foods)	$77.3 million	$1 billion	$923 million	$841 million	a. _____
Staples Inc.	$106 million	$1.2 billion	b. _____	$603 million	c. _____
Dole Food	$26 million	$1.2 billion	d. _____	$656 million	e. _____
Borders Books	$43.2 million	$964 million	$921 million	$817 million	f. _____
Ivax Pharmaceutical	$75 million	$690 million	$615 million	$217 million	g. _____
Pfizer	$1.9 billion	$6.9 billion	$5 billion	$5.8 billion	h. _____

Answers: a. 1.10 *b.* $1.1 billion *c.* 1.82 *d.* $1.2 billion *e.* 1.83 *f.* 1.13 *g.* 2.83 *h.* 0.86

Final question: The Foolish Flow Ratio is only one of many, many different checks to run on your company. Keeping that in mind, *which are the six most attractive companies, by flow ratio, in the table above?* Please write them in order from greatest to sixth-greatest.

1. _____ 2. _____ 3. _____

4. _____ 5. _____ 6. _____

Did you write: (1) Microsoft, (2) Coca-Cola, (3) Pfizer, (4) Starbucks, (5) Hershey, and (6) Borders? Good, you're right!

Great-performing long-term stocks, all.

Shareholders' Equity

If you've taken the time by now to call up one of your favorite companies to get its financial statements, you may be looking over a real live balance sheet even as we speak—er, write. Good! If so, you'll notice there's actually a final section of the balance sheet that we haven't yet mentioned. It's listed under liabilities, though it's a horse of a different color: "shareholders' equity."

Shareholders' equity is the owners' piece of the business, as distinct from the debt (long-term and short-term) that supports the biz in the form of liabilities. Fools spend little time looking at this particular section, except occasionally to calculate the "debt-to-equity ratio"—simply a company's total liabilities divided by shareholders' value. Shareholders' equity is simply total assets minus total liabilities.

Should a company eventually want or need to borrow money, it's helpful to have lots of equity and little debt—creditors like this. But since Fools generally avoid investing in businesses that make many appeals to creditors, we'll gracefully end this section here. In fact, before you knew it, we began *and* completed the balance-sheet section, like *that*. (Snap!) OK, to the income statement. Forward, march!

THE INCOME STATEMENT

Four times a year, public companies step into the Wall Street spotlight and announce their past three-month financial performance. Instantly, Wall Street begins sorting through the numbers, calculating ratios, and divining new valuations for the entire business. Quarterly earnings reports are like baseball scorecards or medical statistics. Laid out on the page, they can tell us about resiliency or disintegration, a healthy consistency or erratic performance. And a surprise in profits, on the upside or downside, can send stocks soaring or tumbling as Wall Street revises its expectations.

We presented the balance sheet first because we consider its importance to be underrated by investment researchers. You see, the investing community concentrates most of its attention on the income statement. It is here that you'll find out how much chocolate Hershey sold, how much it cost Hershey to manufacture and package that chocolate, how much it cost the company to distribute and promote that chocolate, and—ever important—how much money it made selling that chocolate.

Before these figures are announced, Wall Street's analysts and experts have already made predictions about what sales and earnings for the three-month period should be (we'll discuss this later). So, when these figures actually do get announced, investors race to compare the sales and earnings results to Wall Street's predictions for the quarter. The longer-term investor, who most often beats the market, usually takes a good while to think before making any assumptions about the quarterly report. Needless to say, while wild trading activity often ensues after an announcement, the most money can be made by assessing the strength and viability of the business in the years ahead.

There's your preface to the income statement. Now let's scrutinize the statement for Messages Incorporated and then break up the parts. Sneak a peek, use it as an eye chart if it is completely unclear, and let's meet back at the bottom to make sense of the scribble.

MESSAGES INCORPORATED, INCOME

(In Thousands)

	1999	1998	CHANGE
Income			
Revenues	97,000	50,000	94%
Less cost of sales (goods)	46,500	21,000	121%
GROSS PROFIT	50,500	29,000	74%
Operating Expenses			
Selling/general/administration	27,500	12,000	129%
Research/development	4,500	6,000	(25%)*
TOTAL OPERATING EXPENSES	32,000	18,000	78%
INCOME FROM OPERATIONS	18,500	11,000	68%
Interest income	1,080	1,000	8%
Total income before taxes	19,580	12,000	63%
Less income taxes	6,700	4,100	63%
NET INCOME	12,880	7,900	63%
Earnings per share	$1.07	$0.79	35%
Shares outstanding	12,000	10,000	20%

* The parentheses indicate a negative number, i.e., a *decrease* of 25%.

There we are. Now let's talk about it.

Revenues and Cost of Sales

We start with *Revenues,* or sales, which is, as one might expect, the total dollar value of all products and services sold over the course of the year. Those numbers appear as the first line on the statement, which explains why an increase in rev-

enues is often referred to as "top-line growth." Messages fared well this quarter. Sales almost doubled, to $97 million from $50 million the year before. If the word "almost" is too vague, let's whip out our calculators. If we divide the current year's sales of $97 million by the $50 million in sales the year before, we see that sales grew to 1.94, an increase of 94 percent. On average, a mature business might grow sales by 5–15 percent per year. Because Messages is a relatively small and new operation with a titillating product, the growth has been more rapid. Hey, let's stand up and shout: 94 percent growth over last year is awesome. People clearly want more messages!

There may be more to the story than has yet been told, however. What if the company is selling those messages for very little money—perhaps not enough money to cover the cost of manufacturing them? Consider this workbook for a second. If Simon & Schuster charged a mere 25 cents for it, it might sell 15 million copies. S&S would also happen to lose millions of dollars in the process. So, while sales can rise dramatically, you'll next have to study how well the company is keeping expenses under control.

Among the costs of running a business, companies pay money for raw materials and the manufacturing labor to assemble them, and these items fall under the category of *Cost of sales.* Now one might expect, with sales of tasty fortune cookie messages on the rise, that costs would also be significantly higher. Yep—cancel the surprise party—the cost of those sales did rise, from $21 million last year to $46.5 million this year. Tap, tap, tap on the calculator, and you'll see that this cost rose 121 percent for the year. That beats out the sales growth of 94 percent. And so, while the company may still be making money (and we'll see that it is), the rate of its profitability has declined. Hey, there are a few somersaults of mathematical logic there. Are you with us? Not too tough.

Now let's look at some ways to assess the company's profitability.

Gross Profit and Gross Margins

MESSAGES INCORPORATED, GROSS PROFIT

(In Thousands)

	1999	1998	CHANGE
Income			
Revenues	$97,000	$50,000	94%
Less cost of sales (goods)	$46,500	$21,000	121%
GROSS PROFIT	$50,500	$29,000	74%

Gross profit is the cash left after the cost of sales has been subtracted from revenues. First, look at 1998. Off $50 million in sales, the company garnered gross profits of $29 million. And thus, the company had what is called "gross margins" of 58 percent. Can you guess what gross margins are? Yep, simply the percentage in gross profits relative to revenue ($29 million ÷ $50 million = 58%). In our experience, any company with gross margins above 50 percent is running an extremely inexpensive, or light, business. We like that. And that was the case for Messages in 1998. How about 1999?

In 1999, the company drove gross profits higher, to $50.5 million on sales of $97 million. The rise in gross profits was substantial, up 74 percent. Many investors would wildly celebrate this climb. Ahh, but you'll note that *gross margins* actually *fell* (50.5 ÷ 97 = 52%, below 1998's 58%). So, while sales and earnings rose, the level of profitability actually went the other way. Why did that happen? Maybe competition has prompted the company to cut prices. Maybe the only way that Messages can grow rapidly is by buying more expensive machinery and materials, thus driving higher its cost of doing business. Whatever the reason, the investing community may get jittery, even if the end result was more gross profit for the company. You'll definitely want to study the gross margins of any company you consider for investment.

Before we go on to *Operating expenses,* do you understand the relationships among sales, cost of sales, gross profits, and gross margins? It can tangle you up the first time through, but the concepts are pretty simple.

Operating Expenses and Operating Margins

MESSAGES INCORPORATED, INCOME

(In Thousands)

	1999	1998	CHANGE
Income			
Revenues	97,000	50,000	94%
Less cost of sales (goods)	46,500	21,000	121%
GROSS PROFIT	50,500	29,000	74%
Operating Expenses			
Selling/general/administration	27,500	12,000	129%
Research/development	4,500	6,000	(25%)
TOTAL OPERATING EXPENSES	32,000	18,000	78%
INCOME FROM OPERATIONS	18,500	11,000	68%

We'll start with the top one of the four entries, *Selling, general, and administration expenses,* or SG&A. Even before defining that, we can't help but notice that it has exploded skyward in 1999—up 129 percent, to $27.5 million for the year. Scary, eh? Well, it might be, if you knew what the heck SG&A expenses are. So, let's find out.

Selling, general, and administration expenses include things like salary expenses— paying for software programmers, the overpaid management, and the underappreciated cleaning crew. It also includes the incidental costs of running the business. The huge expenses for the company's accountants and lawyers would fall into this category, as well as the expenses for keeping the lights on and the water flowing at Messages' headquarters. The costs associated with keeping the company's salespeople on the road looking for new opportunities fall under SG&A as well. These expenses don't involve the material product being sold itself, but arise from much of the business surrounding the product.

Now drop down a line to *Research and development costs.* These are the expenses that fund Messages' scientists working overtime in the company's two New Mexico laboratories to develop the next great medium for message distribution. Will it be Messages chewing gum, melting on your tongue, not your fingers? Has Messages set up a high-tech system for the delivery of notes between bar patrons? Or is Messages developing encryption decoders for the CIA? Whatever the mission, these are all research and development (R&D) costs to the company.

Hey, it looks like we have some financial relief for Messages here. They successfully cut R&D costs by 25 percent. The company had to pay out only $4.5 million for research this year. Hmmm, but is that all good? Not necessarily. Problems will arise if Messages resides in an everchanging industry where new products in the pipeline are crucial to enduring success. Take the pharmaceutical industry. Drug makers can't sit still just because they created a concoction that successfully treats stomach acid. They must plow profits back into R&D to go in search of *the new.* In Messages' case, by shortchanging its research and development efforts, the company successfully trimmed short-term costs but may have compromised its future. Falling R&D expenses are generally not something investors love.

OK, now add up SG&A and R&D (gotta love the acronyms!—by the way, what *does* "OK" stand for?) and you'll come up with the *Total operating expenses* of the business. About now, if

you haven't before, you should begin realizing how difficult it is to run a successful business, even in America. Even as sales rise dramatically, the material cost of those sales, the marketing and promotional expenses, and the ongoing expense of research and development can narrow profits down to not more than a razor's edge. And we haven't even gotten to taxes yet!

Now study the line dedicated to *Income from operations.* From operations in 1998, Messages made $11 million. In 1999, the company boosted operational profits to $18.5 million. But we can't hoo-haah and celebrate yet, right? We have to calculate "operating margins." While gross margins represent money remaining after merely the cost of the product (or "cost of sales") is removed, operating margins show the profitability after all of the daily expenses of running the business (sales, general, and administrative costs) are subtracted as well. You calculate the operating margins by dividing income from operations (shown on the balance sheet) by total revenue. Perhaps read that again, slowly, good Fool, and then use what you've just learned and the numbers below to calculate the 1998 and 1999 operating margins!

CALCULATE OPERATING MARGINS

	1999	1998
Revenue	97,000	50,000
Income from operations	18,500	11,000
Operating margins	_____%	_____%

Answers: 1999, 19.1%   1998, 22%

To repeat: Earlier we subtracted the cost of the sales from the sales revenue itself to obtain gross margins, and now we have subtracted the operating expenses as well to get the operating margin. How do you get the margin? You divide the income from operations by total revenue to get the operating margin. It's a mouthful, but not difficult.

There's only a little more before we get to the end of the income statement. Most companies also enjoy a dollop of income (or expense, in high-debt situations) from interest on the company's cash sitting in the bank. For the years 1998 and 1999, Messages took in $1 million and $1.08 million, respectively, in interest payments; thus the final total for *Income before taxes* was $12 million in 1998 and $19.58 million in 1999. Now, close your eyes. Now open them. Poof! Who's that elderly gentleman in a white top hat, garbed in red and blue, and spangled in stars? It's Uncle Sam, and he's here to collect income taxes!

INTEREST AND TAXES	1999	1998	CHANGE
Interest income	1,080	1,000	8%
Total income before taxes	19,580	12,000	63%
Less income taxes	6,700	4,100	63%
NET INCOME	12,880	7,900	63%

The tax man takes his 34 percent cut, and Messages is left with 1999 profits, or *Net income,* of about $12.9 million, an increase of 63 percent over the previous year. Because earnings sit at the bottom of the income statement, after all costs have been removed, it's often referred to as "the bottom line." Stand up where you are (airplane, cafeteria, crowded theater, prison) and say it with us to be cool, "Messages Incorporated had $12.9 million on the bottom line in 1999. Fire!" Got a few stares, eh? Sweet!

Profit Margins

You've mastered the gross margin, you've conquered operating margins, and now your fans want to see if you can figure what Messages' "profit margins" (also known as "net margins") are. We'll set you up helpfully, once again.

CALCULATE PROFIT MARGINS

	1999	1998
Revenues	97,000	50,000
Net income	12,880	7,900
Profit margins	_____%	_____%

Yes, to get the number you're looking for, you simply divide the final net income by the sales, and, voilà, Fool, you've just calculated the net margins. In 1998, Messages had net margins of 15.8 percent. In 1999, the company showed net margins of 13.2 percent. Just as we noted above, even as the company is selling more and more product, the level of final, bottom-line profitability on each sale is falling. The investing community much prefers to see rising margins, and so should you. The Coca-Cola Company— one of the great businesses on the planet—has driven up its net margins from 10 percent to more than 20 percent over the last decade. Wall Street has rewarded Coke investors with a ten-year growth rate of 30 percent per year on the price of the stock. Over the past decade, Coke investors have doubled their money every 2.5 years, en route to making 14 times their money (as of this writing) since 1987. Not bad, eh? Investors love to see rising profit margins. Keep your eyes fixed on them, dear reader.

Earnings Per Share

Think we're done with the income statement?

Almost, but not yet. Now we have to figure out *Earnings per share*. If you hold ten shares of stock in Messages Incorporated, you'd like to know how much profit is backing each one of your shares. This is particularly important because in many quarters, the total number of a company's shares that are publicly owned (a.k.a. shares outstanding) changes. Some companies use cash to buy back shares in the marketplace and retire them, thus increasing the value of those shares that remain. Most companies, conversely, release more and more shares with time: They dole out employee and executive options, or use shares to acquire smaller companies, or sell more shares to the public in a secondary offering. Thus, you'll need to keep your eye not just on the total profits, but more important, on the profits per share. Let's check out what Messages has been up to.

MESSAGES INCORPORATED, INCOME

(In Thousands)

	1999	1998	CHANGE
NET INCOME	12,880	7,900	63%
Earnings per share	$1.07*	$0.79	35%
Shares outstanding	12,000	10,000	20%

* Net income and shares outstanding are in millions, while earnings per share is always an absolute dollar amount. Dividing net income by the shares outstanding gives you the earnings per share.

Over the course of the year, Messages issued 2 million more shares. Did it acquire a competitor? Did it sell more shares to the public via an investment firm in New York? Nope. You can't tell from this chart, but in this case Messages Incorporated had 2 million stock options exercised by its management team and employees. Messages staffers essentially sold some stock that had been granted to them as compensation. Selling of this nature is not necessarily a bad thing, but something to keep your eyes on.

With those additional shares, the company's profit increase of 63 percent became, for shareholders, an increase of only 35—measured in earnings per share. (Though the company pie was much bigger this year, a few more people got a slice of it.) To calculate earnings per share, remember, you just divide the total amount of bottom-line earnings (net income) by the total number of shares outstanding. Voilà, the company had $1.07 of earnings per share (EPS) this year, versus 79 cents in EPS last year. Now you'll know what investors in our online areas are talking about when they say, "Hey, Apple Computer missed estimates by 10 cents." They didn't miss Wall Street's expectations by a mere dime, no! They missed them by 10 cents *per share*. And were that to happen to Apple, with its 126 million shares outstanding, that would translate into underperforming estimates by $12.6 million ($0.10 × 126 million). That dime sounds a lot more important now, doesn't it?

There you have Messages Incorporated's income statement for 1998 and 1999. While the company reported sales growth of 94 percent, a good deal of that growth was lost on new expenses. Company profits increased only 63 percent, and the bottom-line earnings growth for shareholders was just 35 percent. Deteriorating margins dragged down what might otherwise have been stratospheric gains, and a 20 percent jump in shares outstanding was a black eye for shareholders, too.

Quiz: The Income Statement

OK, let's see how good you are. Can you nail all seven of these questions?

1. If Messages reported revenue of $126 million in the year 2000, versus $97 million in 1999, sales would have risen how much?
   a. 15%   *b.* 30%   *c.* 43%   *d.* 130%   *e.* Who cares? All I know is this is more money than I have.

2. If cost of sales was $65 million in 2000, given $126 million in revenue for the year, what would the gross profit be?
   a. $61 million   *b.* $32 million   *c.* $191 million   *d.* $19 million   *e.* 48.41269%

3. So then, gross profit margin for 2000 would be
   a. 61%   *b.* 58%   *c.* 48%   *d.* 52%   *e.* You figure it out. You wrote this confusing book.

4. Selling, general, and administrative expenses for 2000 came in at $33 million, a 20% increase over the $27.5 million the year before. Looking at question 1 for the sales figures, in 2000, SG&A expenses relative to those in 1999 were
   a. lower   *b.* higher as a percentage of total sales   *c.* lower as a percentage of total sales   *d.* none of the above   *e.* all of the above

5. Remember that in the year 2000, Messages announced sales of $126 million. Let's say earnings for the year were $14 million. What's the company's net margin?

   a. 10.2%   *b.* 4.9%   *c.* 9.4%   *d.* 11.1%   *e.* I hate this quiz and I'm burning your damn book.

6. Given your answer to question 5, do you think Wall Street will be happy with Messages' performance in the year 2000?
   a. Very much so, yes.   *b.* Nope, it doesn't look good.   *c.* You haven't given me enough info.   *d.* I skipped the section on profit margins.   *e.* I already burned your book.

7. Messages' net income came to $14 million in the year 2000. If this great American business had 12.5 million shares outstanding, earnings per share would then be
   a. $1.05   *b.* $1.12   *c.* $1.17   *d.* $0.89
   e. My answer cannot be heard over the roar of flames.

Answers: 1. b   2. a   3. c   4. c   5. d or e   6. b or c   7. b

   In all seriousness, dear Fool, if you got any of these seven questions wrong, you should return to the beginning of this section on income statements. It's only a few pages, and getting it right might prove the difference between investing in a company with $17.4 million in net income and investing in another company with −$17.4 million in net income (known here as "net *losses*"). And compounded over the rest of your life, the gains you can expect if you understand the income statement—and the balance sheet—can be dramatic. Don't exhaust yourself trying to figure every single last thing out about a company. But yes, you should get all seven of the above questions right before proceeding.

   And once you've done so, Fool, onward! To the statement of cash flows.

STATEMENT OF CASH FLOWS

You have a firm grasp of the balance sheet; you've tackled an income statement; and now to put it all together we bring . . . the statement of cash flows. Cash flow, huh? What we'll be measuring here is the directional flow of monies into and out of Messages' business. We're tempted to play a trick on you and say something like, "This stuff is easy! You'll have it down in no time." But the truth is that cash flow statements are tricky beasts. Too many investors never look at them.

OK, so, take your first glance at Messages' statement of cash flows. Chances are, you're going to be confused as heck. But we'll get to untangling it after the full presentation. Without further ado, vvvv-walla!

MESSAGES INCORPORATED, CASH FLOWS

(In Thousands)

CASH FLOW	1999	1998	CHANGE
Cash Flow from Operating Activities			
Net income	12,880	7,900	63%
Adjustments to Reconcile Net Income to Net Cash			
Depreciation	1,200	800	150%
*Effects of Change in Operating Assets and Liabilities**			
Accounts receivable	(20,000)	(5,000)	300%
Inventory	(10,000)	(4,000)	150%
Accounts payable	3,300	2,000	65%
Accrued expenses	8,000	4,000	100%
NET CASH provided by (used in) operating activities	(4,620)	5,700	N/A

* The number represents the increase or decrease from the prior year. The parentheses or lack thereof reflects whether the item is added (no parentheses) or subtracted (with parentheses) when calculating cash flow.

This is the abridged version of the cash flow statement for Messages. The full treatment would feel like chalkboard line punishment, and while it's important, let's just stick to the top half planted before us. While it won't fetch much at the art gallery, it is certainly worth a look to see how much money came in, and how much went out, over the course of the past year. Earnings and cash flow are not the same thing. A company can report a loss in their income statement yet still have accumulated a positive net difference in cash from doing business. How so? Read on.

Net Income

The first item on this shortened statement of cash flows is *Net income*. For those with a photographic memory, or if you're simply smart enough to thumb back to the previous "Income Statement" section and find the net income figure for 1999, you will see that that figure and this figure are both indeed the same $12.88 million. If only the whole statement were that easy to grasp. Mind bender oncoming. Do not operate heavy equipment while trying to think through the remainder of this section.

Depreciation—What's That?

Below the restatement of $12.88 million in net income, you see the item *"Depreciation"* under the line *Adjustments* blah blah blah. It's listed at $1.2 million. "Depreciation" is the key word there, and generally you know that it means a sinking or declining in value. So why is $1.2 million *added* here? (*Deductions* are indicated by parentheses.) Well, because cash does not actually leave the company's coffers when depreciation is recorded.

Messages Incorporated has accounted for the declining value of all of its equipment—much as you might recognize the declining value of your sharp new sports car. However, those "expenses"—which you'll find on the balance sheet—aren't real *cash* losses; they're just value losses. The company already paid for that equipment, the cash is already gone, so the depreciating value isn't a cash loss today. The mission of the cash flow statement is to track the flow of dollar bills. Thus, we need to add back in the $1.2 million in equipment value that was deducted on the balance sheet.

You are with us, yes? OK, good. On to the next loop-de-loop on the roller coaster.

Accounts Receivable

Do you remember on the balance sheet (page 104) how accounts receivable *rose* by $20 million in 1999? If not, well, they did. And do you remember how we claimed that, even though they're listed as current assets, with the company expecting to collect the cash in the year ahead, we nevertheless took rising receivables as a sign of weakness? OK, well, here comes further explanation of that. On the cash flow statement, we're tracking the dollars in the here and now; we're studying the present flows of cash. Because Messages doesn't yet have that additional $20 million that is in "accounts receivable," we have to subtract it out of their net income. That's going to hurt. Why? Well, you see what's happened here, do you? The company announced sales of $97 million and earnings of $12.88 million. But in those sales and earnings, there are millions in cash that the company has yet to collect. If that seems like a good thing, remember that Messages has already announced to the world that it has all those sales and earnings. Collecting the money is just a formality to Wall Street; to the company, it may be a challenge—if there are products returned, refunds, or insolvent business partners. So, that additional $20 million in receivables in 1999 is significantly going to damage the present state of cash flows. Messages' business is starting to look even wobblier.

Inventory

Receivables were bad enough, but we're not yet done subtracting.

In 1999, the company showed inventory growth of $10 million, to $20 million total, if you go back and look on the balance sheet. And you guessed it. Though that inventory is listed as a current asset—since the company plans to sell it as finished product in the year ahead—it isn't yet cash. The cash flow statement, then, deducts that $10 million out of net income. And if you're thinking that's just too cruel to handle, remember that in a number of industries, businesses are unable to sell their inventory at various times. They have to dismantle it and sell it as scrap—if even that! So, the listing of inventory as an asset on the balance sheet can be as misleading as the accounts receivable figures.

Because it ain't cash yet, inventory gets subtracted out as well.

Accounts Payable and Accrued Expenses

Ahh, after all those subtractions, it's time for an addition or two. Let's sweeten up the statement by reflecting the monies that the company has saved by not yet paying all of its bills. *Accounts payable* increased $3.3 million and *Accrued expenses* grew $8 million. Both are liabilities that have yet to turn into an outflow of *cash*. You grasp that concept, yes? The cash river flows both ways. We stick net income at the top; add back depreciation; pull out all the current assets that aren't cash; add back all the current liabilities that haven't been paid—and we end up with an understanding of flow of cash through operations. Is

this company really making money? Or is it announcing earnings in the form of receivables, or riding heavy inventories—factors that aren't shown on the income statement? In the case of Messages, let's see!

Final Tallies

The end result of all our tallying falls down on the line *Net cash provided by (used in) operating activities*. This reveals whether the company wound up with more or less cash from their business operations over the course of the year. Don't look now, because in Messages' case, the results—a negative amount, as the parentheses indicate—weren't inspiring.

	1999	1998	CHANGE
NET CASH provided by (used in) operating activities	(4,620)	5,700	N/A

The company is consuming more cash than it is taking in. In 1998, cash flows were positive, by $5.7 million. But in 1999, they got loose with their receivables, let inventories spiral up, and ended up with negative cash flow of $4.62 million.

This should send flags and flares in the air and sound sirens. Negative cash flows are not necessarily the end of the world. At times, companies *want* to increase inventories. For example, a retail manufacturing company has to increase its product count before Christmas. They don't want to sell out of Elmo dolls, so they mass-produce them. And when the balance sheet for that quarter arrives, the company may show a tremendous rise in inventories, yet a rise that isn't problematic. This is where your knowledge of the business comes into play. Not all of this stuff is quantitative.

All of that said, more often than not, rising receivables (rising more quickly than sales) and bulging inventories are problematic, and you'll want to avoid companies (particularly unproven companies) with negative cash flows from operating activities.

Other Sections on the Cash Flow Statement

The cash flow statement doesn't end with operating activities, but you can. The two remaining sections on a cash flow statement—investing and financing activities—aren't critical to investing. We can blow them off for now, though they're fairly straightforward and are also largely hooked into the balance sheet. But don't ignore this statement altogether. The results of cash flows from operating activities are critical.

It's Time for a Parting Quiz!

OK, let's see how well you know your stuff.

1. Net income from the statement of cash flows will match net income from the income statement.   T   F
2. On the cash flow statement, depreciation is subtracted from net income.   T   F
3. Accounts receivable and inventory items in the cash flow statement are taken from the income statement.   T   F
4. A negative amount (reflected by parentheses) on the operating activities line shows that a

company spent more money to run their business than they made from it.   T   F

Answers: 1. T   2. F   3. F   4. T

To clarify 2 and 3: Depreciation (2) is actually added back to cash. The accounts receivable and inventory numbers (3) are drawn from the balance sheet, not the income statement.

OK, so this wasn't as painful as expected, was it? We've just successfully covered the balance sheet, income statement, and statement of cash flows. If you're like many, there's a pretty good chance you had no idea what payables were when you started, or why inventory growth at a business can be a bad thing, or how to calculate earnings per share, or whether a company with positive earnings on the income statement was actually making money over on the statement of cash flows.

Now, we don't expect all of this to have formally settled in, finally congealed, and be unremovable from your head, barring surgery or a bad skiing accident. For many of you, this is just the beginning, and you really should take an hour or two and go back over this chapter to be absolutely certain that you grasped it all. From here, you're going to want to get your hands on the financial statements of some companies out there. How about Starbucks, Nike, America Online, Nordstrom, and TCBY—that yogurt place? It might be interesting to see how they're doing, eh? Just grab their phone number from a product label or store clerk, give their investor relations department a call, have them send you an investor's packet, and sort through the statements. You'll be startled. Not all businesses are rock solid. Some are greatly mismanaged. Yes, some of the very products and services you use are managed by people who may end up destroying the business. Of course, for most others, studying them, following them, and investing in them will prove a greatly profitable venture for you in the years ahead.

Now, get your hands on your calculator, take a few deep breaths, run a lap around the block, call your uncle and brag to him how much you know, fix a large glass of lemonade, take another couple of deep breaths, make sure you're still holding that calculator, and get ready for the next chapter. 'Cause when you turn the page, we're going to start learning how to value entire busi-nesses and determine which companies will make for great investments and which won't. Re-member, had your family invested $3,000 into Coca-Cola in 1919, when it went public, and then followed the company's financial reports and rightly held on to the stock throughout, your stock would be valued above $300 million—after paying down all taxes. Wow.

You'll want to learn how to value companies. You'll want to find the next Coca-Cola and Micro-soft. And, who knows, the next ones may be Coca-Cola and Microsoft. Let's see!

CHAPTER 8

Now, What Do I Want to *See* in Those Numbers?

By now, you're probably amazed at your own Foolishness. You've balanced your own budget, paid down short-term debt, and put a solid savings plan into play. You've even split your long-term savings between an index fund and the Foolish Four. You now have a strong base for the beginning of your investing career, or for your entire investing career. You're comfortable now, yes? And it wasn't nearly as hard as that college buddy of yours who turned investment broker told you it would be, was it?

So, now it's time to ask, "Where do I go from here, and why have I just spent two days working my way through all those numbers?" Simple. Because you want to do more than just beat the market. Yes, the index fund and the Foolish Four are plenty profitable, but even after you learned how to manage them you kept reading and scribbling and learning?

You discovered that you like this stuff, that you want to learn about business. You want to value individual stocks. You want to determine whether or not to buy more of the stock of your employer. You want to own the greatest companies on the planet, hold them for decades, and turn a couple of thousand bucks into a couple of million bucks by the time you retire, or your kids retire, or their kids. Well, to get there, you've already found that you only need to add stuff like 6 + 17 successfully (23). You only need to know how to multiply 12 × 2.6 properly (31.2). And how tough *is* it to divide 178 by 14 with a calculator (12.7)? Sure, you'll occasionally need to take a couple of square roots, like the square root of 2.5, but a calculator can do that for you in a jiffy (1.58). The future of your financial situation rests more in those calculations than in working triple overtime next month or inheriting a whole mess of money from your great-uncle Cornelius. So, is it time for you to begin investing in individual stocks aside from the Foolish Four? Let's see.

Three Quick Quizzes

Quiz #1: Why invest in individual stocks?

a. Because I might make a lot of money in the next year.
b. Because there's no other alternative. I have to be in stocks.
c. Because if I'm methodical, I can beat the index funds, which beat the majority of managed funds, and individual stocks of great companies mixed with the Foolish Four approach makes great sense.

Your answer here is *c*. Chances are you won't make much money at all in your first year of investing. And there certainly are alternatives to common stock. Index funds are a great way to begin investing. Nope, we believe the right answer is that, with method and resolve, private investors can handily outperform the market over the long term.

Quiz #2: Why analyze individual companies?

a. To understand how business works and to locate the best investment options.
b. Because I have to; I'm paying $40,000 per year to get this freakin' MBA.
c. I don't have to; I can make enough money just buying hot stocks and selling them a month later, doing my Wise stock chart analysis and watching the phases of the moon.

The Foolish reply is *a*. We're making these too easy. We obviously don't think that you need an MBA to be introduced to business, and we think it's a very bad idea to apply to investing what is called "technical analysis"—studying the movement of the stock price with charts rather than understanding the merits of the business for the long term.

Quiz #3: Pick your preferred way of life:

a. Spending 30 minutes every eighteen months on investing, mixing the Foolish Four with an index fund, smiling at all the hullabaloo over managed mutual funds, and going on with life.
b. Spending a few hours a week researching companies, starting an investment club with your entire family or a close group of friends, and trying to beat the historical 23 percent annual returns of the Foolish Four.
c. Spending 2.5 minutes a year, buying the index fund, and knowing you'll beat the majority of mutual funds on the planet.

As you probably guessed, there's no wrong answer to this one. It's just a matter of personal choice. So let's now try to determine whether you'd be happy with *b*, researching companies, perhaps being a part of an investment club, and trying to outdo the Foolish Four.

Can I Really Beat the Pros?

Here's Quiz #4 for you, if you like: *Is it really possible for an individual investor to outperform the Wall Street professionals, who manage billions of dollars?* We'll answer this one: Simply, obviously, easily yes. They may have teams of researchers; they may buy up reams of business information; they may even have the power to dramatically affect (read: manipulate) pricing in the marketplace over any short period of time, but despite all this, the big mutual fund families and brokerage houses ain't ten-ton gorillas, and you ain't their banana.

Bigger isn't better in investing. If you were managing a $500 million mutual fund, you'd probably have a lot of anxious shareholders holding you accountable every week. And you'd have a host of SEC guidelines to abide by—which would dictate that you couldn't invest in just five great companies (like General Electric, Microsoft, Coca-Cola, Merck, and Intel). No, you'd have to buy dozens of companies, and you'd probably feel compelled to buy hundreds of companies. If you were willing to trade frenetically and generate huge commissions, big Wall Street firms would reward you for those commissions. But would that necessarily be beneficial to your investors? Their management fees would rise; their taxes would rise; and their overall return would most likely go down! This is precisely the reason that at least 80 percent of all mutual funds consistently underperform the market—*every year.*

Believe it or not, when it comes to beating the market, the big institutional investor is at a substantial *dis*advantage to the small private investor, for reasons related both to how *they're* compensated (can you say, *"conflict of interest?"*), *and* for the logistical nightmares they face in trying to manage such large sums of money.

What You Want to See on on a Balance Sheet

If you're committed to finding great companies and investing in them, it's time for us to state clearly what you should actively seek out on America's financial statements. We've talked about inventories and receivables. We've championed those businesses that avoid long-term debt and increase profit margins. Here now is what you should hope to find when you're studying the report of a company that you're considering for investment. (This will also effectively serve as a review of the terms and numbers introduced in the last chapter.)

Once again, we're going to call on the help of our fictitious friends at Messages Incorporated to aid us in our explanation. Below is the company's balance sheet.

MESSAGES INCORPORATED BALANCE SHEET
YEAR 1999 COMPARED TO 1998

| | (In Thousands) | | |
	1999	1998	CHANGE
Assets			
Current Assets			
Cash and equivalents	24,000	20,000	20%
Accounts receivable	34,000	14,000	143%
Inventory	20,000	10,000	100%
Prepaid expenses	1,500	1,000	50%
TOTAL CURRENT ASSETS	79,500	45,000	77%

(continued)

| | (In Thousands) | | |
	1999	1998	CHANGE
Fixed Assets			
Property and equipment subtotal	12,000	6,000	100%
Less depreciation	1,200	800	50%
TOTAL FIXED ASSETS	10,800	5,200	108%
TOTAL ASSETS	90,300	50,200	80%
Liabilities			
Current Liabilities			
Accounts payable	6,500	3,200	103%
Accrued expenses	18,000	10,000	80%
TOTAL CURRENT LIABILITIES	24,500	13,200	86%
Long-term debt	0	0	0%
TOTAL LIABILITIES	24,500	13,200	86%

Here's what you should be looking for . . .

1. Lots of Cash

Cash-rich companies don't have trouble funding growth, paying down debts, and doing whatever the heck it is they need to, to build the business. Increasing cash and equivalents is good. Messages has $24 million in cash.

2. Very Little or No Long-Term Debt

We don't like companies that grow at a healthy pace by borrowing a lot of money. The risk here is that today's successes are compromising future opportunities—when they'll have to pay down that debt. Certainly, long-term debt *can* be used intelligently. But in our experience, the companies in the strongest position are those that don't need to borrow to fund the development of their business. We certainly prefer those companies with a great deal more cash than long-term debt, for obvious reasons. Messages has no long-term debt.

3. Low Amounts of Inventory

Fools prefer companies that don't have to carry much inventory. The products should race out the door. One way to measure this is to study the company's total number of days' worth of inventory on hand. It's a simple calculation: Just (*a*) divide the total amount of sales in one quarter of business by the total amount of inventory. Now (*b*) divide 90 days by that number (90 days is the total number of days in a three-month period). This is the company's "inventory turnover." Let's check Messages Incorporated. Here are the numbers you'll need:

sales during the most recent quarter:
$39 million

inventory: $20 million

So, we (*a*) divide $39 million by $20 million, and come up with _____. Yes, 1.95. Now we divide 90 days by 1.95, and we see that Messages can turn over its inventory in 46 days. Was that clear? We hope so. It's a useful calculation to run, whose trend you should track over time.

What we want here is a lot of sales and just a little bit of inventory. This means that the product is hot and that the company speedily rolls new inventory out the door. Ideally, we like to see companies with less than fifteen days of inventory. With forty-six, Messages doesn't cut the mustard here. But if the number is trending downward over time, that's forgivable. Impressive, even. Finally, it's important to remember that different industries often have different "norms" as far as inventory (and accounts receivable, our next section) practices are concerned.

4. Low Accounts Receivable

At first, it might seem a good thing to have a lot of people out there owing you money. But if you aren't charging much or any interest on that money—as is the case with many company receivables—this is distinctly a bad thing. Accounts receivable rising faster than sales growth often indicates a softness in product demand, since companies are selling their stuff and allowing buyers more generous terms of payment. This can inflate sales and earnings, while substantially harming cash flows. The result can be misstated profitability. We're going to run a very

similar equation to the previous one on inventory as we try to determine how many days of receivables the company is carrying.

Thus, (*a*) divide sales of $39 million for the quarter by accounts receivable of $34 million. You'll get 1.15. Now (*b*) divide 90 days by that figure to obtain the total days of receivables. Your answer is ____. Yes, 78 days of receivables. We look for companies with less than thirty days of outstanding accounts receivable. At seventy-eight days, Messages would appear to be misstating sales and earnings—what is called "stuffing the sales channel" with product that they aren't being paid for. Flashing red light here. Though now is where your business knowledge comes in again. Perhaps most of Messages' sales are in Japan, where businesses typically take ninety days to pay. While 78 days is unusual and worth caution in *most* cases, there are exceptions.

5. High Accounts Payable

This one runs contrary to our thoughts about short-term debt in your *personal* finances, where it can be an extremely bad thing, because you'd pay a high interest rate on that debt, 16–18 percent for most credit cards. But this isn't true in the business world, where accounts payable do not penalize the company with meaningful interest payments. Business contracts have a provision for the number of days a company can put off payments, and the best businesses can put off these payments for many days. As we just learned, Japanese businesses are notorious for batting expenses as far away from today as possible. We prefer companies that have a near one-to-one relationship between accounts payable and accounts receivable. In the case of Messages, we aren't going to be happy. The company has $34 million in receivables (money yet to come in) and only $6.5 million in payables (money yet to go out). Hey, this must be good—$27.5 million more coming in than going out. Good, right? Ah, but the company has already accounted for the $34 million in receivables even though it hasn't been paid yet, so there's no upside here. Additionally, because high interest is not being paid to the company on its receivables, it is in a disadvantageous position. And it doesn't yet have that cash to work with or invest in its business. Another red light flashes.

6. A Low Foolish Flow Ratio

Our final measurement is the Foolish Flow Ratio. Here, as you learned earlier, you simply subtract out cash from current assets, then divide that figure by current liabilities. You'll prefer the flow to be below 1.25, which would indicate that the company is aggressively managing its cash flows. When this ratio is low, you know that inventories are down, receivables are down, and payables are up. This is a perfect mix when a company has loads of cash and no long-term debt. Why? Because it indicates that while the company (1) could afford to pay bills today and (2) doesn't have to worry about rising receivables, it is in enough of a position of power to hold off its payments *and* to collect all dues up front.

Messages has current assets of $79.5 million and $24 million in cash. So, subtract the latter from the former, to arrive at $55.5 million. Messages has $24.5 million in current liabilities. Divide the $55.5 million in noncash assets by the

$24.5 million of liabilities, and you'll arrive at a flow ratio of 2.26. We consider this high. Another red light whirs on the balance sheet. It must be noted here, however, that larger companies generally have lower flow ratios due to their ability to negotiate from strength. Thus, don't penalize your favorite dynamically growing small-cap too much for a higher Foolish Flow Ratio.

Are any of our balance sheet guidelines hard-and-fast rules? Nope. We can imagine reasonable exceptions for each. As mentioned earlier, a company can run inventories very high relative to sales in a quarter, as it prepares for the big Christmas rush. Wouldn't want too few moon boots going into mid-December, right? So, inventories may be seasonally inflated (or deflated), in anticipation of great oncoming demand. And accounts receivable might be a tad high simply by virtue of when a company closes its quarter. Perhaps the very next day, 75 percent of those receivables will arrive by wire transfer. Here, the calendar timing of the quarterly announcement hurt your company. And rising payables can, of course, be a very bad thing. If the company is avoiding short-term bills because it can't afford to pay them, look out! Finally, flow ratios can run high for all the reasons listed above.

Having qualified our assertions, we still believe that the best businesses have such high ongoing demand that inventories race out the door, product distributors pay for the merchandise up front, the company has enough cash to pay off its payables immediately but doesn't, and future growth hasn't been compromised by present borrowing. Look to companies like Coca-Cola and Microsoft to find these qualities fully realized.

WHAT YOU WANT TO SEE ON THE INCOME STATEMENT

Once again we turn to our friends at Messages Incorporated to investigate what we should hope to find on the income statement of any company whose stock we're considering.

MESSAGES INCORPORATED, INCOME

(In Thousands)

	1999	1998	CHANGE
Income			
Revenue	97,000	50,000	94%
Less cost of sales (goods)	46,500	21,000	121%
GROSS PROFIT	50,500	29,000	74%
Operating Expenses			
Selling/general/administration	27,500	12,000	129%
Research/development	4,500	6,000	(25%)
TOTAL OPERATING EXPENSES	32,000	18,000	78%
INCOME FROM OPERATIONS	18,500	11,000	68%
Interest income	1,080	1,000	8%
Total income before taxes	19,580	12,000	63%
Less income taxes	6,700	4,100	63%
NET INCOME	12,880	7,900	63%

Here's what you should be looking for . . .

1. High Revenue Growth

You'll want to see substantial and consistent top-line growth, indicating that the planet wants more and more of what your company has to offer. Annual revenue growth in excess of 8–10 percent per year for companies with more than $5 billion in yearly sales is ideal. Smaller com-panies ought to be growing sales 20 to 30 percent or more annually. Messages posted 94 percent sales growth for 1994. Outstanding.

2. Cost of Sales Under Wraps

The *Cost of sales (goods)* figure should be growing no faster than the *Revenue* line. Ideally, your com-pany will be meeting increasing demand by sup-plying products at the same cost as before. In fact, best of all, if your company can cut the cost of goods sold during periods of rapid growth, bravo! It indicates that the business can get its materials or provide its services cheaper in higher volume. In Messages' case, cost of goods sold rose by 121 percent in 1999, outpacing sales growth. A red light just blinked from the income statement.

3. Gross Margins Above 40 Percent

We prefer to invest in companies with extraordinarily high gross margins—again, calculated by (a) subtracting cost of goods sold (cost of sales) from total sales, to get gross profit, then (b) dividing gross profit by total sales. That line was a brainful, eh? OK, let's check out Messages.

Sales	$97.0 million
Cost of goods sold	$46.5 million
Gross profit	$50.5 million
Gross margin	_____

Getcher calculator buzzing! Divide gross profit by total sales to get gross margins. For Messages, you'll end up with 52 percent. This indicates that there is only moderate material expense to the Messages business. It's a fairly "light" business. Very nice.

Not all businesses are this light, of course. Many manufacturing companies have a hard time hitting this target. Does that mean you should never invest in them? No. Does it mean you should have a slight bias against them in favor of other higher-margin companies? Yeah.

4. Research and Development Costs on the Rise

Yep, we actually want our companies to spend more and more on research every year, particularly those in high technology and pharmaceuticals. This is the biggest investment in the future that a company can make. And the main reason businesses spend less on R&D one year than the last is that they need the money elsewhere. Not a desirable situation to be in. Look for R&D costs rising. Of course, though, not all companies spend much on R&D. A kiss is still a kiss, a Coke is still a Coke.

Generally, the best way to go about measuring R&D is as a percentage of sales. You just divide R&D by revenue. You want to see this figure trend upward, or at least hold steady.

5. A 34-Percent-Plus Tax Rate

Make sure that the business is paying the full rate to Uncle Sam. Due to previous earnings losses, some companies can carry forward up to a few years of tax credits. While this is a wonderful thing for them, it can cause a misrepresentation of the true bottom-line growth. If companies are paying less than 34 percent per year in taxes, you should tax their income at that rate, to see through to the real growth. Messages paid exactly 34 percent in taxes on earnings in 1999. Brush by this one, then.

6. Profit Margins Above 7 Percent and Rising

How much money is your company making for every dollar of sales? The profit margin—net income divided by sales—tells you what real merit there is to the business. We prefer businesses with more than $5 billion in sales to run profit margins above 7 percent, and those with less than $5 billion to sport profit margins of above 10 percent. Why go through all the work of running a business if you can't derive substantial profits out of it for your shareholders? In the case of Messages Incorporated, net margins are running at 13.3 percent ($12.88 million earnings ÷ $97 million in sales = 13.3%). Excellent.

Another way of thinking about this is that in a capitalistic world, high margins—highly profitable business—lure competition. Others will move in and attempt to undercut a company's prices. So companies that can post high margins are *winning;* competition is failing to undercut them.

WHAT YOU WANT TO SEE ON THE CASH FLOW STATEMENT

Far and away the most important thing to find out from the cash flow statement is whether the line *Net cash provided by (used in) operating activities* is positive or negative. If a company is cash flow negative, it means that these guys are burning capital to keep their business going. This is excusable over short periods of time, but by the time companies make it into the public marketplace, they should be generating profits off their business. If a company you are studying is cash flow negative, it's critical that you know why that's occurring. Perhaps it has to ramp up inventories for the quarter, or had a short not-to-be-repeated struggle with receivables. Some companies are best off burning capital for a short-term period while they ramp up for huge business success in the future. But if the only reason you can find is that their business isn't

successful and doesn't look to be gaining momentum, you should steer clear of that investment.

You now have a fine checklist of things to look for (and hope for) on the balance sheet, income statement, and statement of cash flows. Few companies are ideal enough to conform to our every wish. But we believe that if, in your investments, you deviate from the superior qualities above, you should have a clear understanding of why you're doing so. The best businesses show financial statements strengthening from one year to the next. For smaller companies with great promise and for larger companies hitting a single bad bump in the road, shortcomings in the financial statements can be explained away for a brief period. But when you do accept these explanations, be sure you're getting the facts. You want to thoroughly understand why there has been a slipup and do your best to assess whether or not it's quickly remediable.

All of that noted, let's practice again on some calculations. In the next chapter, we'll begin digging in closer toward valuation. You'll note that, up until now, we've merely outlined the ideal characteristics, without ever putting a price tag on them. That's coming. But first, let's make sure you've nailed down our basic concepts.

Quiz: Basic Concepts

1. Assume that the S&P 500 rose 10.29% last year. Which of the following would you expect to be the performance of the average managed mutual fund for the year?
   a. 12.49%   *b.* 19.42%   *c.* 10.34%   *d.* 9.11%

2. Which of the following situations is preferable?

	CASH	LONG-TERM DEBT
a. Loperfido World	$145 million	$11.4 million
b. Jefe Airlines	$891 million	$3.9 billion
c. Befumo Beachwear	$11 million	$4.6 million
d. Hoop-It-Up Inc.	$321 million	$0

3. What is Befumo Beachwear's gross margin, and do you like it?

Sales	$85 million
Cost of goods sold	$35 million
Gross profit	$50 million
Gross margin	_____

4. Calculate the Foolish Flow Ratio for Hoop-It-Up Inc. *Ist das gut?*

Cash	$321 million
Current assets	$853 million
Current liabilities	$615 million
Foolish Flow Ratio	_____

5. What is the sales growth for Loperfido World?

SALES, 1997	SALES, 1998	SALES GROWTH
$584 million	$618 million	_____%

6. Given the size of Loperfido World, is that sales growth substantial enough to put you up on your office desk, cheering?
   Yes   No

7. Take a look at Loperfido's growth in research and development. Is this a good trend?

1994	$9.4 million
1995	$12.5 million
1996	$22.4 million
1997	$34.5 million
1998	$51.3 million

Yes   No

8. Calculate Loperfido's net profit margins for 1998.

Sales	$618 million
Cost of goods sold	$246 million
R&D expenses	$51 million
SG&A expenses	$237 million
Total operating expenses	$534 million
Total operating income before taxes	$84 million
Provision for taxes	$31 million
Net income	$53 million
Earnings per share (EPS)	$0.58
Shares outstanding	$91.4 million
Profit margins	_____

9. In question number 8, do you understand every single term?
   Yes   No

10. If you knew that gross margins for Loperfido's *in 1997* were 46.4%, what would you be thinking while looking over the *1998* statement?
    a. Gasp, gross margins have remained the same, and that's not a good thing.
    b. OK, so we're making money out here. Good job!
    c. I haven't a clue what you're talking about, Fool.
    d. I'm not happy about this; gross margins are falling.

Answers: 1. *d*   2. *d*   3. 58.8%. Yes.   4. 0.87. Yes. Good.   5. 5.8%   6. No   7. Yes   8. 8.6%   9. Yes   10. *d*

Without being too preachy, we're telling you that if you got any of these ten questions wrong, you should work your way back through this chapter. It will take you only an hour or so, and it might result in a substantial difference in your savings ten years from today.

And if you nailed them all, Fool on. Let's go fishing for some companies!

CHAPTER 9

Locating Winning Stocks

FINDING THE MARKET-BEATING GIANTS

Remember when we sent you searching through your refrigerator and your neighborhood, looking for great businesses? Well, of course that's the first place we search for *market-beating companies*—among those businesses that sit all around you. Giant consumer businesses that provide us with the stuff we need in our daily lives often make for wonderful investments. Campbell Soup? That's been a great investment. The Gap? Another great investment. Coca-Cola? Perhaps the greatest business and greatest investment of the twentieth century. Truly, most of the great investments you'll make in your lifetime are no more than an arm's length away.

For this reason, it bewilders Fools that so many Americans rely on hot tips from phone-calling brokers and cocktail party "gooroos," that so many people invest in obscure mining com-panies or shady limited partnerships. They've been misled into thinking that obscurity, not simplicity, is the mother of ingenuity and great profits. Pshaw! Among Warren Buffett's key holdings are Coca-Cola, Gillette, Disney, and American Express. Buffett did not create his holding company empire by searching for obscure businesses about which he knew very little, hoping to get lucky. Instead, he looked around at the products and services he knew something about, used simple mathematical principles to help him evaluate the merit of the business, and treated investing as a lifelong endeavor. Want a reason to get out your calculator and do a little homework every time one of the companies that you encounter every day catches your eye? Berkshire Hathaway, an insurance corporation that is essentially an investment company for Buffett, is valued at over $90 billion as of this writing. Let's see just how we can follow this example.

WHAT SHOULD YOU BE LOOKING FOR?

1. Consumer Brand

The first question you'll need to ask yourself is, "Is this a name-brand company?" There are literally hundreds of products and dozens of companies that provide you with brand-name stuff—from soda to antifreeze, from newspapers to personal computers, from cold medicine to dairy products. You'll want to start by listing the favorite products you use, much as you did here previously. Then note the parent company of the product. Here are five examples. After them, list six of your own.

PRODUCT	COMPANY
Doritos	Pepsi
Windows95	Microsoft
ESPN	Disney
American Express card	American Express
Saturn	General Motors
_____	_____
_____	_____
_____	_____
_____	_____
_____	_____
_____	_____

2. Best in the Business

Now we're going to ask you to make a qualitative judgment call. Are the companies that you've listed above the best in their business? Possibly, you have

no idea. But guess what? That's the second challenge facing you. For now, just list the lead competition of each of your companies. Do not worry about who competes directly with the product you like; instead, concentrate on the largest direct competitor of the company. What do we mean by that? Well, we started by listing Doritos. We then noted the company, Pepsi. But now, we place to their right their most substantial competitor—Coca-Cola—which does not make any snack food products. We're looking for the largest threat to the entire business. In that case, Coke is it.

Please list what you consider to be the largest competitor to each business you've listed.

COMPANY	COMPETITION
Pepsi	Coca-Cola
Microsoft	IBM
Disney	Time Warner
American Express	Visa
General Motors	Chrysler
_____	_____
_____	_____
_____	_____
_____	_____
_____	_____
_____	_____

Now think through your list again. Do you think you have the premier brand between the two? In _our_ case, we're going to supplant Pepsi with Coca-Cola, even though we know that might make a lot of people unhappy at Pepsi headquarters in Texas. At present, Coca-Cola is the leading brand. Please circle only the six top brands on your list.

Now, heck, let's try to shorten our list.

3. Repeat Business

From here you'll want to narrow your list down to only those companies that you regularly do business with or come into contact with. What you will find is that typically the very best businesses on the planet are those that constantly deal with their customers and repeatedly make a positive impression. The single greatest example of this is Coca-Cola, which gets free advertising each and every time you open up a big red can. Microsoft greets millions of people each day when they flip on their computer. You almost can't watch athletics on television or even walk around any city without being submerged in Nike swooooshes. And these have naturally been among the better companies to invest in. They make contact with their customers every month, week, or, ideally, day.

Please now shorten your list to include only those companies that meet your eye at least once a month. Cross those that don't make it off your list.

COMPANY

Coca-Cola

Microsoft

Disney

American Express

General Motors

_____

_____

_____

_____

_____

_____

Now, you have our five stocks and a collection of your own. Let's run a few numbers!

4. Profit Margins Above 7 Percent

Aha, remember profit margins? Among these very large consumer businesses, we're going to demand profit margins of at least 7 percent. This means that, after taxes, they make seven cents in earnings on every $1 of sales. We don't want to hitch our wagons to businesses that haven't figured out ways to generate substantial profits. When a businessman buys a major-league baseball team, he wants the value of that team to increase through the sale of more season tickets, more hot dogs and soda, more T-shirts and ball caps. The value of the team increases as the profits increase. So, too, with your investment in a public company. So let's make sure your chosen companies are earning at least 7 cents on every dollar.

How?

Three ways: (1) Sign online to The Motley Fool and ask. It's free. (2) Call up your full-service or discount broker and ask. (3) Call the company directly, with the phone number off product labels, and ask their investor relations department what the company's profit margins are. That's what they're there for, so don't hesitate.

We did the first one, and here's what we came up with.

COMPANY	PROFIT MARGIN
Coca-Cola	22%
Microsoft	28%
Disney	8%
American Express	12%
~~General Motors~~	~~3.6%~~
_____	_____
_____	_____
_____	_____
_____	_____
_____	_____
_____	_____

Lookie there, GM is scratched out, four of our five businesses are still alive. It almost makes you wonder if we knew the characteristics in advance of our submissions! OK, so how many companies are remaining from your original list?

5. More Cash Than Debt

We also don't want to invest in companies that are forced to shoulder loads of long-term debt to fund new ventures. This is perhaps the trickiest of all our demands, since in many cases, larger companies can borrow money at very low rates.

Additionally, there are instances where companies pay out billions of dollars in acquisitions to maximize future growth, feeling very strongly that eliminating the debt won't be difficult. When Disney acquired Capital Cities/ABC, which owned ESPN as well, it did so believing that in the decades ahead it could pay down that debt with the substantial monies made from those businesses.

So, it almost seems unfair to cross Disney off the list, just because today it has more debt than cash. But we're looking for the *strongest* consumer businesses on the planet. In most cases, they have so much cash saved up that they don't have to borrow for acquisitions. Additionally, they're so aggressively run that they don't like to ever think they'd have to spend a fortune to buy out a competing or adjacent business. We're going to stick to our guns and cross off those large consumer businesses that have more debts outstanding than moola in the bank.

And how do you determine how much cash and how much debt your selections have? Follow the same suggested steps above: (1) Fool, (2) broker, (3) company. OK, excellent, you got the information. Draw a line through any that don't meet the criterion of more savings than borrowed money:

COMPANY	CASH	DEBT
Coca-Cola	$1.9 billion	$949 million
Microsoft	$9.0 billion	$0
~~Disney~~	~~$1.1 billion~~	~~$12.8 billion~~
American Express	$8.4 billion (equity)	$6.3 billion
_____	_____	_____
_____	_____	_____
_____	_____	_____
_____	_____	_____
_____	_____	_____

6. Past Performance

This final one is truly contrary because we live in a world where everywhere legal disclaimers must state that "past performance is no guarantee of future results." It seems some corporate executives got a little bold with their predictions for growth, and some activist shareholders felt that was unfair, and some enterprising lawyers found ways to profit off the debate. The consequence has been an ever so slight move away from believing that great companies remain great over time, while weak businesses often weaken. We think it makes a good deal of sense to know exactly how well companies have performed when you invest in them.

Certainly there are damaged businesses that, after a difficult decade, turn everything around. Our online portfolio's greatest investment to date, Iomega Corporation, turned everything around when General Electric–trained management took over in 1994. The stock rose more than 1,000 percent over the next three years, after a dismal preceding decade. Yes, there are exceptions. But a good general point of reference is how well the company has done over the past ten years. We like to see market-beating performance.

So how do you figure how well your companies have done over the past ten years? You got it: (1) Fool, (2) broker, (3) company. You got the numbers already? Great. Fill 'em in!

COMPANY	10-YEAR TOTAL PERFORMANCE
S&P 500	+197%
Coca-Cola	+1,300%
Microsoft	+6,400%
American Express	+176%
_____	_____
_____	_____
_____	_____
_____	_____
_____	_____

We do not think it's a good idea to cross companies off this list unless they've dramatically underperformed the S&P 500. Chances are, if the business is as strong as the first five items would indicate, the company's stock has been on fire lately. In fact, as of this writing, American Express—the one company on our list that has underperformed the market over the past ten years—has tripled in value over the past three years, blasting ahead of the market. So, past-ten-year performance is important just to provide you with some context. It's not a must.

Concluding Thoughts on Market-Beating Giants

Let's take a look at the final three stocks that made it through our Foolish Gauntlet of Five, Microsoft, Coca-Cola, and American Express. Each of these businesses is familiar to almost every American; each is best of breed in its industry; each has frequently repeated contact with its customers; each has healthy profit margins; none has more debt than cash; and all have performed remarkably over the last five years, with only American Express slipping up and underperforming the market for the decade.

The reason these are great stocks and great companies is that the principles outlined above make sense. These companies generate extraordinary earnings by serving people across the planet on a regular basis. With any stock on your beginning list of five that made it through the gauntlet, think very seriously about doing more research on the business and adding it to your portfolio for the long run if it passes muster. The very best place for you to start—and possibly finish—as an investor in common stocks is with those companies that you and everyone know, that you believe provide useful products and ser-vices, that are fiscally responsible, and that have been successful.

With a bit of money in an index fund, a bit of money in the Foolish Four, and a bit of money in large-capitalization consumer heavies, we don't necessarily think you will ever need anything else in your investment portfolio. With these, you'll be invested in the five hundred companies on the S&P Index; you'll have four multinational giants with billions of dollars in sales; and you'll have a handful of name-brand giants pumping out growth for you across the globe.

Why go anywhere else? Well, of course . . . to learn more and to seek even better opportunities. From here, that will mean smaller companies with substantially greater risk but enormous possibility for reward. Beyond this point lie trapdoors and treasure chests. Proceed at your own risk.

FINDING SMALL-CAP GROWTH STOCKS

You're a glutton for this stuff, eh?

One of The Fool's favorite dishes happens to be investing in smaller companies. Of all nations, America most champions the start-up entrepreneur and the small business. Small businesses in America continue to create more jobs than conglomerates ("upsizing" in the face of so much downsizing), and the growth in new technologies has only increased the desire to build better mousetraps and solve the various problems that face us every day—among them, pollution, hunger, disease, despair, and complacency.

Large companies can have a way of plodding on with automatic business models, aspiring to monopolistic control far more than concerning themselves with designing solutions for a better world. That's often the responsibility of their smaller brethren. Dynamic bantamweight companies in the United States pop up to build new technologies, provide services at less expense, and create innovative products that no conglomerate would bother with. It is these smaller companies that have historically provided the strongest investment returns on the U.S. markets, as they can exhibit a rate of growth in earnings that blows away larger companies. Small-capitalization businesses do bring with them the ongoing possibility of disintegration and bankruptcy. But they also are many Fools' favorite fare because, find the right one or two small companies and your portfolio can explode on the upside. America Online, an absolute monster stock for the Fool Portfolio, has appreciated over 900 percent during a three-year period, growth that did extraordinary things to our initial investment of $5,000. How did America Online do it? It started with a small base of sales and exploded them by attracting millions of new subscribers.

But finding great small companies that turn into great big companies isn't easy. It often feels like looking for your best friend among seventy-five thousand fans at the latest boring Super Bowl. If you haven't been given any clues about where to search, you'll be embarking on a nightmare journey. Ah, but here we aim to provide you with some of those clues. Thankfully, many of the same principles that turned up the greatest large companies (consumer familiarity, profitability, past performance) hold true for superior small-caps. But other qualities become more important: How big is too big? How fast should sales be growing? What indications are there that management is solid? These and other questions are critical.

To help answer them, Fools use a few simple screens to narrow the field of over ten thousand

public companies to a few dozen with the potential to blast out their business reach. Throughout this section, we'll be using Messages Incorporated to examine what to look for, and we've left space for you to start evaluating companies of your own choosing as well. We'll be using eight filters, or "screens," and again the aim is to help your eyes focus in on what counts and to narrow the field of ten thousand fillies to just a few powerful steeds.

Screen #1: Market Cap Under $1 Billion

Foolish small-cap investing looks for certain preliminary features in a company that make it *just right*—not too big and not too small. Too big, and the potential for significant return on investment may have passed. Too small, and the company may not have the critical mass to stay competitive and grow. This first screen is all about market capitalization—or total company value—which we presented earlier. Refer back there to see if you got all the quiz questions right! For you slackers, market cap is simply the stock price multiplied by the total number of outstanding shares. You can get this last number from the company's income statement. Here are the numbers for Messages. Perhaps you'd like to try this out with one of your own companies:

	SHARE PRICE	TOTAL SHARES	MARKET CAP
Messages Incorporated	$24	12 million	$288 million
Your company	___	___	___

What we're looking for here is stocks with a market capitalization under $1 billion.

Screen #2: Sales Below $200 Million

To further keep us among the properly sized small public businesses, we look to companies with sales below $200 million per year, which are therefore generally undiscovered by Wall Street. Because institutional investors have so much money to invest, they can't buy shares of smaller companies without either buying the company outright or putting their eggs in so many different baskets that they can't keep an eye on 1 percent of them. Thus, smaller investors have a chance to get in before the big fellas do. And if your instincts and research are right, these companies will continue to grow to the size that institutions can buy into. When that happens, you have the simple principle of supply and demand at work. Huge money pours in, the number of purchasable shares remains the same, and the price will rise—sometimes dramatically.

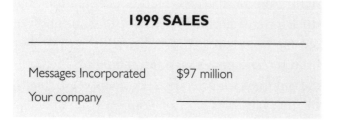

1999 SALES

Messages Incorporated	$97 million
Your company	

Screen #3: Share Price Above $5

Five-dollar stocks can seem awfully attractive. After all, you can buy more shares! The reality is, of course, that no matter how many shares of stock you have, you'll have made the same dollar investment. And if you have 1,000 shares of a $3 stock that falls to $1 per share, that's far more painful than holding 150 shares of a $20 stock that falls to $15. *The total dollar investment is what matters most.*

So, why avoid companies with stocks trading under $5 per share? Because many of them got there for a bad reason—they dropped!—and at that price they'll unfortunately tempt many people into gambling on their colorful stories. While *real* businesses are churning out steady cash profits, many of the nickel-and-dimers are busier promoting their stocks, trying to lure newbie investors into taking a chance on their dubious business prospects. And because brokers get paid based on how many trades they make and how many shares they trade, they love to pitch the penny stocks at you.

Many of these companies are low-grade promotional businesses. It's estimated that three-quarters of all stocks trading under $5 per share will one day end up worthless. And almost all of these businesses are unfamiliar to you. Avoid this group forever and we think you'll be better off.

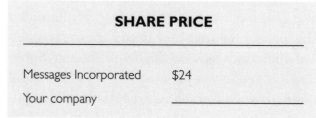

SHARE PRICE

Messages Incorporated	$24
Your company	

Screen #4: Earnings and Sales Growth of at Least 25 Percent

Across the spectrum of ten thousand public companies in America, you'll find sales growing at all kinds of rates. Some companies will see sales declines, while others are more than doubling their revenues; but look closely and you'll see that most companies' sales are growing at a rate of

5 to 10 percent annually. Since we're specifically looking for those smaller companies at the strong end of the spectrum, we like to study companies with at least 25 percent growth in *sales* over the past year. (There is some reason to think that the bar should be raised even higher, to study only the highest-growth businesses.)

Additionally, we like to find operations whose *earnings* off those sales are growing at comparable rates—ideally, faster. Earnings growth that outpaces a very rapid climb in sales is an excellent situation because it indicates that while the company is selling truckloads more stuff, it is—simultaneously—finding ways to do so more profitably.

	SALES GROWTH	EARNIINGS PER SHARE GROWTH
Messages Incorporated	94%	35%
Your company	_____	_____

While it isn't ideal to see the rise in earnings not keeping pace with the rise in sales, if both are rising rapidly, we'll sometimes choose to overlook the decline in the rate of profitability—or at least find out *why* this is happening before dismissing a prospect. Messages' earnings growth looks frightening, though, compared to sales growth.

Screen #5: Net Profit Margin of at Least 10 Percent

Companies with profit margins in excess of 10 percent are a rare breed. But that's precisely what we're looking for when we go out in search of the limited group of smaller companies that warrant

our investigation. If they're earning 10 cents for every dollar of sales, these smaller companies might be taking market share away from larger companies while generating healthy profits. What you'll want to find is companies that are also growing these higher margins to loftier heights. Profitability drives the value of the overall company, and thus the stock price. As a shareholder you'll always be rooting for the earnings growth rate. We don't think you should accept any small business as a potential investment unless it's maintaining these high margins. You're too good for the rest, Fool!

	MESSAGES INCORPORATED	YOUR COMPANY
Revenues	$97 million	_____
Net income	$12.88 million	_____
Profit margin	13%	_____

Screen #6: Cash Flow Positive

The next of our Foolish filters is based on the cash flow statement. All we're looking for here is that companies have positive cash flow from operations. This is simply a check to see if the company is burning money, rather than making it.

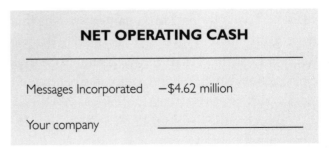

NET OPERATING CASH

Messages Incorporated	−$4.62 million
Your company	_____

Yikes! This is the unfortunate sign that we talked of earlier when discussing Messages' levels of receivables and inventory. Negative cash flow is excusable only in companies ramping up into phenomenal growth. Unless you have a good reason to believe that your company is burning cash to fuel a growth spurt, you should discard it and hold to your standards!

Screen #7: Relative Strength of 90 or More

Investor's Business Daily offers a statistic for every public company that we find extremely useful. It's called "relative strength," and it works just like the grading system used on you in high school. A 95 is smashingly excellent, a 25 is time to burn your report card. What do the numbers mean? They speak to how well a particular stock has performed relative to the rest of the market. A number of 95, for example, means that the company has outperformed 95 percent of all public companies traded on all U.S. exchanges over the past year. The number 25 would indicate outperformance of a mere 25 percent of the companies; this company has lost badly to the stock market.

Our screen requires that a company have a relative strength ranking of 90 or higher. Why? Because the cream usually congregates at the top. Typically, those small-caps that have been succeeding have the greatest chance of further success. Trying to buy very small companies that have gotten hammered by the market is, we think, an extremely dangerous game. So, buy a copy of *Investor's Business Daily* and search out stocks with relative strength of at least 90; make your search easier. (Oops! Look at Messages Incorporated!)

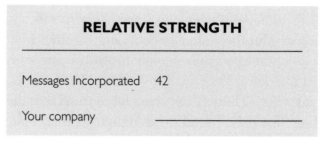

RELATIVE STRENGTH

Messages Incorporated   42

Your company   _____

Screen #8: Insider Holdings of 15 Percent or Greater

Knowing that management holds a significant stake in the company's stock is an added assurance that they care enough to do their best and that they have confidence in the company's future. Look for at least 15 percent of stock to be held by insiders. While it's a little difficult to find up-to-date ownership information, fairly accurate data can be found in the company's annual report and in the *S&P Stock Guide*. These figures are on the Internet, as well. Finally, you can call the company directly and ask them for an ownership profile.

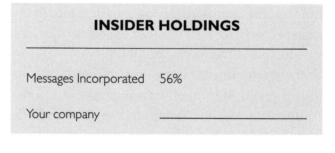

INSIDER HOLDINGS

Messages Incorporated   56%

Your company   _____

Insider Buying and Selling

If you were the CEO of a company and had three kids to put through college, two mortgages, and an unpaid second honeymoon, where would you most likely get the money to pay for it all? Very likely, you'd sell some shares of the company you own. What's more, you'd probably do this somewhat often, even though you might not really want to—after all, you believe in the company, but you've got to pay those bills. Then again, when the stock happens to hit a low point, it makes sense to buy it on the cheap, since you know the company's doing well and the share price will improve. For these reasons, the Foolish investor pretty much ignores insider selling. We do pay attention to insider buying, which says more about management's sentiment than their selling. Selling can occur for too many reasons to draw any solid conclusions from it. Buying occurs for only one reason.

Concluding Thoughts on Small-Caps

Unfortunately for Messages Incorporated, the company failed two of the critical screens that we use to limit the enormous number of small public companies we consider buying to just a few. Sta-tus as cash flow negative and a stock performance that has outperformed only 42 percent of the market over the past year are both unacceptable. As many things as there are to like about Messages—rapid sales growth, a great business concept, strong management ownership—their balance sheet is far too unstable for us, and per-haps that's why it has only outperformed 42 per-cent of all stocks in the past year.

But that's not going to stop us from trying to value their business fairly. We'll close by asking you:

Is there a present value for Messages' busi-ness? If so, name it:

$ _____ million

Don't have a clue? Well, Fools, then it's valu-ation time!

CHAPTER 10
Valuing Your Company

At this point, you may be saying, "Whoa there, you didn't tell me enough about where to find all those statistics—the speed of sales and earnings growth, the profit margins, that stuff. Help me out, Fools."

What you first need to know is that 99 percent of the information you need about a company is presented in its quarterly earnings statements and its annual report. The financial statements are made public every three months when the company has a conference call to explain its performance—which often is illegally limited to an exclusive group of Wall Street analysts (you'll be hearing more about this as we combat it in the months and years ahead). Anyway, following earnings the marketplace swirls with investors and traders trying to place an immediate fair value on the company.

Every three months, when earnings come out, companies like our mythical Messages Incorporated see their stocks passed around like a hot potato. So much attention is focused on those new numbers that stock prices gain volatility. *Should you be extremely and immediately con-cerned about the performance of your company every three months?*

Yes   No

Our answer—a circle somewhere in the middle. You should not be *extremely* concerned or even *immediately* concerned. But you will want to study the financial reports of your company, and thoroughly. And to do so, you should be certain to call the company and be placed on its mailing list for quarterly financial reports. But don't bother trying to beat the analysts at their game. Instead, study the financials as they're released, and attempt to decipher what the numbers are really saying. If you have a portfolio comprising index funds, the Foolish Four, and some consumer giants, and now you've added one or two good, well-managed, small-capitalization companies, you shouldn't be concerned about any three-month performance period. You're already set up for the long haul. Just remember that you have more time than you think.

But hey, how do you determine if management is "good"?

The financial performance of the company says an awful lot. Still—and you should expect to read this often through the remainder of the workbook—if you're not online, you're making a huge mistake. While you can get printed financials sent to you, and while you can subscribe to *Investor's Business Daily* or the *Wall Street Journal* to keep up with your earnings reports and business news, there's no place other than online where you can ask questions about business and investing and get hundreds of responses.

The Motley Fool, whether you're on the Web (www.fool.com) or on America Online (keyword: FOOL), houses thousands of simultaneous conversations twenty-four hours a day. An investment club in Seattle, Washington, is sharing its ideas on the financial strength of Starbucks coffee with the world, possibly right now. The result is a giant, searchable database of ideas on thousands of companies, investment strategies, and portfolio-management techniques dating back four years now, with reams of fresh new information coming in every day. To invest Foolishly, you'll want access to these thousands of ideas—some of which will be ingenious, others common, others badly flawed. But you'll learn so much quicker if you see it all.

Let's get back to the numbers. The mailman has arrived with the financial statements from the last three-month period that you requested from a company you're studying. You've sorted through the balance sheet, the income statement, and the statement of cash flows. You think you've got a sturdy company, but you haven't a clue whether the company should be worth $240 million, $290 million, $350 million, or something well short or long of that. You'll notice that just

between the highest and the lowest value, there's a range of 46 percent. That range could make your $5,000 investment in a small-cap worth over $7,000 or less than $3,000. Obviously, you'll want to figure some fair value to the business that makes logical sense.

Valuation—are you ready? Great. We're going to immerse ourselves in a pond of ratios. *Splash!*

What Are Ratios and Why Use Them?

In this chapter we'll be looking at various "ratios" that are widely used to help investors gauge the financial health of a company. Very simply, a ratio is *a comparison of two numbers, expressed as a percentage.* For example, if you bought a stock at $20 and it's now at $25, it's now worth $25 ÷ $20 = 1.25 = 125% of its original value, and your profit is 25%. If, on the other hand, it's now trading at $15, it's only worth $15 ÷ $20 = 0.75 = 75% of its original value, and you're down 25%.

Why use ratios to express performance instead of the real numbers? Because percentages iron out the different sizes of the numbers being used across comparisons.

For example, take two companies that each had $100 million in revenues last year. If they both grew sales by 20 percent, did they grow by the same dollar amount? Yes, *they did*—they both grew by $20 million. But if one company, instead, had $500 million in sales the year before, while the other one had $100 million, and they both grew sales by $20 million, the latter grew by 20 percent—but the former by only 4 percent. Using ratios allows us to compare companies of radically different sizes and understand how their growth rates affect their value.

Practically speaking, we'll be using ratios to get a sense of whether a company is relatively strong or weak, overvalued or undervalued according to a standard benchmark. While it's not *that* easy, it isn't hard. Your seventh-grade math teacher actually asked you to do harder things than this. We're only going to be tossing two ratios at you: the price-to-sales and the price-to-earnings ratios. And be forewarned, if you haven't encountered this stuff before, your head may be swimming with new terms, acronyms, or figures the first read through. Give it a second and third look, though, and these ratios will put you in position to begin assigning fair prices to stocks.

1. THE PRICE-TO-SALES RATIO

The price-to-sales ratio (P/S) values companies on the basis of their last full year of sales. What two numbers make up the ratio? We'll be comparing a company's *current market value (market capitalization)* with its trailing twelve months of *sales.* Did that sentence bewilder you? It shouldn't have. This stuff is checkers, man; it's tic-tac-toe. Let's try two examples, then have you do one.

Let's start with Messages Incorporated. We need to figure the company's capitalization, as we did before. Start with the stock price, $24 per share. Now multiply that by the 12 million shares outstanding. We've done this before: $24 × 12 million shares = $288 million. That's the current market value given Messages Incorporated, or its *market capitalization* (or market cap).

Second, we'll need the last full year of *sales.* Let's use the $97 million from 1999. Now we simply need to divide the market cap of the company by that sales figure—to come up with 2.97. The price-to-sales ratio for Messages is 2.97.

	MARKET CAPITALIZATION	12-MONTH SALES	PRICE-TO-SALES RATIO
Messages Incorporated......	$288 million	$97 million	2.97

OK, so the price-to-sales (P/S) ratio is 2.97. What the heck does that mean, this notion that Messages trades at three times sales? It means that for every $1 of sales, the investing community is assigning a value of $2.97 for the company. The market here is assessing the worth of each dollar of sales. This usually sits at $1 or higher, but for some companies—say, a small software business that is about to be undercut by Microsoft—the marketplace of investors says, "No, each dollar of your sales is worth only 50 cents, because we expect you to be stunted by Microsoft's entry into your business."

Imagine a small software company with the same sales figures as Messages, but trading at 0.50 times sales instead of 2.97 times sales.

	MARKET CAPITALIZATION	12-MONTH SALES	PRICE-TO-SALES RATIO
Mr. Software	$48.5 million	$97 million	0.50
Messages Incorporated......	$288 million	$97 million	2.97

Lookie there, even though both companies have the same amount of sales, the market values one at $288 million and the other at $48.5 million. Those different valuations make one enterprise worth millions more to its founders and investors than the other.

The price-to-sales ratio granted can take into account the competition, the amount of debt a company is carrying, the prospects for future sales and earnings growth, including all the margins that we learned about, and the perceived value of management. You will certainly want to know the P/S (that's the first time we used the acronym) of any company you're studying closely. And you can sound cool at cocktail parties, saying stuff like, "The market likes Messages Incorporated much more. They're trading at 3 times sales. Mr. Software is in trouble, probably doesn't even deserve its one-half-sales multiple." Then skewer that olive with a toothpick, for effect. Of course, then you need to explain what you just said, otherwise you're being Wise, not Foolish!

2. THE PRICE-TO-EARNINGS RATIO

Perhaps you've heard your dad on the phone at some point gabbing about the price-to-earnings ratio of particular stocks he's studying. "I've been watching Mr. Software, and the company is trading at a P/E of 21. In the meantime, Messages is trading at 12 times earnings. I can't believe I bought that dog." Yada, yada, yada, you had no idea what he meant.

In just a few minutes you will.

The P/E ratio is just a way to compare a company's stock *price* with the amount of *earnings per share* it has. Reread that sentence until you understand it, and you'll realize that the comparison makes perfect sense. Right?

What we're doing is comparing the annual earnings that the company makes for each share of stock existing with the value that the marketplace is assigning to each of those shares. Let's take Messages.

Net income	12,880
Earnings per share	$1.07
Shares outstanding	12,000

That's from their 1999 income statement. And their stock is trading at $24 per share. So, what's the calculation we need to make? Huh? You know, yes? That's right. We divide the share price by the earnings per share: $24 ÷ $1.07 = 22.4. Messages Incorporated has a P/E ratio, then, of 22. Just as investors said above that Messages was trading at 2.97 times sales, they'll now rightly say that the company is trading at 22 times earnings, too.

Why run this ratio? Well, you're attempting to place a value on an entire company by looking at its profits. When you buy shares of ownership in a restaurant, you want that eatery to make more and more money, to expand, to attract more customers, to be a glitzy stop where celebrities schmooze. The restaurant's profits will then increase, the ownership stake in those profits will increase in step, and you'll have made good money by guessing that the restaurant where Juliette Binoche or Harrison Ford eats will gain in popularity.

So the value of a stock is tied to a company's growth in profits, right? Then what better starting point than the P/E to compare total profits per share to the price of a stock? In Messages' case, is the P/E ratio of 22 high, or low? Excellent question. It is the eternal question of investing. It was the same question people were asking about Mr. Software's price-to-sales ratio (P/S). At 0.5 times sales, was Mr. Software cheap with Microsoft entering its business? Should the company have been trading at a P/S that more closely resembled that of other software companies—

from 4 to 10 times sales—or was the company staring a bankruptcy judge in the eye, with Microsoft's foot planted squarely on its head?

The only way to determine whether a price-to-sales ratio and a price-to-earnings ratio are fair is to make judgments about the future prospects of the business. Business analysts on Wall Street are paid thousands each year to assess the short- and long-term potential of businesses within an industry. We'll be looking at those in a jiffy, but let's get you cracking on the calculation of a few P/S and P/E ratios.

CALCULATE PRICE-TO-SALES RATIOS

	PRICE PER SHARE	TOTAL SALES	MARKET CAPITALIZATION	PRICE-TO-SALES RATIO
Messages	$24	$97 million	$288 million	2.97
Mr. Software	$8	$97 million	$48.5 million	0.50
Tattooland	$67	$142 million	$394 million	2.77
Giaobashi	$11	$32 million	$452 million	14.12
Pennsylvania Steel	$143	$1.4 billion	$241 million	0.17
Alfonso Lucky's	$21	$549 million	$742 million	a. _____
FoolMart	$25	$245 million	$643 million	b. _____
PG's Putters	$78	$812 million	$1.9 billion	c. _____
Young Programmers Co.	$12	$15 million	$54 million	d. _____
Just for Dogs	$91	$140 million	e. _____	3.41
Just for Automobiles	$241	f. _____	$117 million	1.29
Nightlights Co.	g. _____	$610 million	$430 million	0.70

OK, a couple of quick questions for you before we give the answers.

What are the possible explanations for the giant discrepancy in P/S ratios between Pennsylvania Steel and Giaobashi? . . . Yes, exactly, the market of investors believes that Giaobashi has substantially better growth prospects than does the steel company. With only $32 million in sales, investors are tagging the Far Eastern enterprise with a value of $452 million. Your charge would be to review whether those expectations overrate or underrate the company's potential.

Second question: Were you able to figure out the stock price for Nightlights Co.? . . . Nope. That column was useless here. We're just trying to fool you, Fool, and to keep your mind sharp.

Answers: a. 1.35 *b.* 2.62 *c.* 2.34 *d.* 3.60 *e.* $477 million *f.* $91 million *g.* unanswerable

Let's work on some P/E ratio calculations.

CALCULATE PRICE-TO-EARNINGS RATIOS

	PRICE PER SHARE	EARNINGS PER SHARE	P/E RATIO
Messages	$24	$1.07	22
Mr. Software	$8	$0.56	14
Tattooland	$67	$2.00	34
Giaobashi	$11	$0.20	55
Pennsylvania Steel	$143	$17.21	8
Alfonso Lucky's	$21	$1.57	a. _____
FoolMart	$25	$0.89	b. _____
PG's Putters	c. _____	$2.20	34
Young Programmers Co.	$12	$0.36	d. _____
Just for Dogs	$91	e. _____	18
Just for Automobiles	f. _____	$19.68	12
Nightlights Co.	$16	g. _____	21

OK, dear reader, one question before the answer key. Why do you think Giaobashi is trading at a much higher multiple off earnings than Just for Automobiles? Why would the market value Giaobashi's earnings so much more richly than those of the auto accessories company? Think on this for a second. . . . OK, yep, the answer is that the market expects the Asian outfit to grow much more rapidly than Just for Autos. Investors are assigning a higher value on those earnings because they expect them to race higher. Time will tell whether the investing community believed too much, too little, or just enough in Giaobashi's ability to flood the Far East with scratch-and-sniff games of chance.

Answers: a. 13   *b.* 28   *c.* $75   *d.* 33
e. $5.05   *f.* $236   *g.* $0.75

Now that we know how to calculate these ratios, we must look together to the future.

THE P/E RATIO AND FUTURE EXPECTATIONS

The point of our examination of the current health of companies—that rather thoroughgoing review of what to look for on the balance sheet, income statement, and cash flow statement—is to determine how well positioned the company is to capitalize on its strengths, to take market share from its competitors, and to assume a leadership position in its industry.

A company that is financially strong today is far more likely to continue to outgrow its competition than one with mediocre or subpar financials. For example, as you look back at the Messages Incorporated balance sheet, you have to think that the pileup of fortune-cookie-message inventory may force the company to significantly discount prices in the year ahead. Not good. And you have to wonder whether the growing accounts receivable may indicate that, say, its Australian partners are holding off their payments until they determine the success of the product. Both circumstances put the company in a weakened financial position.

You've learned to review everything from accounts payable to gross margins, to get a read on a company's financial state. Then we showed you how to take a gander at two ratios, price-to-sales and price-to-earnings, to get a sense of how the market is valuing different companies. Now it's time to take both of those and use them to assess the future of the companies you are following, companies like Messages Incorporated.

Analyst Expectations

Today's stock prices are predicated on the future earnings growth of the business. If you could travel forward twelve months in time, you could study the financial reports on a couple of dozen companies, see what directions their earnings have taken, return back to today, and make an absolute fortune on the market. If *only* we knew definitively what would happen to the underlying financial positions of the public companies we

follow and invest in! This is our essential challenge—to estimate future business growth. And while Fools strive to make assessments based on their own knowledge of a company and an industry, that can be a daunting task. You say you have two kids, a fifty-hour-per-week job, car payments, and a bad back that won't stop nagging you? Aha! Chances are you won't be running all over the country visiting factories, talking to management, interviewing customers, appraising social trends, and predicting the technological advances that will change our world. We'll even bet that you won't be dropping in on Boeing's plant in Seattle to interview them about their production plans for the year ahead.

Lucky you, though, that Wall Street pays out a good deal of money to business analysts charged with making predictions about the future of entire industries and their companies. For instance, each big investment firm in Manhattan has an expert on the automobile industry, a guy or gal who treks back and forth between Detroit, Manhattan, Tokyo, and beyond. They race around like children on a treasure hunt, asking questions, noting down clues, and building maps. Their predictive models read like a long list of "If . . . then" statements from eighth-grade computing class: If Chrysler sells 1 million more minivans than it did last year, then the company will make this much more money, which translates into this much more in profits per share, which would result in the stock price climbing this much. "If that happens, then this might happen." That's what it's all about, the life of the stock analyst.

After the analyst has gone out hoping to build informed determinations on the growth of an industry and the companies competing in it, she then returns home and writes up lengthy, sometimes unreadable, reports about the future prospects of individual businesses. Because of their better access to company management, analysts often pull together some valuable insights. But because they wasted two years in business school, their predictions are often enough flawed and heavily jargonized! Finally, because these analysts are employees of investment houses that have vested interests in seeing particular companies succeed, you never can quite tell what their motivations are. And that means that if you use analyst reports to invest—and we think that you should—you should always compare the actual results of your business with the predictions that the analyst previously made to see how strong her assumptions were. And you should tend to pay more attention to the numbers than the words in analysts' reports.

Does that sound like a good deal of work? Well, it is and it isn't. It *is* because if you're invested in six smaller companies, you're going to need to follow their partnership announcements, reports from Wall Street, and their earnings performance. Your kids, job, car, and bad back make doing all that extremely difficult. But it *isn't* a lot of work, because once you learn what is valuable and what isn't, you can begin to focus on your few small-cap stocks for just a few days four times a year (when they announce earnings). If it all seems too much, though, then you just learned your threshold. Apply what you've learned about index funds, the Foolish Four, and consumer giants; spend no more than a handful of hours on investing each year; hang out with us online; and go about your merry way—walloping the expensive and submediocre gaggle of managed mutual funds.

Aha. If you're still reading, then you should know that the most important piece of informa-tion that analysts provide is their estimation of a company's growth rate in earnings. Analysts usually carry their earnings per share estimates two years or more forward. So you'll see something like this:

EARNINGS PER SHARE

	1998 A	1999 EST.	2000 EST.
Mr. Software	$0.56	$0.64	$0.71

The *A* after 1998 indicates that those earnings have already been announced ("actual"). The *Est.* stands for "estimated" earnings. In this instance, the Wall Street analyst following Mr. Software believes that the company will generate 64 cents of earnings per share in 1999 and 71 cents of earnings per share in 2000. To remind you of what that means, consider that Mr. Software has 6.1 million shares outstanding, a stock price of $8 per share, and therefore a company value of $48.8 million. Now, if the analyst is pegging it for 64 cents in earnings per share, how much in total earnings does that amount to?

Come on, you know this! Here are some tidbits of info:

6.1 million shares $0.64 in earnings per share

To calculate this, simply mutiply the total shares by the earnings per share: 6.1 million × $0.64 = $3.9 million. If the company keeps the same number of shares, then the analyst expects it to make $3.9 million in profit over the next year. Got that? Great. Let's practice a few, then.

CALCULATE ESTIMATED EARNINGS

	SHARES OUTSTANDING	EST. EARNINGS PER SHARE	EST. TOTAL EARNINGS
Messages	12 million	$1.29	$15.5 million
Mr. Software	6.1 million	$0.64	$3.9 million
Tattooland	5.9 million	$2.57	a. _____
Giaobashi	41 million	$0.47	b. _____
Pennsylvania Steel	1.7 million	c. _____	$32.3 million

You're probably thinking about just skimming over that, peeking at the answers, and reading on. Hey, come on! It took us some effort to put that table together.

Answers: a. $15.16 million *b.* $19.27 million *c.* $19.00

OK, so there you have the analyst's total earnings and earning-per-share estimates for the years ahead. Are they going to be right? More than 95 percent of the time they'll be off by a little bit (and sometimes a lot!). (So's the weatherman.) But generally they'll be in the ballpark. And you, the investor in small-caps, will want to know just exactly where that ballpark is.

There are three places to locate earnings estimates, and we're going to challenge you to track them down for the companies that you're following or are invested in. The first place you can find them is at The Motley Fool Online, where all earnings-estimates data is free. The second is a call to the company itself, which may be able to furnish you with Wall Street estimates. And the third is a direct call to your discount or full-service broker, who may be able to dig the numbers up for you. Here's the challenge . . .

Using whatever resources are available to you (the library, the newspaper, the company, *your broker, or The Motley Fool on the Web or AOL), write down three analysts' opinions on your company. They can be numerical estimates or just qualitative comments from the "expert."*

1. _____

2. _____

3. _____

Do not continue reading this book until you've dug up three opinions on your company, either from Wall Street analysts or from discussing the company's merits on The Fool Online or in your investment club.

Hey, do not continue reading until you've done so!

Hey, we see you. We're sitting three chairs behind you in the coffee shop. Look back. See us? No. No, two tables over. Ahhhh, yep. That's us. We're tracking you. Go back to the three spots above and enter in analysts' opinions.

Fine. Now we need to determine the rate of growth off those estimates.

THE GROWTH RATE

By the end of this section, you'll better understand the importance of analyst earnings estimates and you'll be forming opinions about whether a P/E of 22 is too high for Messages Incorporated or not.

A company's stock trades at a price that is a multiple of its present earnings, and usually the greater the expected earnings growth, the higher the multiple. Why's that? It's because investors believe the future value of the stock will reflect the future earnings growth of the company. The higher the expected earnings growth, the higher current multiple they'll grant. If you ever get dizzy about earnings growth concepts, just remember that you want to own the restaurant where Juliette Binoche and Harrison Ford and friends eat every Thursday night. You want successful businesses for which there is great demand and that will make ever-increasing amounts of money from operations. You want the San Francisco 49ers football team. You want Eric Clapton's next three recordings. You want the Tiger Woods of your industry.

Quiz

Which type of company would you rather own?

a. one that consistently posts better earnings and whose stock plows steadily higher
b. one that has been making the same amount of money for six straight years, has little sense of enterprise, and has a stock that is trading near its low, at virtually the same price it was ten years ago

Darn, that one was pretty easy. But simple concepts are essential to beating the market, and it's a continual wonder to us just how many people buy into situation-*b* companies thinking they're "buying low to sell high." High usually

never happens with these! You want to find companies that have consumers hungry for their product and that have a systematic approach to generating profit off that demand. And with your analyst's projected numbers in hand, you can calculate the estimated growth rate of earnings going forward. This number will be critical to your valuations.

A company's earnings growth rate is much like a child's growth rate. Infants can nearly double in size in a single year. The chances of a fifty-two-year-old man doubling his height next year are, well, slim. (We're paging through our *Guinness Book of World Records* right now.) Much of what we're going to be doing in the next few chapters has, as its direct analogy, the growing rate of your ten-year-old daughter or son. If your child grows from fifty inches to fifty-five inches tall next year, he will have grown by 10 percent. We'll be making just that kind of calculation when studying the growth rate in profitability of public companies.

Generally, investors like to look at one-year, three-year, and five-year growth rates to get a sense of the short-, intermediate-, and long-term expectations for a company. Let's look at a one-year growth rate example first.

Messages Incorporated's One-Year Growth Rate

Messages' predicted earnings for 2000, according to our mythical analyst J. Theodore Verrill, are $1.29 per share. Over the past twelve months, Messages has posted earnings per share of $1.07. Consider Messages as you would your young son. What's the growth rate from one year to the next?

$1.29 ÷ $1.07 = _____, or _____%,

for a growth rate of _____%. Poof! We beat you. It's 20.5% growth. Let's round to 21%.

If you've mastered this one-year growth rate calculation, the rest are only a little tougher. To get comfortable with the calculation you just ran, please stand up in your chair and, while juggling three cats and a flaming torch, tell the world, "Messages Incorporated is expected to grow earnings by 21 percent over the next year." Excellent. Extremely Foolish of you. Now quickly get a hose and put out the cats.

Ready for the next challenge? OK, suppose the analysts have generated earnings estimates for the next *two* years. Let's say that analysts are projecting $1.74 in earnings per share for Messages in the year 2001. What's the *total growth* from the present state?

Well, $1.74 ÷ $1.07 = _____, or

_____%, for a growth rate of

_____%. Poof! We beat you again. It's total growth of 63%, rounded up from 62.6%.

Time now to step up to the most difficult growth rate calculation you'll be forced to make. What is important to us as investors is the annualized rate of growth of the companies we follow, rather than the total. In order to assess the fairness of a company's present P/E ratio, we need to know its estimated per year rate of growth. You're possibly confused by that language, and probably confused as to why we'd care about the annual growth rate. But stop asking why, and let's just get the calculation done!

Before we proceed, though, we're going to welcome back an acronym (be nice to him). We generally hate acronyms, but over time some of them stick and make it easier for authors to write their silly books. Fools all, henceforth when referring to earnings per share, we'll often be writing "EPS." So we're really dealing with two important acronyms in this section, EPS and the P/E ratio. Can you make a little mnemonic song out of those two in your head? . . .

Armed with those abbreviations, let's look again at Messages.

EARNINGS PER SHARE

	1999 A	2000 EST.	2001 EST.
Messages Incorporated.........	$1.07	$1.29	$1.74

What we're searching for now is the annual EPS growth rate, and to find it, we'll need to put our first square root into play. Yep, you've come 153 pages in this workbook using nothing but fifth-grade mathematics. Here's where we enter sixth, laying a square root on you. To get the smoothed-out, annual rate of growth over any number of years you must *divide the last number by the first*, then *take a root of that number*, using the root matching the *number of years measured*. Got it, right? We hope *somebody* did.

Fine, fine, so it wasn't the clearest explanation. Let's just try our example. With Messages, we must divide the EPS estimate for 2001 by the actual EPS in 1999. Then, because we're looking at a *two*-year period, we must take the *second* (or square) root of that number. If it were a three-year period, we'd take the *third* (or cubed) root. So what's the projected annual growth rate of Messages from the two years 1999 to 2001?

Divide 1.74 by 1.07, then take the square root of the resulting number.

Step 1. 1.74 ÷ 1.07 = 1.63

Step 2. square root of 1.63 = 1.276

Step 3. 1.276 = 127.6% (earnings each year, compared to previous year)

Step 4. 27.6% = growth rate per year

Thus, Messages is projected to grow each year into 127.6 percent of what it was the year before—a growth rate of 27.6 percent per year over the next two years.

If you're going to invest in small-cap businesses, it's pretty crucial that you understand how to calculate growth rates. So, we'll run another by you. Take your five-year-old son, Blake. Blake is thirty-eight inches tall today. If he sprouts to fifty-five inches over the next *three* years, what will be his annual growth rate?

Step 1. 55 ÷ 38 = 1.45

Step 2. cubed root of 1.45 = 1.13

Step 3. 113% (size each year, compared to previous year)

Step 4. 13% = growth rate per year

Blake will grow at an average, annualized rate of 13 percent per year if he hits fifty-five inches in three years.

We can continue calculating growth rates all day long, including the growth rate of our waistlines for sitting here and rambling on and on and on. Instead, though, we'll give you several to tackle yourself. You'll need a scientific calculator to plug through all these roots. If you don't have one, hey, plink down $20 for one. (If you're a Windows computer user, the ol' Windows calculator works just fine, here.)

Good luck with these, Fool.

CALCULATE GROWTH RATES

	1999 A EARNINGS	EPS EST.	YEARS OUT	ANNUAL GROWTH RATE
Messages	$1.07	$1.29	1	21%
Mr. Software	$0.56	$0.71	2	13%
Tattooland	$2.00	$2.92	2	a. _____
Giaobashi	$0.20	$1.43	3	b. _____
Pennsylvania Steel	$17.21	$21.23	2	c. _____
Alfonso Lucky's	$1.57	$1.92	1	d. _____
FoolMart	$0.89	$1.32	2	e. _____
PG's Putters	$2.20	$4.17	4	f. _____
Young Programmers Co.	$0.36	$3.21	9	g. _____
Just for Dogs	$4.98	$6.12	1	h. _____
Just for Automobiles	$19.68	$23.12	2	i. _____
Nightlights Co.	$0.75	$1.25	2	j. _____

Answers: a. 21%   b. 93%   c. 11%   d. 22%   e. 22%   f. 17%   g. 28%   h. 23%   i. 8%   j. 29%

THE FOOL RATIO (PEG)

Unless you successfully navigated the preceding work sheet, you really shouldn't be pressing on into small-caps. You've learned an awful lot about financial statements, about the characteristics of good business, about why not to invest in managed mutual funds, and about the basics of your own financial position. It would not be a good thing if you compromised all of that hard work by investing in small-cap stocks without fully understanding the calculations you have to make and the expectations you should set in order to invest successfully in largely unknown companies. If you don't thoroughly understand the following concepts, turn back. Or reread your Fool Lib, from earlier. Then consider the following mine-field of words (and please just ignore the subliminal hints):

accounts payable   gross margins
cube roots   interest income

    Fool

operating profits   SG&A expenses
inventory turnover

    Fool

EPS   profit margins   current liabilities
Warren Buffett

    Fool

cost of goods sold   analyst estimates   P/S ratio

    Fool

operating cash flows   long-term debt

Do you have supreme (Fool) confidence in your (Fool) definitions of the terms (Fool) above? Have you gone back and corrected any mistakes you made on work sheets? Do you really believe that you'll be able to research and *invest* in small-capitalization companies rather than take a spin at their wheels and pray for the best (read: gamble)?

If so, proceed on tiptoe past this line.

The Fool Ratio

It is now time for us to learn about the Fool Ratio, which will help you fairly value small businesses as they grow to the sky or dry out and die in the valley. Our ratio concentrates on the relationship between the *earnings growth rate* and the *price-*

to-earnings ratio. Like any model, this one has a few weaknesses, which we'll discuss at the end of this section.

What better way to start than just to define the concept?

The Fool Ratio holds that a small-capitalization company is fairly valued when its *annual earnings growth rate* equals its *price-to-earnings multiple.*

If you've read this far, you've suffered through some mind-bending sentences from us, but this one might take the cake. Before we explain it, provide examples, and set you on your merry way—calculating Fool Ratios with the best of them—take another look at the definition:

The Fool Ratio holds that a small-capitalization company is fairly valued when its *annual earnings growth rate* equals its *price-to-earnings multiple.*

Do you have any clue what that means or why that might be so? Take a shot in the space provided below. What do you think the definition *means*?

_____

_____

_____

_____

_____

Interesting reply (for those of you who wrote, "I haven't a clue," hey, we find that interesting, too). (As if we can really see what you wrote! Come on!) OK, it's time for us to step out, define, detail, perhaps even defend the Fool Ratio!

Let's start simply by asking why companies grow. Companies grow because customer demand increases, hopefully allowing the company to operate in greater volume with greater efficiency, generating for it an increasing amount of profits. If you started a coffee shop tomorrow, you'd want people to come, buy stuff, and put money in your cash register. This would enable you to hire more staffers, put out more advertisements about your business, and then possibly—poof!—open a second coffee shop across town. Before you know it, you're the founder of Starbucks coffee, and your business in the public marketplace is valued at nearly $3 billion. Nice job, that didn't take much effort! So:

1. Companies become more valuable as they increase their profits and expand.

The second concept we'd like to share is the idea that investors affect the value of companies. As more and more people covet an ownership position in a certain company, as the demand grows and the supply doesn't, the price of the stock increases. So:

2. One reason stocks rise is because more investors want to buy shares than sell them.

The third concept (of six) we'll play pitchmen to is the idea that these two forces converge for a reason. As a business increases its profitability, investors sit up and take note. If earnings blast through the roof, investors line up on telephones or online services in all points on the globe and buy, buy, buy! Conversely, if earnings

growth stagnates or, gasp, reverses into decline, investors trip over themselves trying to sell. The stock falls. So:

3. Combine the first two: When earnings consistently rise, investors line up to buy the stock.

If you grasp those three concepts, zing, here comes the next one. The fourth is that the investing community is fanatically obsessed with trying to predict the rate at which profits will rise for companies in every industry. Teams of analysts are employed to predict earnings-per-share growth in the years ahead, and if they get it right, it can earn billions of dollars for mutual funds, pension funds, banks, brokerage firms, and private investors around the planet. The market focuses an awful lot of attention on analyst predictions for the future earnings of entire industries and individual companies. So:

4. Because earnings growth drives a stock's price, the investing community carefully tracks the predictions for a company's future earnings made by Wall Street analysts.

The fifth concept is just as logical: The rate at which earnings grow in the *future* is and should be primarily reflected in the *present* value of any public company, in the present price of its stock. If a company is expected to grow earnings from $100 million to $150 million over the next twelve months, stock investors are going to drive up the value of the company to partially or wholly reflect that expected $150 million in earnings. If the company beats that estimate, expect the stock to rise further. If the company falls short of $150 million in earnings, expect the stock to fall. So:

5. *Expectations for future earnings growth are usually factored into the present value of every stock.*

Time for our last point. To fairly price a company you must look at its existing financial state as reflected in the financial statements (our earlier lessons in the workbook), calculate earnings growth rates (our recent lessons), and find a way to relate the two together to divine a fair value (the remainder of this chapter). A company's underlying financial strength and its future earnings growth are your twin towers of valuation. So:

6. *Hey, Fool, when valuing a company, you must account both for its present state of affairs and its potential for future earnings.*

Before we dive into the Fool Ratio, please reread those six concepts. They may not sound terribly exciting, but it's amazing how few investors—experienced investors, even—actually grasp them. They provide you your foundation for intelligent stock analysis.

Excellent. Now it's time to return back to our original definition of the Fool Ratio:

The Fool Ratio holds that a small-capitalization company is fairly valued when its *annual earnings growth rate* equals its *price-to-earnings multiple.*

You're probably getting closer to grasping that definition. The last piece of the puzzle is the P/E multiple. Remember that a P/E multiple reflects the amount of money—the price—that the market is willing to pay for the profits, the company's earnings. A P/E ratio of 23 says that

investors are willing to pay $23 per share for every $1 of a company's earnings. Why? Because they expect that $1 in earnings to grow. Someday soon it'll be $2 in earnings. Then $4 in earnings. And each bump up will represent millions, tens of millions, hundreds of millions, even billions of dollars of additional profit at the company. What we need to do is to relate the rate of speed of that earnings growth to the present P/E multiple that the market has assigned the stock.

And here she comes, the Fool Ratio. Our dear ratio holds that for a stock to be fairly and fully valued, the P/E multiple should equal the annual earnings growth rate of the company. This means that if Runklemania has $1 in earnings per share and is projected to earn $1.25 per share next year, with that estimated annual growth rate of 25 percent the company should trade at 25 times earnings. The earnings of $1, multiplied by 25, tell us the stock is fairly priced at $25 per share.

Didja catch that? Sure, so let's walk through a trickier one.

	1999 A	2000 EST.	2001 EST.
Messages Incorporated	$1.07	$1.29	$1.74

Here we'll need *first* to calculate the annual rate of earnings growth. *Then* we'll need to apply that as our multiple back against trailing earnings of $1.07.

So, first:

square root of $(1.74 \div 1.07) =$

square root of $1.63 =$

$1.276 = 127.6\%$

$27.6\% =$ annual rate of earnings growth

Our annual growth rate is 27.6%. That acts as our multiple of $1.07 of earnings. So, our fair price for Messages today . . . *ka-ching!* is 27.6 × $1.07, or $29.53 per share. The beauty of carrying out this calculation is that we've included future earnings estimates into our valuation. Future estimates are what we've used to calculate a growth rate, and now we're simply using that growth rate to put some value on the current share price. Nifty, eh? It's now time for you to try a few.

CALCULATE A PROJECTED FAIR PRICE

	1999 A EARNINGS	EPS EST.	YEARS OUT	ANNUAL GROWTH RATE	FAIR PRICE
Messages	$1.07	$1.74	2	28%	$30
Mr. Software	$0.56	$0.71	2	13%	$7
Tattooland	$2.00	$2.92	2	21%	$42
Giaobashi	$0.20	$1.43	3	93%	$18
Pennsylvania Steel	$17.21	$21.23	2	11%	a. ____
Alfonso Lucky's	$1.57	$1.92	1	22%	b. ____
FoolMart	$0.89	$1.32	2	22%	c. ____
PG's Putters	$2.20	$4.17	4	17%	d. ____
Young Programmers Co.	$0.36	$3.21	9	28%	e. ____
Just for Dogs	$4.98	$6.12	1	23%	f. ____
Just for Automobiles	$19.68	$23.12	2	8%	g. ____
Nightlights Co.	$0.75	$1.25	2	29%	h. ____

Time for the answer key revealing our fair prices. We hope you nailed them all.

Answers: a. $189   *b.* $34   *c.* $19   *d.* $37 *e.* $10   *f.* $114   *g.* $157   *h.* $22

Believe it or not, you're fully responsible for having completed the crucial column of the spreadsheet above. And you've now landed some fair prices—which we're going to be very careful about and refer to as *loose* fair prices—for a dozen stocks.

The Fool Ratio Applied

The final component of the Fool Ratio is its application. Our hope, when looking to buy small-cap companies, is to *locate those whose loose fair price is approximately one-half the existing share price,* leaving plenty of room for—hopefully—appreciation. With our ratio, we're aiming to locate stocks trading at $30 per share that look to be fairly priced at $60 per share, stocks trading at $10 that seem to be worth $20, and so on. When we divide the existing price by the fair price, we get our final important ratio, it reflects the P/E to the growth rate, and tells us what percentage of the fair price is the present share price. For instance, a stock trading at $10 with a fair price of $20 has a Fool Ratio of 0.50. A company with a fair price of $30 and a stock trading at $30 has a Fool Ratio of 1.00.

In our search for uncommon values among small-capitalization businesses, we look for stocks with a Fool Ratio of 0.60 or less. So let's take a look at our companies and calculate.

CALCULATE THE FOOL RATIO

	SHARE PRICE	FAIR PRICE	THE FOOL RATIO
Messages	$24	$30	0.80
Mr. Software	$8	$7	1.14
Tattooland	$67	$42	1.59
Giaobashi	$11	$18	a. _____
Pennsylvania Steel	$143	$189	b. _____
Alfonso Lucky's	$21	$34	c. _____
FoolMart	$25	$19	d. _____
PG's Putters	$75	$37	e. _____
Young Programmers Co.	$12	$10	f. _____
Just for Dogs	$91	$114	g. _____
Just for Automobiles	$241	$157	h. _____
Nightlights Co.	$16	$22	i. _____

A quick question for you before we get to the answers. Look at Tattooland's ratio; it's 1.10. Does the stock appear overpriced, or underpriced?

j. _____

Answers: *a.* 0.61   *b.* 0.75   *c.* 0.61   *d.* 1.31
e. 2.02   *f.* 1.20   *g.* 0.79   *h.* 1.53   *i.* 0.72
j. overpriced

What to Do with the Fool Ratio

Look back up at the previous page and you'll see that we've now determined that Messages is trading at 80 percent of its apparent fair value. That's not terribly attractive to us. And since there are so many other undervalued stocks out there, we should and will commit to investing in companies that present uncommon bargains. With a 0.80 Fool Ratio, Messages won't make our buy list. Which stocks will we be researching? Well, if they weren't mythical, we'd be sending away for the financial statements from Giaobashi (Fool Ratio 0.61) and the rapidly growing chain of dining and entertainment emporiums, Alfonso Lucky's (Fool Ratio 0.61).

Given that we're starting to make value judgments about the difference between little numbers like 0.50 and 0.80, it's probably time to trot out a table laying out some of our thinking here. To that end, here are our Fool Ratio guidelines.

Below 0.60: Look to buy. When the Fool Ratio is 0.60 or lower, we'd consider buying a company that is in strong financial condition, is well poised to execute its business plan, and appears prepped to meet or beat earnings estimates.

From 0.60 to 0.75: Be patient. With a Fool Ratio from about 0.60 to 0.75, this sort of company has to have mint-condition financial statements for us to consider buying it. Why? Because we think that as the valuation gets higher, investors should demand better underlying financial might.

From 0.76 to 1.00: Pass for now. A stock with a Fool Ratio from 0.76 to 1.00 is a pass. If we already own this sort of company, we hope it's en route to a ratio of 1.00, fair value! If not, it's generally one to pass by, particularly if there is any weakness in the financial statements. In certain rare situations—namely, if the company is the industry leader of a new dynamic growth industry—we may still buy even here. But that is rare.

From 1.01 to 1.50: Consider selling. A stock whose Fool Ratio is 1.00 or above is usually fully, fairly valued. This is what we hoped for, but now that the day has come, the stock may not have much growth left. It's often time to sell. A hearty handshake, a warm thank you, and we're outta there! However, if the company appears to be on the road to large-cap status, or long-term industry domination, we sometimes will hold. Again, it's important to recognize that every rule may have its exceptions.

From 1.51 up: Learn about shorting. During our travels, we'll happen upon companies whose Fool Ratio is 1.50 or above. For whatever reason, these companies appear seriously overvalued to our Foolish eyes. Before we dismiss these companies, though, we like to find out why the stock is so beloved. Maybe the market is right and the future prospects are drop-dead gorgeous. Or maybe the stock has run up on over-enthusiasm. Because it's a riskier investment for aggressive investors, we don't go into "shorting" at all in this workbook—it's an investment strategy that has you counting on a stock to fall, not rise. You'll have to come to our online area to learn more of that! (We also treat the subject in our *Motley Fool Investment Guide*.)

Time for a few final thoughts on Messages and its valuation. It's a curious blend of strong growth, brand-name strength, and impressive profitability, right along with some now obvious blemishes in its financial complexion. For instance, the sales growth is awesome, but because a good deal of those sales and earnings have been booked but not collected, we must ultimately put Messages low on our list of attractive stocks. Companies that are cash flow negative give us the willies. Add to it that Messages is trading at a Fool Ratio of 0.80, and it's just too expensive for us. We'll keep our eyes on it, though. Heck, we've spent enough time studying the darned company!

If this were a typical get-rich-quick financial book—complete with guys in suits pointing at you on the cover to come get that easy cash *now*—we might have made Messages out to be the great investment prospect of the twenty-first century. Instead, we've presented a company like so many others, complete with strengths and weaknesses, and some subtleties not immediately apparent to the fool (small *f*) who gives the company only a cursory glance. Most stocks are like Messages—with pluses and minuses requiring that you consider and weigh them before making an investment decision. Our aim in these pages is to present you good tools with some Foolish guidance as to how to use them.

Proceed with Caution

Much as it pains us to admit that our Fool Ratio isn't all powerful, it isn't. Not every company can be valued using it. This tool is based on the assumption that a company is a small- to mid-cap and is in a growth business.

There are several industries upon which the Fool Ratio should not be unleashed—automobiles, agriculture, banks, insurance companies, airlines, utilities. They just aren't typically upward-spiraling growth industries, or are cyclical, and most of the companies are too big for the Fool Ratio anyway. Other valuation approaches are required to make informed investing decisions on them. For now, you would probably want to invest in them only if their stocks fall into the Foolish Four grouping.

YOU'RE NOT DONE YET

Among the last places—but an important place—to look for more information is the company you're considering. Search through its materials once more to get a sense of the growth (both present and future), and perform the Foolish financial assessment. Write down four or five questions that you have about the business, call up their investor relations department, and just ask.

What Are They Saying?

Read your company's annual report and write down three growth goals that management has set for itself in the next year.

1. _____

2. _____

3. _____

Now write down three items that your research has turned up that indicate a company you're interested in is in good financial shape. After that, write down up to three items that may either indicate or lead to financial problems down the line if they are not addressed.

Strengths:

1. _____

2. _____

3. _____

Potential problems:

1. _____

2. _____

3. _____

This short list of thoughts is an excellent way to stay on top of the companies in which you've invested. Refer back to it every time the company announces a new quarter of earnings. And think about updating it each quarter, too.

The Most Important Opinion—Yours

The last (and first) place to go is into your own mind and heart. It is now your turn to step up and be counted. When all the numbers have been crunched and all the available information has been digested, it always comes down to what *you* think is going to happen, what you believe to be true. Ignore the gooroos, ignore even the opinions of good people you meet online or in an investment club. Make the decision yourself; it's one you'll have to take credit or responsibility for in the future.

Hey, you may agree with the company's or the analysts' viewpoints, or you may have come to very different conclusions. The crucial point—the Foolishness of it all—is that you do your own research and come to your own conclusions. And so far, you're doing just that. We'll hope you continue to avoid the overpriced services on Wall Street.

Oh, but before you make your final decision, you must create one more important work sheet.

The Final Page

If you've done good research, you may end up owning particular small-cap companies for the rest of your life—as they blossom into large-caps and begin ruling the universe!

Given this, we recommend that you create a work sheet dedicated to each company that you buy. This one-page summary should be your own personal "Analyst Report." Include what you deem appropriate—from earnings estimates to product comments to questions you need answered to what you love about the business to what you'd say to management at the next shareholders' meeting. If you're going to invest hundreds or thousands of bucks in this company, you should have a one-sheet report of your own.

Hold on to this sheet. It tells you *why* you're doing what you're doing. It can't help but keep you Foolish; it will show you how much you've learned today, and remind you in a few years how much you had yet to learn.

Stock valuation considered, let's segue again into another one of those subjects you may have thought you'd never consider in your entire life: portfolio allocation!

CHAPTER 11

Allocating, Following, and Buying

SO MANY STOCKS, NOT ENOUGH BUCKS

You've managed to get this far in our Foolish tome, scribbling your answers, rereading when necessary, and occasionally dreaming about what you'll do with a bunch of loot twenty years from now. Now it's time to get practical about how much money you have to invest and how much new money you can add each month or quarter.

Remember, Fool, that any money you'll need in the next three years should *not* be invested in the stock market. The market is too volatile. Over any three-year period, the Foolish Four could fall 10 percent, the index fund 20 percent, and your small-cap stocks 30 percent. Or worse. If that happened to the money you needed for tuition, mortgage payments, medical purposes, or basic necessities, look out, Martha, the tree's going to fall. Don't treat the market as a money machine, waiting for you to shake money out of it every few months or years. Nope, the stock market is your long-term savings vehicle, your thirty-year depository. Used correctly, it'll have you retiring to run your own minor-league baseball team, or to go sailing on the *Fool-E-2,* or to help rebuild a burned-out neighborhood in your city. If you invest for decades to come, you'll recognize that it doesn't really matter how much money you start with or even whether you start *today.* What will matter is that you know what you're doing when you begin and that once you start investing, you never stop.

OK, take a moment and flip back to your personal balance sheet on page 26. Turn things over in your mind a bit, and then please enter again here how much money you have to invest for more than three years and how much money per quarter you can realistically add to the stock market:

Starting money $_____

New money per quarter $_____

Great. Now let's determine how to allocate it.

If virtually all that you can save is tied up in your company retirement plan, that's fine. That's great. You're like many people. However, as you're getting your financial house in order, you may find you have more to invest. And you've now soaked up enough Foolish teaching to number among your possible investments the Foolish Four stocks, the index fund, a few consumer giants, and one or two small-cap companies you've recently analyzed. But now you have to figure how much money goes where. Remember that investing is not a one-time-only thing, and you don't have to buy an entire portfolio all at once. In fact, most likely you'll buy a few stocks at a time, building your portfolio as money becomes available. So don't feel like you have to get all your starting money into stocks *today*. As you do add, you'll aim to maximize your profit potential while limiting your dependence on any one particular stock.

Voilà! The Eternal Foolish Allocation to the rescue! Each of the investing opportunities you've identified fits into one of several categories. On the basis of the relative risk and the time commitment these categories require compared to their potential reward, we've assigned each a percentage range below. As always, these are simply guidelines to provide a starting point; your interests and skills may lead you to a different allocation. The point is to invest according to your risk tolerance—the Eternal Foolish Allocation (EFA) is a means to keep you on track. Here's the classic EFA—whoa, yuck, we slipped and created our own acronym!—for the first-time investor. In the following sections, we will be talking exclusively about investors with $5,000

or more to invest. For those of you who have collected less than that, begin now to acquaint yourself with these ideas. However, your best bet is to read our upcoming section on *dividend-reinvestment plans*. Anyway, here's the low-risk Fool Portfolio Allocation:

LOW-RISK FOLLY

ALLOCATION	$5,000 INVESTED
30%—index fund	$1,500
50%—Foolish Four (2 of them)	$2,500
20%—consumer giant	$1,000

Two things to note here.

First, you'll be weighting 80 percent of your portfolio into a combination of single mutual fund (index) and only two or three of the four stocks (Foolish Four). Can you do that? When you can only afford a few of the Foolish Four, you should just buy the top-yielding stock or two, as long as it isn't *also* the lowest-priced stock of the group. If it is, move down to the next highest yielder. For a refresher, please return to the Dow Dividend Approach section. Are you not sufficiently diversified? Yes, indeedy, you have plenty of diversification there. You could even put all of your money into the index fund, and over the long term you'd be fine. It holds ownership positions in five hundred stocks, probably 450 holdings more than Warren Buffett has with the billions of dollars he invests at Berkshire Hathaway. The index fund alone diversifies you enough to cover you. Beyond that, your Foolish Four stocks are conglomerate behemoths, housing loads of subsidiary companies under their umbrellas. You get plenty of reach with that group as well.

Our second point for you to note is that your

commission costs should total 2 percent or less of your overall investment. If you are paying a $20 commission at a discount broker, then you should try to put no less than $1,000 into any stock.

MODERATE-RISK FOLLY

ALLOCATION	$5,000 INVESTED
50%—Foolish Four	
(2 of them)	$2,500
50%—consumer giant	$2,500

One thing to note here—the index fund is gone. While we love the index, Fool, we earnestly believe that you can be better than average at everything you set your mind to do. A mix of high-quality name-brand companies and beaten-down giants should put you in position to do just that.

HIGHER-RISK FOLLY

ALLOCATION	$5,000 INVESTED
30%—Foolish Four	
(one)	$1,500
50%—consumer giant	$2,500
20%—small-cap	$1,000

If you have just $5,000 to invest, here you'll be purchasing a single small-cap stock. Hey, you better know what you're doing there, Fool. If you were to lose 50 percent on the small-cap, or $500, you'd be kissing 10 percent of your original investment funds good-bye. Ouch! That said, if you have decades ahead of you, you'll make those losses up and more—and you can learn a great

deal about business and financial statements by making that first small-cap investment.

GREATEST-RISK FOLLY

ALLOCATION	$5,000 INVESTED
20%—Foolish Four	
(one)	$1,000
40%—consumer giant	$2,000
40%—small-cap	$2,000

If you're going to move money away from the mechanical Foolish Four approach and into long-term holdings in consumer giants and small-cap growth stocks, you'd better have mastered everything in this Foolish Workbook; have read our latest book, *You Have More Than You Think;* have read through *The Motley Fool Investment Guide;* and have been investing for at least a few years. The greater your exposure to small-cap stocks, the more you'll need to know about financial statements and estimated earnings growth, and you should be ready to endure more potential volatility and short-term pain than with any of the other allocations. Until you're well and ready, it may be best after all, fellow Fool, to keep *all* of your $5,000 in the Foolish Four—in all four stocks. But . . . you think you want to try other investments? Let's see if you should.

Pick Your *Eternal Foolish Allocation* with *M&M's*

To get a feeling for your Foolish Allocation preference, go to the kitchen and get four cereal bowls and a bag of M&M's. Count out one hundred of 'em. Now label the bowls according to the list above—*Index Fund, Foolish Four, Consumer Giant, Small-Cap Growth Stocks.* Come on, grab a bag of M&M's and a few bowls and do this. It's a Foolish way to approach this.

Before separating out the M&M's by bowl, bear in mind your preferences for safety and convenience. Consider how much time you have to devote to investing. Consider how able or unable you'll be to stomach high losses when the market gets punished. Can you hold your stocks through a market decline of 10 percent or 25 percent? How about 40 percent? We hope the answer to all three is yes, because chances are the market will drop comparable amounts a handful of times in the next couple decades. But if you want to minimize the amount of volatility and short-term drag, obviously you'll want to be heavily in the index fund and the Foolish Four, with maybe a couple of consumer giants and no small-caps.

Now take a few minutes and break out the one hundred M&M's bowl by bowl according to your own chosen allocation percentages. You needn't count out the M&M's exactly; use the bowls as a visual guide to help you express your own tolerance for risk. We know this'll take some effort, but trust us, your eyes will be opened by doing so. First, you'll have your initial Eternal Foolish Allocation. Maybe you have fifty M&M's in the index fund, thirty in the Foolish Four, and twenty in consumer giants. Maybe you eliminated an entire category. Whatever you came up with, this is a nice starting point for deciding how to spread your investing dollars out among your current choices, given your current interests and investing skills.

Only three steps left to this exercise.

1. With your M&M's allocated, count them out and translate the percentages into dollar amounts. For example, if you've put forty-five M&M's in your index bowl, that's 45 percent of your investing dollars. Multiply your total money to invest by 0.45, and there's how much you might choose to invest in the index fund. Repeat this for each bowl.

2. Now, write down on a piece of paper the names of each of your companies. Drop those slips into their appropriate bowl—your four Dow stocks in the Foolish Four bowl, your consumer heavies into the consumer giants bowl, and so on.

3. And now for the final step. Look out over your bowls and ask yourself why you didn't just jot this out on paper. This entire exercise was a waste of time! Extract all the M&M's from the bowls and quickly munch them down, wondering how you got tricked into a silly exercise by the Fools. The final step was designed to humble you! Hurry up, put the bowls away before anyone sees. Oh, and by the way, we can't believe we got you to stand up in public places and say things like, "Messages Incorporated has grown its earnings per share at a rate of 35 percent last year." That's *too* much! Wish we could have been there.

All right, enough fun. It's not like we're resisting being silly ourselves—just look at our book covers! Anyway, back to business.

The Eternal Foolish Allocation is simply a device to help you address the issue of risk in investing. It doesn't have to be swallowed whole or achieved instantly. Even if you do put it into play, you'll need to reassess your allocation over time, as you add more money, as some of your investments thrive, and as others barely survive. Your first allocation may include no M&M's in the small-cap-stocks bowl. Maybe you'll add some in a few years.

Or perhaps you invested in some small-caps early on but later realized you didn't have the time necessary to track them. Move M&M's out of the small-cap bowl as your portfolio grows.

A couple of notes before we depart this section. First, we used only the example of $5,000. If you have substantially more than that, spread your money out further, into more investments. However, don't invest in too many companies at once. Generally, *five to fifteen stocks is all that any Foolish portfolio will ever need.* That guideline holds true whether you have $6,300 to invest or $630 million. Buy more than fifteen stocks and you won't have enough time to watch them all, you may not have enough money to invest significantly in them, and you'll probably start to dilute the strong performance effectiveness of your best investments. Remember, you want to *out*perform the S&P 500, which you can duplicate just by buying the index fund. If you're trying to beat it with common stocks, you should not be aiming to run your own index fund.

Second, in this section and elsewhere, we've used the phrase "small-cap growth stocks." However you need not limit yourself to small-cap growth alone. If you have a hankering for mid-cap or large-cap growth stocks like Cisco Systems or KLA-Tencor or Glenayre Technologies—companies that lack a huge name brand and don't sell directly to consumers, but are still great long-term performers—go for it! The main point is that this category represents more volatile growth stocks, small-cap or otherwise.

FOLLOWING UP ON YOUR INVESTMENTS

Stand up where you are and raise your hand if you think that *none* of the information you've collected about your company will ever change and that the stock will perform just as it has in years previous.

We'll hope that you didn't just raise your hand, because change in business is as inevitable on the stock market as it is in life. And it's all so unpredictable! If you want to see how difficult trying to forecast the future really is, write down a few predictions of what will happen in your life and in the lives of some of your close friends and family, then pull those guesses out in a few years. You'll find that it's extremely difficult to match them up, and this is for something you really *know*, like your friends and family (at least we hope and assume that you know your family better than your stocks). Here, for the fun of it, let's make some predictions.

The Foolish Crystal Ball

Make a few predictions about what you think that you, your family members, and your close friends will be doing five years from now. Mark down where you think everyone will be, what they'll be primarily focused on, and whether or not they'll have read our Foolish books by then!

You: _____

_____

_____

Your _____: _____

_____

_____

Your _____: _____

_____

_____

Your best friend: _____

_____

_____

Your other best friend _____: _____

_____

_____

Tuck this book away and then bring it out again in five years, and we think you'll see that it's extremely difficult to predict events and interests over a sixty-month period, even for what you know best. The same thing is doubly or triply true of the stock market. Even if your company continues to do well, there's no guarantee that another business won't come in and do it better. And there's no guarantee that the market for your company's products will continue to flourish. When was the last time you bought an eight-track cassette, dear Fool? How about a horse-and-buggy?

So, what does that mean for you?

It means that periodically you'll need to check in on the consumer-giant and small-cap businesses in which you've invested. Are they beating Wall Street expectations? Are they pleasing their customers, driving profits ever higher, and sitting on a stock that has consistently beaten the S&P 500?

How often should you track your companies? Ideally, four times a year, each time the company's earnings reports are released. This is when you get the best information on how they're spending money, executing their business plan, and meeting the challenges of the competition. You needn't live in a vacuum between statements. Read the paper, watch TV, go to the store, and keep an eye on news that may affect your

company's fortunes. And if you have access to the Internet, join the band of thousands of Foolish investors who are, no doubt, writing articles about your stocks both as we type this and as you read it.

Keep in mind that not all news or every opinion requires action. Even bad news shouldn't necessarily have you calling your broker a minute after the market opens. Take the time to see how your company responds. It's one thing for a company to blunder; it's another for a company to encounter a new challenge. A drop in the stock price is simply the market's panicked guess at how the news will affect the company. We expect that you picked good, strong businesses for the long run. That's especially good reason not to panic at the first sign of bad news. What you're looking for is continued growth on calm seas, and strong, clear-sighted navigation through stormy waters. So, before you buy stocks, take your time. And when you're holding them, do the same, fellow Fool.

Is It All Over Yet?

This said, investing is about more than just making your original selections. Your goal as an investor is to maximize your investment returns. Once a company you've invested in has achieved the goals you set for it—and doesn't appear to still have the growth potential it once did—why not say good-bye and jettison it out of your portfolio? Of course, here it's important to have new investment opportunities waiting in the wings. In our Fool Portfolio, we usually don't sell a stock until we have a better one to buy. Don't stop investing your time just because you have no savings left to invest. Your adventure into common stocks *can* proceed without capital.

A Short To-Do List

1. Put the companies you own into a manila folder. Mark down the dates that they'll be announcing earnings (you can call the company and ask, or get the info online) and jot those dates in your business calendar.

2. In another folder, put the companies you looked at but decided not to own. Note their prices when you considered them. Plan to review them every year.

3. Start a folder of new companies or industries that you'd like to investigate and research. When you have new money to invest, return to this folder and begin your next search mission.

STARTING AND MANAGING YOUR OWN ACCOUNT

You're now ready to set aside money for investing over the long haul, you've designed an allocation model for yourself, and you're committed to doing a bit of stock research each month. Despite the temptation to fire up the old jalopy, race over to the New York Stock Exchange, and place your orders *today*, lend us an ear as we consider stockbrokers and market mechanics. We think we may just be able to make these otherwise drearily gray topics interesting. Give us a shot!

Getting Ready to Buy Stocks

Contrary to all the action taking place on the stock exchange floors, or on Nasdaq trading terminals all over the country, most investors never need to go farther than their telephone to communicate their buy and sell wish lists. That's where a brokerage house comes in. While we are extremely skeptical of the commission-frenzied financial industry, a broker is still necessary to facilitate the order process and see to its fulfillment. You'll just want to shop around for the least expensive one.

Thumb through any financial magazine and you'll see ads for brokers. Dozens of 'em. Sometimes these magazines run feature stories comparing various discount and full-service brokers—a generally worthwhile read, even if their leading advertisers may always seem to win the comparison game! The ultimate Royal Taster, however, is you. You should probably round up a few attractive brokerage candidates—from names that friends have recommended to online- and offline-advertised brokerage houses. Call them, request information and an application, and start asking a lot of questions online and at your investment club.

The Different Sorts of Brokers

Brokers come in all flavors and sizes; finding what works best for you is critical.

Full-service brokers are usually the most anxious for your business. These brokers, oddly enough, are often compensated on the basis of how many trades they make in your account. This is why brokers call you during dinner (and breakfast and lunch) pitching you the next big winner. When you buy or sell stocks or mutual funds with a full-service broker, poof! they collect a transaction fee—often quite a stiff one. For this reason, we avoid the big investment firms and their brokers—or are they calling them "financial advisors" now? More than just a telemarketing nuisance, they usually underperform the market's average returns. Why? Because they're focused on getting you to trade, not on buying the highest-quality companies and then holding on to them for a lifetime. Doing the latter would turn their collective stomach—not to mention ruin their business.

Even though we recognize that the full-service industry has been trying to clean up its act, we still can't recommend full-service brokers with any enthusiasm, because it *has been* an *act*. For at least a few more years, as of this writing, full-service brokering will continue to prove disadvantageous to small investors.

If you've been listening, you've probably already narrowed your list to *discount brokers* and will have a few informational brochures arriving at your house soon. While the commissions they charge will weigh heavily on your opinion, don't forget to look at the entire picture. What is the minimum amount to open an account? What services does each offer? Are they open around the clock? Do they pay competitive interest rates on your money? Compare additional fees, too. Some may charge a postage and handling fee on top of every commission (ugh). Different brokers will charge different fees for services like transferring stock or wire transfers. In essence, find a company that offers the most cost-effective solution to serve your particular needs. Online, The Fool offers a discount brokerage center for your perusal.

Making Your First Investments

Once you've actually set up your brokerage account and funded it accordingly, you're ready to make your first few investments. Huzzah and welcome!

While your local newspaper will publish the closing prices for common stocks, there are actually two share prices for every stock at every point in time. There is the "bid," which is the price you'll get when you sell a stock. And there is the "ask," which is the price you pay when you buy a stock.

Quiz Time!

Think about it for a second. Will the bid price or the ask price always be higher?

Bid   Ask   Neither

We'll answer this in a jiffy.

Let's look at an example. While the final trade of the day for Microsoft may have been $129⅞ a share, there were two other prices at the time. In this instance, the bid price was $129¾ and the ask price was $130.

If you wanted to *buy* Microsoft, the best price available to you was $130 per share. You'd buy 100 shares, for $13,000. On the flip side, the best price you could get if you were selling shares of Microsoft was $129.75 per share. Were you to sell 100 shares of Microsoft here, you'd take in $12,975.

The difference in these prices is known as the "spread." And this spread in prices is one way that market makers earn a living. Who are "market makers"? They're the fellas who take and carry out the orders you give to your discount or full-service broker. Unlike the broker, these market makers keep an ongoing inventory of numerous stocks. They play banker in the process, and therefore expect to be compensated for the risks involved in holding a ton of stock for you to buy from. Naturally, the more obscure the stock, the thinner is its trading volume, the more risky it is for the market maker to hold it, and thus, the wider the spread in pricing. Sometimes you'll stumble across stocks bidding $10 and asking $11. That 10 percent difference is substantial. Were you to buy $10,000 worth of that stock, the spread alone would put you at a $1,000 disadvantage. Yowch!

Ultimately, for the long-term investor, giving up $⅛ or $¼ in the spread to buy an attractive stock (as well as paying a reasonable broker's commission) will be insignificant. However, it is indeed important to recognize these trading costs and know that you'll want to keep them to a minimum.

Oh, in answer to our bid-ask question. The asking price will always be higher than the bidding price. You'll always get less money back for selling than you'd get buying it at the same time. If the reverse were true, ask yourself what would happen!

Running a Sample Trade

Let's follow a single trade.

Below is a confirmation slip, probably similar to the one you will receive when you buy or sell a stock. On it, you'll find the name of the stock you bought or sold, how much of it you bought, at what price you bought it, and how much in full you paid for it. Take a look at this one.

CONFIRMATION SLIP

	BOUGHT	PRICE	COMMISSION	TOTAL
Rodman's Hair Inc.	500 shares	$25¼	$29.99	$12,654.99

Pretty self-explanatory stuff, eh?

So You're Anxious About Placing That First Order?

Maybe you think you might sound stupid. Maybe you're wondering if it really is such a good idea for you to take your financial future in your own hands, to become master of your own destiny. Wasn't it nice before, when a broker could screw things up for you, and you could blame him, struggle on with your life, and do so with the smug satisfaction that comes from pass-

ing the buck? No, it wasn't! But, there's certainly no need ever to rush. Let's take a minute here, tap into someone's cellular phone with our scanner (they thought these conversations were private!), and listen in on a stock order. Let's listen:

"But I really *do* love you, Homer. . ."

Wrong channel. Here we go.

"Hi, I'd like to place an order to buy some stock."

"Your account number, please."

"It's 952-22-3231."

"Name, please."

"Abby Normal."

"Yes, Ms. Normal, what order would you like to place?"

"I'd like to buy 200 shares of Messages Incorporated, ticker symbol M-E-S-S."

"Messages is currently bidding $19¾ and asking $20."

"Yes, I'd like 200 shares, but I'd like to place a limit order there at $20."

"Thank you, Ms. Normal. Let me read you back your order to confirm." (Reads it back.) "OK, we'll call you back when the transaction is completed. Anything else?"

"Hmm, I've been thinking about that volatile stock, Tattooland. Any thoughts on it?"

"As you know, Ms. Normal, since we're a discount broker, we don't offer any advice or recommendations."

"Darn. OK! Well, I think I'll hold off on Tattooland for now. Thank you!"

"Thank you. I will add, by the way, since I'm a closet Fool who parks all day at the www.fool.com Web site without my boss knowing, that you really should conduct all your own research and make your own decisions. It's the only way, Ms. Normal, that you'll ever derive any real education or true satisfaction from your investments! But there, I've gone and said that on a taped and monitored line! Ah well, another blow for freedom in the Fool Revolution!"

And with that we'll click off our scanner and review.

The call began with the person stating her account number. Routine. Then the discount broker confirmed her name. Routine. Then Abby ordered 200 shares of Messages Incorporated and spelled out the ticker symbol for the broker.

(Had she not studied the balance sheet?!) Routine. But then Ms. Normal said something unusual. She said, "Yes, I'd like 200 shares, but I'd like to place a *limit order* there at $20."

Huh?

Well, at the moment, Messages was bidding $19¾ and asking $20 per share. Normal placed a "limit" order at $20, setting her boundary line there. In doing so, she directed the broker not to buy any shares above $20. So if the stock moves up in between her phone call and the placement of the order, Abby Normal may not buy any Messages.

If you want our Foolish take, we question the logic of limit prices for any long-term investor. Too many times a stock you like at $20 hits $20¼, then suddenly $22, and never returns home to $20. In general, we think you should avoid limit orders and just buy the company, not the one-day stock price, expecting that if things go well the quarter point won't make a difference. Consider just buying at the market price.

Trying to shave a fraction may eventually cost you a great opportunity. It's happened to us! We've learned.

Anyway, placing your order is that simple. Your broker will call you back once the order has been filled. Some brokers may just put you on hold for a minute, then come back with the confirmation of your market-order execution. Then, a couple of days later, a confirmation slip will show up in your mailbox, buried underneath a few pounds of unsolicited junk mail—more trees wiped out for low-grade promotions. Ack!

But there's your confirmation slip! Congratulations, a holding is born.

A Little Jargon

Here are some terms you might expect to hear or use when talking with your discount broker. Please note that any brokerage worth its salt will be friendly and helpful, answering any questions (however simple) in a kind and thoroughgoing manner.

"Market order, please." A market order is one that will be executed right away at the current price, without limit if it rises during the purchase.

"I'd like a limit order at $20." Unlike market orders, a limit order carries a price that represents either the most an investor is willing to pay for a stock or the least he is willing to receive for the sale of that stock.

"Ten-4 Rubber Duck, Convoy spotted a Smokey." Remember when CB radio jargon was cool? This has no bearing on your stock market order. It may still save you a speeding ticket, however, so we figured we should include it. Right?

"I'll make that a good-till-canceled limit order, please." Also known as "GTC," this is a request that a limit order remain active until it is executed. Ms. Normal's limit on Messages at $20 per share can sit there for weeks waiting to get filled, if it's a good-till-canceled order.

"Make it good for the day only." You guessed it. This limit order designation is good only on that trading day.

"How 'bout that Motley Fool?" While not *guaranteed* to help you win friends and gain influence, few things are more likely to do so. Provocative, anyway, at the very least.

THE FUTURE OF BUYING STOCKS

Nowadays one can place stock orders without ever saying a word. We don't want to downplay Alexander Graham Bell's achievement, but for the many who prefer the convenience of placing stock orders without delay or chatter (there are other times to socialize), punching numbers on a telephone or computer keyboard is ideal. Today you can do everything electronically, from entering your account number to selecting a stock to buy to getting an update on the total value of your account.

Investors can now place orders around the clock. And the costs of doing so are falling substantially. Between 1994 and 1997 online, we've seen discount brokerage fees fall from $75 per trade to $5 per trade. This outstanding trend (*achievement*, really) has allowed more people to buy into the stock market and left more funds on the table for the private investor. Touch-Tone and computer trading have seen huge gains in popularity. And we expect that growth to continue.

The greatest growth is coming directly from online services, where thousands of investors talk about their investments and place orders with a mouse click. Dozens of discount brokers have set up shop on the World Wide Web to provide services to their customers. Internet access opens up a more visual presentation of the transaction and account information, but far more important, it provides access to everything from current news items to earnings estimates to analyst reports to public debate on business and investing.

The entire stock market is headed onto the Internet.

Direct-Purchase Investing

An alternative, extremely inexpensive way to invest also deserves mention here. Today, a growing number of companies, in an effort to increase their base of long-term shareholders, offer opportunities for you to buy stock directly from them without having to pay transaction fees for each trade.

These programs are most commonly called "dividend-reinvestment plans," or DRiPs—one of the worst acronyms in all human existence—though we regularly refer to them as "direct-purchase plans." These are offered by over a thousand companies. A direct-purchasing investor would, for instance, buy shares directly from the Coca-Cola Company and have the opportunity to submit additional funds each month to increase her position. All without paying a fee! By going directly through the company's transfer agent, these plans have made building investment positions cost-effective for investors with little initial capital. In many plans you can invest as little as $25 per month.

Individual investors like all of us are apparently beginning to matter more and more to public companies. In an era of focus on increasing shareholder value, these companies realize that one way to do that is by increasing shareholder satisfaction. By making it easier for someone to own and add to company stock through the years, these plans are literally creating long-term investors. That is also why some companies are rewarding their shareholders with perks. Every holiday season, Wrigley's sends free gum to its investors. Chomp, chomp. Other companies will send coupons or discounted products to their share owners.

Now, a free chew or a low-cost investment is a terrible reason to buy a stock. However, if you have researched first and then found that these attractive add-ons also exist, then sure, buy through the direct-purchase plan and chew that Doublemint gum to your heart's content. There is power in being an individual investor. Heck, use it.

Some Drawbacks to Direct-Purchase Investing

This manner of investing isn't for everyone. It isn't as perfect as a slice of cool Key lime pie on a salty hot afternoon. For starters, one cannot time one's additional investments. A company will purchase your stock for the plan on a monthly, sometimes quarterly, basis, and the money must be sent to the transfer agent well before then. Additionally, some companies will send you your shares and you'll be responsible for keeping them safe in a file cabinet or safety deposit box, or with the transfer agent. And the administrative hassles can be a bear. Each time you add more money and each time your company pays a dividend that it reinvests for you, you'll have an entirely new purchase price that'll have to be recorded for tax purposes. Thus, your "cost basis" will vary as often as every month. Thankfully, there are a slew of computerized financial programs that will track this for you, but it's still something worth considering. Online, The Fool offers a real-money direct purchase portfolio with a goal of building $500 and an additional $100 invested per month into $150,000 in twenty years. Get online and see if direct purchasing is your cup o' tea, or a good idea for your child's college fund.

And there you have it, a brief review of portfolio allocation and follow-ups, and a walk through making your first trade. After working through all these workbook pages, you might be discouraged to hear this, but . . . we think *the single greatest mistake you can make from here on in is acting too hastily.* There's no rush to get fully invested, especially if many of those investments would be in low-quality companies or holdings that you won't have the time to track. Pull back the reins a bit as you roll through the final chapters of this book. In the world of common stocks, haste makes more waste than you can imagine.

As we enter this Foolish workbook's home stretch, we still have some loose ends to tie, as well as a few new topics to cover. Let's get right to it then, with a chapter on tracking your investment returns, when to hold and when to sell, and whether investing is bringing additional value to your life beyond money, or eating up large blocks of your free time and interrupting your sleep at night. Read on, dear Fool.

CHAPTER 12

Perfecting Your Portfolio

Are we to understand that you've now read and reread twice all of the chapters leading up to this section? Excellent! Then we'll further assume that you've either put together a portfolio of stocks on paper that you're following or you've actually invested in a portfolio of common stocks and are ready to evaluate exactly how well (or badly) you're doing.

One of the biggest early mistakes that the authors of this book made in their teenage investment years was buying too many different stocks. No matter how much fun it is to call the broker, no matter how interesting it is to have a new stock to talk about at parties, do not put together an investment portfolio so full of ticker symbols that you are only fleetingly familiar with the company names and businesses. When you get to a point where you don't understand the businesses that you're invested in, either you should pare back your portfolio to a number of holdings that you can follow or you should just drop back to the index fund and Foolish Four. We believe that anyone looking to us for advice can track no more than twenty holdings at any one time, although we prefer the high limit to be set closer to fifteen.

But you know all that!

So, let's imagine that you've taken all our advice (*very* Foolish of you) and put together a stock portfolio. Imagine that you hold these ten stocks.

YOUR PORTFOLIO, EARLY 1998

COMPANY	SYMBOL	NUMBER OF SHARES	BUY PRICE	FEE	TOTAL COST
Foolish Four					
General Motors	GM	66	$60	$29	$3,989
Chevron	CHV	62	$63½	$29	$3,966
General Electric	GE	42	$94¼	$29	$3,988
Du Pont	DD	45	$87	$29	$3,944
Consumer Giants					
Coca-Cola	KO	85	$65	$29	$5,554
Gap	GPS	100	$36	$29	$3,629
Campbell Soup	CPB	60	$42	$29	$2,549
Small-Caps					
Messages Incorporated	MESS	100	$25	$29	$2,529
Mr. Software	SIR	320	$8	$29	$2,589
FoolMart	FMRT	140	$24¾	$29	$3,494
TOTAL				$290	$36,226

Take a few moments looking over this portfolio. You've purchased the Foolish Four up top, putting equal amounts of money in each. In reality, you'll never buy exactly equal amounts, but all of them are within $100 of one another. Below the Foolish Four you've added three consumer giants, all familiar names. Your daughter buys all of her clothes at the Gap, and you love their balance sheet. You are addicted to Diet Coke, and the company is in a wonderful competitive position across the planet. And finally, you've purchased three small-cap companies: Messages, because you read so much about it in the Foolbook;

Mr. Software, because you wanted to buy something going head-to-head with Microsoft; and FoolMart, because you've been buying a lot of stuff in our online store.

There's your portfolio. Now let's briefly consider three aspects of these statistics. (Because we didn't account for pennies, the total numbers will be off by up to as much as one dollar. No biggie.)

1. Consider the dollar and percentage breakdowns by category.

CATEGORY	PERCENTAGE OF PORTFOLIO	TOTAL DOLLARS
Foolish Four	44%	$15,887
Consumer giants	32%	$11,732
Small-caps	24%	$8,612

2. The total commissions you paid on your portfolio come to $290. That represents 0.8 percent of the total portfolio. The largest commission on any single position, percentagewise, was the $29 on your $2,500 investment in Messages Incorporated—1.1 percent of that investment.

3. You own ten stocks. The Foolish Four need to be followed only once every year. Your three consumer giants need checking only four times a year, when they report their earnings. And your three small-cap stocks should probably be studied at least once a month due to the nature of the investment. (Ideally, you know these companies so well that you're constantly de facto checking up on them, without even really thinking about it.)

From an allocation standpoint, this portfolio looks well within the proposed guidelines of the Foolish Workbook. You hold only half of the twenty positions that we consider the appropriate maximum number of holdings for any portfolio up to $1 billion in cash. (Ross Perot, you can stop reading here.) The Foolish Four make up nearly half of the portfolio; the account isn't overweighted in small-cap stocks, but isn't absent them. And there's a nice selection of consumer heavies, selling stuff each day to consumers around the country and the globe. And finally, and important, no investment ran commissions above 2 percent, and the overall portfolio incurred total commission costs of less than 1 percent. It's easier to do this with larger amounts of money—if you have a borderline-minimum amount to invest, you may have to stray from our guidelines.

The allocation looks solid to us. Now let's consider the performance first of Messages Incorporated and then of your overall portfolio.

MESSAGES INCORPORATED IN 1998

Messages closed out the year at $16.50 per share, down from your purchase price of $25. This means that in a single year, your investment in this company has fallen $879, or 34.8 percent. Tough year. Let's tap the numbers into a table here, and if you've made your first investment, you can enter the numbers for that one into your very first tracking list.

FOOLISH STOCK TRACKING LIST	YOUR TRACKING LIST
Date: Today	Date: _____
Ticker: MESS	Ticker: _____
Shares: 100	Shares: _____
Current Price: $16½	Current Price: _____
Current Value: $1,650	Current Value: _____
Purchase Price: $25	Purchase Price: _____
Purchase Cost: $2,529	Purchase Cost: _____

Why did Messages fall so dramatically in value? Did the company announce mediocre earnings? Was it hurt by currency hedging gone wrong on its Asian business? Did management make the blunder of spending inordinate amounts of time trying to correct its losing markets rather than plowing resources heavily into its winning markets? Or was it just a really bad year for stocks? Before we can answer those questions, let's take a look at the performance of the overall numbers for this imaginary portfolio.

YOUR PORTFOLIO AT THE CLOSE OF 1998

The year 1998 drawing to its sorry fictional end, you now download your year-end quotes from The Fool Online, or tap the prices into your computer spreadsheet after talking with your broker, or write them down in a notebook after quoting them in your local newspaper. It's been a difficult twelve months, but you're still holding all of your stocks. You'll be turning over your Foolish Four stocks in 1999, but may not place any other trades. You've kept abreast of the earnings reports of your consumer giants, and you've received every quarterly earnings report and press release from your small-caps in the mail. Very un-Wise of you.

Here's what the first year of investing Foolishly brought you.

OVERALL PERFORMANCE

COMPANY	NUMBER OF SHARES	BUY PRICE	TOTAL COST	PRESENT PRICE	PRESENT VALUE
Foolish Four					
General Motors	66	$60	$3,989	$58	$3,828
Chevron	62	$63½	$3,966	$60	$3,720
General Electric	42	$94¼	$3,988	$95½	$4,011
Du Pont	45	$87	$3,944	$84	$3,780
Consumer Giants					
Coca-Cola	85	$65	$5,554	$60	$5,100
Gap	100	$36	$3,629	$33¼	$3,325
Campbell Soup	60	$42	$2,549	$46	$2,760
Small-Caps					
Messages Incorporated	100	$25	$2,529	$16½	$1,650
Mr. Software	320	$8	$2,589	$5¾	$1,840
FoolMart	140	$24¾	$3,494	$24	$3,360
TOTAL			$36,226		$33,374

Eight of your ten stocks were down for the year. Messages has gotten mauled. Investors have been bailing out on Mr. Software as well. Your two winners are General Electric, up about $23 total for your portfolio, and Campbell Soup, which has made you some $211. Otherwise, everything else has lost you money. Either it's been a horrible year for the U.S. stock market or you've done a very poor job of picking stocks, Fool.

Let's look at your percentage returns for the year.

PERFORMANCE BY STOCK

COMPANY	TOTAL COST	PRESENT VALUE	PERCENTAGE RETURN
Foolish Four			
General Motors	$3,989	$3,828	−4.0%
Chevron	$3,966	$3,720	−6.2%
General Electric	$3,988	$4,011	+0.6%
Du Pont	$3,944	$3,780	−4.2%
Consumer Giants			
Coca-Cola	$5,554	$5,100	−8.2%
Gap	$3,629	$3,325	−8.4%
Campbell Soup	$2,549	$2,760	+8.3%
Small-Caps			
Messages Incorporated	$2,529	$1,650	−34.8%
Mr. Software	$2,589	$1,840	−28.9%
FoolMart	$3,494	$3,360	−3.9%
TOTAL	$36,223	$33,374	−7.8%

In 1998, your $36,223 in savings has lost just short of $3,000, falling 7.8 percent. Messages has lost over one-third of its value; Mr. Software has fallen nearly 30 percent. None of the remaining eight stocks have collapsed. Campbell Soup and General Electric are the only stocks with plus signs in the percentage return column. That's a look at your individual stocks. Now let's take a gander at your performance by categories— Foolish Four, consumer giants, and small-caps.

Studying your portfolio by category requires a series of calculations that will take but a few minutes and will give you a grounded sense of how you're doing and how well you're allocating your funds. Too often investors don't know how their small-cap growth stocks are doing relative to, say, their stock in the one or two conglomerates they own. By breaking them down into groups, you may well learn that you've improperly allocated funds.

PERFORMANCE BY CATEGORY

CATEGORY	TOTAL COST	PRESENT VALUE	PERCENTAGE RETURN
Foolish Four	$15,887	$15,339	−3.4%
Consumer giants	$11,732	$11,185	−4.6%
Small-caps	$8,612	$ 6,850	−20.5%
TOTAL	$36,223	$33,374	−7.8%

Nearly $2,000 of the $3,000 your portfolio lost in 1998 was drained by your small-cap investments. Your Foolish Four investments held up best, followed closely by your consumer giants. At first blush, it appears you've done an extremely lousy job of finding small companies to invest in. And while your larger companies haven't lost you much money, they've still lost you money! What the heck is going on here? Investing is supposed to be about *making* money. What have the Fools gotten you into?!

Well, as much as the numbers above tell us about *your* year, they don't tell us how your investments did relative to the performance of the entire stock market in 1998. If stocks were up 4 percent, you'd be forced to conclude that you had a disappointing year. Of all your investments, only Campbell Soup could be considered a success. Conversely, if the stock market fell 30 percent in 1998, you'd even be able to call Mr. Software a winner. Without the context of the broader market's performance, you'll have little idea of how well or how poorly you are doing. You won't know whether to just move all your money into index funds, because you can't beat the stock market, or to just buy the Foolish Four, or to put all of your money into small-cap stocks because your financial analysis there has been awesome. Without a snapshot of the market's doings, you're lost.

Below are the performance numbers for the S&P 500 and the Nasdaq in 1998. The S&P 500 is used to measure the overall performance of the U.S. market; the Nasdaq is used here to measure the performance of the smaller companies in the marketplace. In a minute we'll be using the two to measure the performance of our portfolio by category. Investors reading the workbook in early 1998 should *not* confuse these figures for a market prediction (unless they end up being close enough to correct that the Motley Fool Inc. can sell itself as a market guru service in the years ahead).

VERSUS MARKET PERFORMANCE

	1997 CLOSE	1998 CLOSE	PERCENTAGE RETURN
S&P 500	962	894	−7.1%
Nasdaq	1624	1317	−18.9%
Your portfolio	$36,223	$33,374	−7.8%

Well, it turns out your portfolio didn't have such an awful year. You lost to the best measure of stocks by less than one percentage point. While you would have done better in an S&P Index fund, you can rest assured that you beat the majority of managed mutual funds in the U.S. in 1998.

You'll also note that the Nasdaq market—which holds more small-cap issues than the New York and American Stock Exchanges combined—got crushed in 1998. The smaller companies fell a whopping 18.9 percent. What you have, then, is a market where the most enterprising companies, the riskiest ones to invest in, got clobbered. The larger companies, with many different products and services and with business across the world, fared much better. But even they declined, by a full 7 percent!

This was clearly a very difficult year for common stocks in the U.S. But it wasn't an extremely rare one. Since 1970, the stock market has closed out seven different years with negative returns. In four of those years, stocks lost more than 9 percent. Every investor in common stocks should be prepared for double-digit decreases in any given year. If you are investing $10,000, you may well lose $1,000 of it over the next twelve months. Our simulated 1998, *while not a prediction of any sort,* is certainly plausible. Be prepared.

Of course, you should also be prepared for a consistent upward journey in the value of the stock market over the only term that really counts, *the long term.* For most of the twentieth century, stocks have climbed at an average annual rate of 11 percent, but along the way, there were some awfully lean years. Investors in one of our favorite companies, Coca-Cola, lost over 65 percent of their investment between 1972 and 1974. But if they remained invested in Coke through those lean times right up until today, the good years more than made up for the bad ones. In fact, an investor who bought in early has been rewarded with 16.5 percent annual growth—far surpassing the market's return. So, our most useful counsel is patience.

Your workbook portfolio is unfortunately down 7.8 percent, but you generally walked in step with the market, so you're fine. Yes, ideally you would have liked to be down only 5 percent, or 3 percent, or even up for the year. Ideally, yes. But you're not. So let's figure what you should do from here.

All Sorts of Returns

Now that you can compute the gain (or—horrors—loss) generated by your portfolio and present it in the form of a percentage (otherwise called a portfolio "return"—as in the return on your invested capital), we should briefly look at different types of returns that you'll want to be calculating.

1. Annual Return. This is the total return measured over a twelve-month period. When you see an "annual return" reported at 10 percent, it simply means that the investment earned 10 percent over the last year.

2. Total Return. Total return represents the *total of price appreciation* derived from an investment. If you started with the sample portfolio and have come to the close of your *first year,* your total return is a negative: −7.8%. (In other words, your portfolio is worth 92.2% of its starting point.) Let's say that *next year* your portfolio rises 10.8%. (Then your portfolio is worth 110.8% of what it was worth after the first year.) Now, what's your "total return" for the two-year period?

1 = portfolio value at starting point

1 × 92.2% = 0.922 (value after first year)

0.922 × 110.8% = 1.022 (value after second year)

0.022 = 2.2% = total return

3. Average Annual Return. This represents the total return expressed as what you would earn for each given year, on average. This is another calculation that might, at first, seem complex. But it isn't. There is going to be some root taking, but we're not talking about drilling at any nerves below your teeth. Let's take an example. Imagine that your portfolio has risen 159% over an eight-year period. Here you would simply take the eighth root of 2.59. The number represents your original investment (1) plus the rise in value (1.59). Type 2.59 into your calculator. Then take the eighth root of it, and you should get 1.126. This indicates that your portfolio has grown at a rate of 0.126, or 12.6%, per year over the eight-year period. To check that, multiply 1.126 against itself eight times and see if you come up with 2.59. Ahh, perfect.

4. Return Versus the Market. The final note we'll throw in here is that you should always calculate your annual, total, and average annual returns alongside calculations of the returns by the S&P 500. How are you doing relative to the overall market? If your stocks are up 26 percent but the market is up 41 percent, you're losing. And if the market is down 18 percent and you're down 11 percent, you're winning. Conventional Wisdom hasn't yet caught up to these simple truths. So, be Foolish instead.

WHERE TO FROM HERE?

After a little more than one year, you'll have some easy and some difficult decisions to make.

Let's start with the easy two. *First,* add as much long-term savings as you can to your portfolio. *Second,* adjust now for the new Foolish Four stocks. Eighteen months after your first investment, sell the stocks that no longer make the Foolish Four cut and buy the new ones that do. Attempt to weight things as before (even amounts in the Four) as best you can, without incurring high commissions. In other words, if you have some holdovers from the previous year, don't pay out high transaction fees trying to align the dollar amounts perfectly.

LATE-INNING NOTE: With the change in capital gains tax laws, we now recommend that you hold your Foolish Four stocks for eighteen months. So, please read the sidebar, Fool!

The New Foolish Four Strategy?

A note for those who knew the Foolish Four when it had a twelve-month holding period: By the time this book hits the superstores, we may be living in a world with a new capital gains tax structure. That new structure should include a long-term tax rate for all positions held longer than eighteen months. Hooray! If that's the case, you'll want to sign on to The Fool Online on the Web or AOL to see if Foolish scientists have worked up all the new numbers for the Foolish Four designed around an eighteen-month holding period.

OK, you've added cash. You've reset your Foolish Four portfolio. And now you have got six other stocks to consider. Start with the consumer giants. You've seen their last twelve months of financial reports. Are they still financially healthy? Is Campbell Soup still growing sales, earnings, and at least maintaining profit margins? Is Coca-Cola paying down debt, holding off its accounts payable, and increasing its savings? How's the Gap doing—four good quarters of earnings? Our suggestion here is that unless you have very serious concerns about the business of your consumer heavies, you continue to hold them. Certainly, for at least one of your heavies, at least at some point in your lifetime, you'll have serious concerns. Consider selling then. But if the company seems headed in the right direction and its financial position is sturdy, we think you should hold.

Your final step is to consider those small-cap stocks. Of your three holdings, two lost badly to the Nasdaq: Messages Incorporated and Mr. Software. Sometimes the investing community has just blown it, overlooking a great value and selling off a stock well below its fair price. But often enough the market has dug through some flaws in the business model. Which one is it for your two dogs? You'll need to ask the following questions:

- Why did Messages and Mr. Software underperform the Nasdaq?

- Are their income statements and balance sheets stronger this year than last?
- Do I feel that these businesses might excel in the year ahead?
- What are their most difficult challenges?
- What are people saying about these companies at The Fool Online?
- Am I having trouble sleeping at night because of these investments?
- Are there better places for this money?

There are another dozen great questions to ask, but these seven should get you on your way.

Remember, just because a stock underperforms its category in a single year, that doesn't mean you should immediately take your money elsewhere. You're an owner of the company and you should evaluate the business, not the stock price. Check through the earlier reading and exercises on financial statements, attempt to determine what went wrong, and consider whether things will get worse or better for the business in the year or years ahead. If things don't look promising, sell and don't look back. Sell at a loss? Yep. If there's a better place for your money, it should be there.

Oh, by the way, we know you didn't pick Mr. Software and Messages. We forced them into your portfolio. Sorry, Fool.

SELLING A STOCK

So, your portfolio lost slightly to the market in 1998. You have your Foolish Four all lined up for the year ahead. You've scoped through your consumer heavies—the Gap, Coca-Cola, and Campbell Soup—and while none of them had a particularly awesome year, you're content that they're on the right track. You believe people of every age will still wear Gap khakis, that people of every age and nationality will still drink Coke, and that in the cold of winter, most people head for Campbell's chicken noodle soup—not another brand. So you're going to hold on to all three of those.

But here you are left with the prickly decision about your small-caps. After looking over FoolMart you're reasonably happy. The company had some inventory problems in the fourth quarter, but its CFO Gary Hill and president Jill Kianka convinced you in their quarterly report that these were one-time problems with three specific products that are falling out of the mix in the year ahead. So you're going to stick with FoolMart, a sweet, pure play on electronic commerce.

But what about that pair of barking dogs, those dachshunds of depreciation, Messages Incorporated and Mr. Software? As they used to say on a silly financial television show: Buy, sell, or hold?

When to Sell

You've reached the most frustrating topic in investing. Everyone has an opinion on when to sell. But while a few key principles do exist, generally you'll have to build a selling strategy that fits your personality. In *The Motley Fool Investment Guide*, we proposed just one sell rule: "When you find a better place for your money, put it there." This generally focuses you on the opportunities that lie ahead rather than the prior performance. Certainly the biggest mistake that investors make is hoping for one of their losers to "just get back to even." If the business looks weak, you should sell.

The Fool Ratio is also around to help you pick exit points. Selling a stock when it reaches fair value is about as reasonable as it gets. (See pages 155–161.) But even there, sometimes you're better off holding a winner that is priced fairly or even overpriced temporarily. If the business is strong, then it will eventually catch up to and rush past the present valuation, pulling the stock up with it. We call that the Motorboat Principle. Why? Have you ever seen a great water-skier slalom outside of the wake, up next to the boat, then fall back into the wake behind the boat? During the fall back, the rope loses its tautness. The skier isn't propelled forward. But then, kapow! Once back far enough, the slalom skier is yanked forward by the motorboat. The stock prices of great companies can get ahead of themselves, but if the business truly is great, eventually it'll yank the stock price up with it.

So far we've offered two ideas—sell if you have a better place for the money and sell when the stock looks fairly priced and the business doesn't seem superior enough to pull it higher anytime soon. That's a decent start. But what other clues are out there? Try asking yourself these questions:

- Is the business stronger this year than last year?
- Does the company appear to be telling the truth to its shareholders?
- Do the reasons I bought the stock still hold true?
- Is the Foolish Flow Ratio improving or weakening? (This is more appropriate to large-caps, just as the Fool Ratio works best for small-caps.)
- Are sales and earnings climbing at a good pace?
- Is Martha Stewart a Fool?
- Will I need this money in less than three years?
- Do I really know enough about this business to be invested in it?

We consider it critical that you ask the last two questions. If you're going to need the money in less than thirty-six months, it shouldn't be in stocks. And if you don't really understand the business you invested in, sell out. On par, you'll do better in an index fund than in businesses that you don't understand. And the first five questions there will guide you to a method for selling. We'll leave you with one last suggestion: Don't base sell decisions on your emotions. You should never rush into the sale of any investment, just as you shouldn't rush into the purchase of any. Take your time, be methodical, be Foolish, and recognize that naturally you'll make selling mistakes in your career. Your aim should be to improve a little bit each time round.

The Sell Game: Don't Look Now!

Since we are focusing on ways to help you sort out how you look at investing in stocks, we want to give you a way of reviewing your stock sales and learning from them. *The Motley Fool Investment Guide* describes a simple technique— a game, really—we call Don't Look *Now!* At the time you sell your stock, record the exit price and the closing price of the S&P 500 Index. Then just basically ignore the stock's price for several months after you sell. Then, three or six months from the date you sold (your choice— whatever length feels right), record the follow-up price for your stock and the S&P 500 Index.

Here's the way to score your results (with a new point-total system if you'd like to maintain an ongoing tally):

- If the stock has risen 20 percent or more over your exit price, that's a *total defeat*! You shoulda held. (Score: −5 points)

- If the stock has risen less than 20 percent but is outperforming the S&P 500, that's a *marginal defeat*. (Score: −2 points)
- If the stock has fallen less than 20 percent and is underperforming the S&P 500, you guessed it—*marginal victory*. (Score: +2 points)
- If the stock has fallen down 20 percent or more from your exit price, claim a *total victory*. (Score: +5 points)

Keep a running score of your performance as a stock seller. After five years of investing, evaluate your performance as a stock seller. What's your total score? You may well find that you bail on your investments much too soon. Or possibly you hold your losers too long. Or maybe you nail *every sale* just right (if that's the case, please send us your strategy via e-mail— FoolWorkbook@fool.com—and if we like it, we'll steal your idea and write a book about it).

Pop Quiz!

It's back to that simple true-or-false game that haunted you in high school science class. Good luck!

1. Don and Dawn Arrington have doubled their money in the stock market over the past three years. They're planning on buying a house with that money in twenty-four months, and they believe they've found a way to double their money every few years in stocks. Given this, it's a good thing that they've decided to keep their money in stocks over the next two years.
   True   False

2. No matter what anyone tells you, if you lose money at the end of any twelve-month period of investing in stocks, you've blown it.
   True   False

3. Most people should just pay management fees to a mutual fund and let the professionals take care of their money.
   True   False

4. The best investors sell out of their positions a lot.
   True   False

5. The Fool says that to be properly diversified, you should have at least fifty stocks in your portfolio.
   True   False

6. A lot of really weird people live in nudist colonies.
   True   False

7. You can begin investing with as little as $100.
   True   False

8. Unless your consumer giant investments are beating analyst expectations, you should sell them.
   True   False

9. Most people have a better chance of winning at roulette than they do of picking investments that will make them money in the years ahead.
   True   False

10. Harrison Ford is a huge Motley Fool fan.
    True   False

The answers to all questions but lucky number 7 are false. Number 7 is true—you can actually begin investing with as little as $50, through the direct-purchase plan we wrote about last chapter. And as for questions 6 and 10, we have no evidence that indicates those are true, so we'll have to mark them as false. If, however, Harrison Ford would like to appear in his next action film wearing a Fool ball cap in the first scene, we'll provide that cap gratis.

ADDITIONAL THOUGHTS ABOUT YOUR PORTFOLIO

You're tracking your portfolio, maybe you've sold a position or two that wasn't meeting your standards, and you're starting to see some results. Over the last eighteen months you've whooped the market, and neighbors have seen you jaunting down to the grocer in—what's that?—a belled, motley cap! You're excited. But still, something seems to be missing. In an attempt to fill that gap, we're tossing out nine ideas for your consideration. Some of these summarize earlier points, while some are new. This section aims to get you to think more deeply in the Foolish investor's mind frame.

1. Is There a Better Way to Track My Portfolio Than on Paper?

Now that your pencil is dulled from scribbling and your handheld calculator is in need of new batteries, you might be wondering if there isn't an easier way to track portfolio returns.

There is, through the use of a computer with the appropriate software.

Many of the online brokers have computer programs that allow you to track the returns of the stocks that you purchase from them, with the simple click of a button. Still other discount brokers have software that will allow you to track returns for your entire portfolio, regardless of where you bought the stock. And finally, you'll be able to find software packages that will track your performance, assemble graphs and charts, and use a calendar to flash reminders of upcoming earnings reports. Two thousand dollars is a lot of money for a personal computer; we expect it'll pay you back that and many times more in the years ahead. A simple package geared just to stock portfolios is FoolSoft's PortTrack program; more info on that and other useful products is available at www.foolsoft.com.

But, hey, computers may not be for everyone—yet. Millions of new computer users would suddenly materialize if the things could be turned on by remote control, connect to the Internet in less than a second, and process video conferences across the planet. Should these people be excluded from being Foolish? Uhhh. Well. Hmm. No. Nope. We thought not. With tools as simple as a pencil, a four-function calculator, and the Foolish work sheets in this book, you can do all of the computations necessary to track your portfolio. They will take more time, and you'll have a greater margin of error in calculations. And we do think personal computers are rapidly becoming necessities. But if you can't stand the thought of getting a computer, getting online, getting digital—the paper, pencil, and counting machine still do work as well as ever.

2. Do My Returns Reflect the Performance of the Market, or of My Individual Stocks?

If you have followed the stock market for a while, no doubt you've heard the dreaded euphemism "correction."

"Correction" is the descriptive word used to describe what happens when the market loses ground. The overall market drops 5 percent or more a few times a year on average. If you own any equities during those declines, it can of course be nerve-racking. Investors invoke the term "bear market" to describe a prolonged "correction." The lines between these two are blurry,

but the term "bear market" refers generally to a downtrend that lasts six months or longer.

Given that the overall market can see fairly dramatic swings over any twelve-month period, you'll need to be absolutely certain that you study the performance of your investments alongside that of the broader market. Remember, your company may be making spectacular progress, but when macroeconomic factors come into play, your company's stock price will be racing upstream at half or quarter speed—possibly losing ground in a strong countercurrent.

It can be frustrating to see one of your companies do nothing over a prolonged period of time. Rest assured that if you've picked a strong company, over the long term things will even out.

Here are some of the factors that can drive the whole stock market and make the actual business fortunes of your companies virtually irrelevant to their share price movement over a short-term period:

Government economic data, such as jobless rates or inflation

Interest rate changes

Election results

International conflicts

Gooroo predictions in glossy financial magazines

A clear trend up or down in earnings reports by conglomerates

The flapping of a duck's wing in Hunan

If you just happen to buy into a company before one of these broad-reaching events trashes the entire market, maintain patience and keep your sense of humor. Just continue to compare your stocks to the market's indices. Even though we've already defined and mentioned the following indices in the workbook, we consider these important enough to give them final mention here.

The Dow Jones industrial average (the Dow) is the granddaddy of 'em all. You hear about this index every night on the news when the anchor looks blankly into the camera and says, "The Dow was up 15 points today." One nationally administered Fool finance class in high school and we'd all know that the Dow index tracks the movement of thirty of the largest blue-chip stocks in America and the world. And even the news anchor would then know that a 15-point Dow move is akin to a four-mile-per-hour breeze coming from wherever. Not news.

The Standard & Poor's 500 Index (S&P 500) is probably our favorite index, the one that tracks five hundred large "bellwether" stocks. Among the list of five hundred sit all thirty stocks from the Dow, and also a load of smaller, more enterprising businesses in a wider range of industries. It's a more precise measure of the market's overall performance. It is also the index that money managers compare their performance to, the index that most money managers lose to each year, and the index that can be duplicated at virtually no cost by purchasing the Vanguard Index Trust 500 Portfolio.

The Nasdaq Composite (the Naz) is the index that tracks all of the stocks traded on the Nasdaq exchange. Because this index tracks smaller companies, many of the high-technology flavor, it is more volatile than the two prominent ones listed above.

You need to use one of these averages, or a combination, as a milestone to gauge how your portfolio is doing. Indices are a very useful tool for placing your wee little investment skiff's performance in context of the entire U.S. fleet.

One final thought. Remember that matching or beating the market over any short-term period involves a high degree of randomness. So don't become discouraged if your portfolio does not immediately beat up on Wall Street your first week, or month, or year. Remember: Unlike Wall Street, you have your eye fixed squarely on the long term. Over time, your position as a small investor will significantly increase your chances of beating the market.

Word Match

a. the Dow _____ the New York Stock Exchange

b. index _____ an index including five hundred stocks, mostly traded on the NYSE

c. the S&P 500 _____ an index including thirty blue-chip stocks, traded on the NYSE

d. return _____ an index including *all* of the stocks on a certain exchange

e. NYSE _____ a grouping of an assortment of individual stocks

f. the Nasdaq _____ income generated from invested capital

Answers: a. an index including thirty blue-chip stocks, traded on the NYSE *b.* a grouping of an assortment of individual stocks *c.* an index including five hundred stocks, mostly traded on the NYSE *d.* income generated from invested capital   *e.* the New York Stock Exchange   *f.* an index including *all* of the stocks on a certain exchange

Matching Puzzle

Commentaries from the media and financial world often overanalyze or misanalyze the effects of news on corporate fortunes. It's really very much simpler, in most cases, than they'd have us believe. Pair the company with the external event that would most affect it.

1. Exxon	*a.* global outbreak of mad cow disease
2. J. P. Morgan	*b.* expensive aviation safety legislation
3. Nike	*c.* the Federal Reserve raises interest rates
4. McDonald's	*d.* war in the Persian Gulf
5. Boeing	*e.* Michael Jordan retires from basketball

Answers: 1. *d*   2. *c*   3. *e*   4. *a*   5. *b*

3. Has My Company's Story Changed?

You're now able to track your portfolio and analyze the performance of your individual holdings against the overall market. Simultaneously, it's important for you to score the performance of your stocks against your own expectations for each.

What does that mean?

Well, we spoke earlier of filling out a single-page report that highlights your own research and sets down some of the main reasons why you've found a good investment. This should include some numerical projections that enable you to directly compare a stock's performance versus your own plans for it ahead of time. This step will help you to assess, on a continual basis, whether or not this stock belongs in your account.

Numbers make your assessments easier to perform, but don't neglect the "story" either. Many different factors could cause you to reassess your company's story. A management change, new and larger competitors, slowing sales, delayed FDA approval—those are just a few of the many items that can change the overall prospects for a public company.

So, Whaddaya Think?

Jot down some thoughts about the management, competition, and strength in products or services of a company that you own (or all of the companies that you own, by Xeroxing this page).

Management: _____

_____

_____

Competition: _____

_____

_____

Products or services: _____

_____

_____

_____

_____

4. Admitting You're Wrong

Sometimes you do all your homework and buy stock in what you believe to be a great company. You love the product and believe in the management. You track it against the market, follow up on all news releases, and dig through the financial reports as they come. Two years later, you still own the stock. Unfortunately, the story has changed for the worse. The stock has gradually fallen, and is now down perhaps 50 percent, cutting in half the amount you plunked into it.

Given that the business is weakened and weakening, it looks like the marketplace is trying to give you a hint.

Dear Fool, remember that some investments just don't work out. The stock doesn't worry about you, and oftentimes the company doesn't worry about you, either—not nearly so much as you may have worried about them. If no end to this underperformance appears in sight, sell the dog. Be thankful that you learned so much about their industry, that you learned a good deal about losing investments, and that you're still in good health! Once you sell, you'll be thankful the puppy has left the house for its new doghouse digs. And ten years from now, if you've been diligent and Foolish with your investments, the bad performance of this one will have been outweighed by two things: (1) the lesson you learned and took from experience, and (2) the money you made after switching the funds into a better investment! A double whammy in your favor. If it waddles like a dog, pants like a dog, and begs for food at dinner like one, it most likely is in fact a dog. Sell it!

5. Whom Should I Listen To Out There?

Planet Earth is well stocked with self-proclaimed experts on every subject. Our financial markets seem to lure these people at an unusually high rate, particularly those who make ridiculous short-term predictions about individual stocks or the direction of the market in general. We refer to these characters as "gooroos."

Most of their predictions are wrong. They don't make money from being right, dear Fool; they make money from just being *there* and being heard. What is lacking is any accountability whatsoever. For years, the big financial newspapers and magazines have printed the short-term predictions of gooroos without printing any follow-up reviewing the performance of those predictions.

What the reader is left with is puffery and self-promotion aided and abetted by journalists who need a quote before their deadlines. Any surprise that the *Wall Street Journal* has been facing a declining subscribership? Their message has often been that if you're not a gooroo you can't make money in stocks. Intelligent readers have tired of all the price guessing that ate up space better reserved for a thorough and objective analysis of business. This continues to stoke the dramatic growth in the popularity of online services, where many have discovered they have more to learn from one another than from yesterday's news.

So, to whom should you be listening for guidance on your money? Above all, start with investment books written by actual investors, like those from Peter Lynch and Philip Fisher. For each that you read, throw out twenty-five business magazines that print covers reading, "Sell Stocks Now!" or, "The Seven Mutual Funds You Need to Own This Summer!" or, "Where's the Market Headed in '98?" None of these topical attention grabbers speak to what should be your underlying interest: the vitality or frailty of particular businesses.

A second source of opinion is the thousands of knowledgeable investors you can meet online today, many of whom own the same investments you do, and some of whom know the company or its industry as well or better. Sign up with an Internet service provider—AT&T or America Online, for example—and surf around Fooldom to participate in discussions about thousands of companies, taking place twenty-four hours per day. You'll also read articles about investment strategies, your big consumer giants, the Foolish Four, getting out of debt, you name it. Free tax help is another outstanding feature, since we have superb full-time CPAs like Roy Lewis answering questions in Fooldom. Something for everyone. But in the end, of course, you should listen to yourself. We've made that point again and again, as it's so integral to what we believe and stand for.

6. How Much Research Is Too Much Research?

Remember to keep records of the resources that you use to make investment decisions, such as newspapers, magazines, and online services. Some of these qualify as deductions on your annual taxes. Review the list with your accountant or tax advisor, or check in to Fooldom to see our list. Also, on occasion you'll want to sift through your various subscriptions and eliminate those that aren't helping much. Save a tree and free your mind up for other things—how much better can it get?

Naturally, alongside your reading of another investment book or two, you should begin to stock up on some other research materials at the outset. Go ahead and scour different publications and Web sites in your first few months of investing. Read skeptically, of course, as always. The answer to the question we just posed is that early on, no amount of research is too much research. As you become more experienced, however, you'll begin to know when to say when. To re-iterate, though, the right financial books—timeless in their teachings—should ultimately prove your greatest foundation. And online information and discussion should ultimately prove your best research resource.

7. The Beauty of Compounded Growth

Worth repeating, perhaps the most important lesson we can leave you with in this workbook, is the principle of long-term compounded growth—a growth that adds more money in years thirty through forty than in all the first thirty years toted up. *Time* is the critical component here—not *timeliness*, as in gooroos making the right market call over the next six months. The amount of time you allow for your investments to grow will radically change the rewards. Let's say you double your money in the market next year—from $2,000 to $4,000—and then remove it altogether to spend on something else, just happy to have "gambled" and won. You'll be kicking yourself fifty years from now, dear reader, because $4,000 compounded at 11 percent annual growth for five decades grows into $738,000. That's the reality of compounded growth.

In the simplest of terms, compounding capital is the money you earn on the money you've earned in previous periods. Remember your first lemonade stand? You scraped together $1 and bought the lemonade mix. You added some water, set up your stand, and away you went. At the end of the afternoon, you may have had $2. (You doubled your money at age eight without ever picking up an investment book!) The next day, you went out and bought two packages of lemonade mix and, with hard work and some luck, ended the day with $4. Then you bought more, opened up a second stand, and maybe before the end of your life, you were an old guy sitting on a porch pitching Country Time Lemonade to America. That's compounding: growth off a growing base of capital. You learned it then. You know it now. Let's muse over a few more numbers.

	ANNUAL GROWTH RATE	NUMBER OF YEARS	PRETAX MONEY
$1,000	13%	70	$5.2 million
$2,000	13%	60	$3.1 million
$4,000	13%	50	$1.8 million
$8,000	13%	40	$1.1 million
$16,000	13%	30	$625,000
$32,000	13%	20	$369,000
$64,000	13%	10	$217,000
$128,000	13%	1	$144,640

As you can see once again, the early bird with the least money got the worm. You simply cannot start soon enough. And, sorry to repeat this once more but . . . hey, it is absolutely ludicrous that our children are not learning the basics of investing and putting away a little bit of money today for their retirement. With so many years in front of them, they have the most to gain! To hammer that home, consider that in the seventy-first year of the $1,000 portfolio, a 13 percent return would yield over $600,000. That's more money than went into all seven of the remaining portfolios—each with more than $1,000 at the outset.

The lesson: Once you've paid down your debts, begin saving and investing today, no matter how little or how much long-term savings you have.

8. *On Becoming a Paper Tiger*

Occasionally we can be absolute experts at contradicting ourselves, so with point 8, allow us to do just that. We do not think that you should begin investing today unless you're secure in your thinking. Why not hone your skills by practicing on paper before you begin your investing career? Then compare the results of your paper portfolio with those of an appropriate index.

There's no rush to investing. Much as we think you'll benefit from getting involved today as an investor in the best companies, you simply are not a Foolish investor if you don't understand what you're doing. You may even actually want to reread the workbook when you're done with it. After all, you aren't reading on meter—it's free!

Take your time; despite the propaganda you may have read elsewhere, Fools don't rush in!

9. *Are You Having Any Fun?*

Education and Folly go hand in hand. None of the tools provided in this workbook will have any real meaning if the destination means more to you than the journey itself (all the living you did to reach the point of being rich). Indeed, if portfolio performance becomes the be-all and end-all of your investing experience, things can go wrong. You might throw all of your money at a "hot" sector and forget what you have learned about diversification. You might subscribe to that "can't lose" publication that tells you how to double your money in thirty days. Finally, you might do well but overlook the importance of your family in the pursuit of your profits.

That's not what we're about, and we expect it's not what you're about. Compounded growth, patience, and the search for great businesses is all about *not* becoming obsessed with your stock portfolio. Don't ignore your family—unless they won't let you have the TV remote control, in which case, grab it and ignore them! Don't spend all of your free time hunched over a copy of the evening news, trying to read the agate type. No matter how much we'd like to see you clicking around The Fool Online for sixteen hours a day, we don't want you there if it detracts from living a full-blown life away from the management of your moola.

Manage your portfolio, NOT vice versa.

CHAPTER 13

Where Am I Going?

Remember those folks we met at the beginning of the book? There were Bob and Carol. Carol's wacky mother-in-law thinks that the only safe place to keep your money is in your tightly clenched fist. Remember Jim and that low-grade mining company he invested in? What about Ronald and Sandy, whose pile of credit card statements is thicker than a phone book? Contrast them with Joanne, who hangs out in her local library, reading up on investing. Let's look in on some of them now and see how they're doing.

A YEAR LATER

Bob and Carol Agee, the young couple with two small children, still find themselves somewhat intimidated by the financial challenges facing them, but they've taken a few steps to reassess and restructure their finances. While they still have lots to learn, their financial bewilderment

has begun to ease. All those foreign terms—"401(k)," "index fund," and so on—emerged from the primordial soup and have actually taken on a now recognizable form.

It hasn't always been easy, but Bob and Carol are beginning to feel a greater sense of control over their lives, because they've decided to confront a few financial demons. For starters, the couple is eliminating fears of Armageddon from their financial strategy. They've decided to focus on the long term and ignore the family rants about market crashes and banks collapsing. Additionally, much to the consternation of Bob's brother-in-law, Bob and Carol have decided to forgo Bob's whole-life insurance plan in favor of a term policy, and have invested the difference in premiums in a stock index fund. They've also assessed their spending habits and have cut back on unnecessary expenses. They now contribute 10 percent of their income toward their savings.

More important, they've committed themselves to taking responsibility for their own financial future, learning more about the historic returns of the stock market over the past six decades. They realize that they're young and that they still have plenty of time to get it right. It's only been a year, and these two have their whole lives ahead of them.

Because of that, Bob and Carol have decided not to pay too much attention to the day-to-day fluctuations in their portfolio. "Up one month, and down the next, it really doesn't matter," says Bob, who is more preoccupied with his fly rod than the stock ticker. "As long as I'm ahead ten years from now, what's the difference?"

THREE YEARS LATER

Jim, the young college grad who grew up raising cattle, learned his lesson after getting burned playing with that penny-stock mining company. Being young and single, he had a higher tolerance for risk than most—but he also knew that it just didn't make sense to gamble with his future.

During his free time between strumming his guitar and hanging out with his fiancée, Alison, he taught himself how to evaluate a company's balance sheet and weigh the risks of investing in it. After saving up a stake of several thousand dollars and grounding his portfolio in several large Dow stocks with high dividend yields, he began investing in selected growth stocks. He chose these smaller-cap companies on the basis of the strength of their management, their command of their respective industries, and the healthiness of their financial statements. He loves low-inventory, cash-heavy, rapidly growing and

very big companies like Dell Computer and Pfizer. But he's also come to love researching unknown agriculture biotech companies, because of his childhood experiences on the family farm in Bradford, Pennsylvania.

While his small-cap stocks haven't beaten the market, his overall investment portfolio is doing quite well. Most important, he knows what's going on with his money. Now the memory of his investment in Trapshooter Reilly seems as if it came from somebody else's life.

FOUR YEARS LATER

Ronald and Sandy have gotten off the credit card treadmill.

Wow, was it tough! They've paid off enormous amounts of consumer debt, and just this past year dug up several thousand dollars for investment simply because they were no longer paying those exorbitant, 18 percent interest rates. When the scissors came out to cut up those credit cards, it was like snipping the strings to their own material-hungry hearts, but the rewards of self-discipline were worth it. Believe it or not, they're starting to sound quite frugal now. They've realized what a waste it was to drive brand-new luxury cars year after year, when the value of those cars dropped significantly in the first year of ownership and continued down in every subsequent year. Their lives are no longer driven by the consumption gods, and all the stress that goes hand in hand with living paycheck to paycheck has diminished accordingly. They don't look as picture perfect as they did, but they're starting to wonder if they're not a lot happier without the glitter.

FIVE YEARS LATER

The quiet diligence and self-reliant spirit of Joanne Kurtz has served her well. She has seen her nest egg grow, and, more important, in her spare time she's learned more about business and finance than most MBA students. Joanne can read an annual report with considerably greater ease than the brokers who cold call her during dinner—so, she actually enjoys their calls for the humor of it! She knows about cash flow analysis and P/E ratios and can tell you things by looking at a company's balance sheet that never get discussed on cable TV.

Joanne has so immersed herself in the philosophy of investing for the long term that her friends asked her to start up their investment club in exchange for free weekly meals for her. And she didn't even ask for that! After paying a small initiation fee and dues of just $25 per month, a dozen members pooled their information and shared their investing decisions. Joanne has led the research on twelve of the sixteen stocks in their portfolio, and over the past three years, the portfolio has grown at a rate of 16 percent per year, while the stock market has risen at 9.3 percent per year.

Meanwhile, Joanne also made what she thought was an extravagant purchase. While grocery shopping one day, she spotted an index card tacked to a bulletin board, and before she knew it, she was the proud owner of a used computer. She knew how to use it for word processing but had never explored the online world. Once she fired up her new modem, she stumbled into a vast conversation with thousands of investors from around the world. Next month, she's flying to Poland to study the Warsaw Stock Market and meet with an investment club there that she met at The Fool Online.

Pretty awesome.

WHAT ABOUT YOU?

We know it's a shame that none of the four examples above blew up over the past five years. The media is all about mayhem and mania, don'tcha know? But if you really look around you in America, the majority of people are living and learning with a great deal of satisfaction. Our sample of four cases isn't that unusual. Americans are starting to manage their own finances, thank you very much, having learned to put simple numbers to work for them.

How about you, Fool?

After a year of Foolish investing, or two years, or five, how are you doing? (True, this is probably your first time through this book, and you probably haven't been putting what you've learned to work yet. That's OK. Just make something up!)

Once you've put your own strategies into play and are learning and earning more from your investments, you'll want to pull back and ask yourself a few questions. Questions like these:

1. Are you better off now than when you started?
2. Are you approaching those goals you set for yourself?
3. Which goals have changed, and why?
4. Should you do anything differently going forward?

Unfortunately, there's no neat mathematical formula for calculating such things. So, how do you know when you're successful?

It's important to sit back and review your progress from time to time. A convenient time for many is once a year around tax time, when they've gathered all their financial materials in one place. You will want to set aside a good chunk of time, alone or with your spouse, to think things over. Make a commitment to review your progress occasionally, to see if you should be buying individual stocks or just purchasing the index fund. Heck, do it right now. Our Foolish Legal Department has already drawn up the papers.

I, the undersigned, knowing that I am but a mere Fool, beaten and buffeted by the Winds of Fate and whipped by the Scourge of Happenstance, in full cognizance of my doubtful abilities to predict all the stuff that might happen to me well in advance of the time it actually occurs, do forthwith and in free concord with all earnest intent, commit my every faculty and sinew toward a periodic reassessment of Progress in my Financial Life, and do hereby contract and bind myself to reviewing the condition of my financial state on a

_____ monthly

_____ quarterly

_____ annual

basis, and will, in due consideration of all the circumstances attending, agree to take whatever action necessary to correct and promote the various endeavors that I have established to further my progress toward achieving every just and righteous end.

Duly attested to this _____ day of

_____, 19_____.

_____ (*signature*)

We will now pause for a moment in profound commemoration of this solemn commitment.

(Please stop reading for a sufficiently awe-inspiring interval.)

You've now made the commitment. You've signed the papers. And we now fast-forward to the arrival of that hour when you're forced to review.

First, pull out the written set of goals you prepared for yourself early on in this book. Read them. Mull them over. Do they make sense to you? Do they still seem valid? Get out a pencil and a piece of paper (or a chisel and a marble slab, if you like to be different) and do your best to answer the following questions.

Big-Picture Questions

Do the goals I've set for myself still seem

appropriate? _____

_____

Were my goals too ambitious? Or not ambi-

tious enough? _____

_____

Have any setbacks or sudden strokes of good fortune occurred to make any of my former goals

seem irrelevant or inappropriate? _____

_____

Did I overlook anything when I set these

goals for myself? _____

_____

How might my goals be changed or im-

proved? _____

_____

_____

Has my financial picture changed drastically due to some unforeseen event (such as an inheritance or a sudden illness)? How have my goals changed in light of such developments? _____

_____

_____

Your Investments Review

Now take a look at your portfolio of investments.

Are the reasons I invested in the particular investment vehicles I've chosen still valid?

_____

_____

Did I expect too much from my investment strategy? Or too little?

_____

What have I learned about my risk tolerance? Am I riding motorcycles without a helmet when I want to be in a Volvo?

_____

What sorts of changes should I make in my portfolio? Should I take on more risk? Less?

_____

_____

Is it time to sell some of my holdings? If so, why? What would be the tax consequences if I did so?

_____

Has my net worth improved, or—shudder —gotten worse? _____

_____

Have I beaten the S&P 500? _____

Personal Questions

Now consider qualitative matters of Foolish glee or misery.

What do I know now about investing that I didn't three months or a year ago? How should my next decisions reflect this new knowledge?

_____

_____

_____

Have my spending habits changed? Have I learned to live within a budget?

_____

Now that I'm a little older, should I adjust my spending and investing habits?

_____

What else do I need to learn?

_____

Where can I go to improve my skills?

_____

Have I lived up to my obligations to my spouse, my family, and my children?

_____

_____

What kind of contribution am I making to others?

_____

What should I do next?

_____

REASSERTING (AND REDEFINING) YOUR GOALS

After you've thought long and hard about your new place in life, given the passage of time and the changes you've made along the way, go back to the beginning of this book. Take some of the quizzes again. Are you getting the same scores you did last time you took them? Are you a more savvy and experienced investor? Review each chapter step by step. Rereading this workbook shouldn't be too much of a pain!

As you proceed, always consider making small changes in your budget. If you are earning more now, how much of this income can you channel toward saving and investing? If you've eliminated your credit card debt, are you now devoting the cash flow you've freed up toward building a better future for yourself and your family? Can you afford to splurge a bit, now that your finances are more secure? ("Absolutely!")

You may have made all sorts of mistakes since your last review. Don't bother hiding from them. Own up to them. Cherish them. They're your mistakes; you've earned them. Making mistakes is often the best way to learn some important lessons. The authors of this book have made just about every mistake in this book! No kidding. Where we may differ from most is that we believe that mistakes should be celebrated, scrutinized, and (hopefully) eradicated. We love that Jim Donatello smilingly can't believe he invested in Trapshooter Reilly, even just a few years after having done so. That's Foolish!

And finally, you may have already realized it, but far from all the stodgy balance sheets and all the number crunching, there is a real joy in the art and craft of designing an investment portfolio for yourself and in tending to this garden—your garden—over the years. Investing is not only a method for improving one's material well-being; it can also be a vehicle for self-improvement. The real return on your investment might not have any dollar signs in front of it.

A Legacy for Your Children

If all our efforts to maximize our investment returns can't help our kids lead better lives, then what's a dollar for? Your money can do a lot for your children. It can provide a secure home in a good neighborhood. It can pay for their books, a computer linked out to the planet, opportunities for travel, a few weeks away at summer camp meeting kids across the country, and a leg up on their college tuition.

Yet while these dollars can make a fine direct gift for a child, we think that far better is teaching your children the value of their dollars and getting them started on their own investments in companies like Disney, Nike, the Boston Celtics, or Rainforest Cafe—companies that they're familiar with and whose businesses they'd enjoy following. You may not have seventy years ahead of you to watch your compounded returns build and build on themselves over the better part of a century, but on average, a child of seven or eight does have seven decades ahead. Consider again the following compounded returns.

SEVEN DECADES OF INVESTING

	ANNUAL GROWTH	TOTAL YEARS	TOTAL RETURNS
$100	12%	70	$278,779
$500	12%	70	$1.4 million
$1,000	12%	70	$2.8 million

It may not seem realistic to you to put away up to $1,000 today for your child's next seven decades. And that's fine, because actually, we don't like the idea of setting up trusts that are divorced from the little guy or gal's daily life. When they get their hands on the money, they may well have no clue what to do with it. A trust fund, however small, in the hands of an untrained (small *f*) fool has all the potential for disaster and no reason for it. Ensure that your kids don't waste money on the state lottery, or run up credit card bills their first year in college, or borrow a lot of money to buy depreciating assets—like a sleek convertible—or invest in unknown mining companies in Vancouver that often enough have been incorporated just to sucker investors.

If you can get your kids following companies that they love—bookstores, baseball stitchers, fruit juice blenders, toy makers, boatwrights—they won't find the subject of saving money and investing it so incomprehensible. Informal Fool studies show that 63.73 percent of adults over the age of twenty-five (median age 41.7, margin of error 1.73 years) don't have a clue about managing their money. This is simply the result of their neither having been taught applicable math in high school nor having received guidance from their parents and grandparents. The easiest way to reverse that trend is to get your kids involved.

But how?

Getting Your Kids Involved

Here are suggestions to help you get started teaching the little whelps about money and investing.

Start by showing your children the wonders of compounded growth. Teach them about the principle of growth off a growing base. Remember that kids, as much as anyone else, love to watch the magic that happens with things that grow, and they take to numbers much better than adults (sadly!). Of course, kids are also the ones for whom compounded growth holds the most potential. So, get your kids on a regular savings plan. Start them out small, perhaps designating a percentage of their allowance for their first share in a direct-purchase plan. One share of Coke ought to be their aim in the year ahead. Why not?!

Allow them to spend some money, too, of course. It isn't realistic to expect kids or adults to faithfully save every dollar that passes through their hands. Saving and investing should be a pleasant part of a happy life, not a painful chore necessitating constant sacrifice. As they get older, your children should broaden their mock- or real-money DRiP portfolio. A weekly or monthly review of stock performance can be a good deal of fun. Is anyone's investment bombing? If so, why? Making your primary aim *to learn* virtually assures that the long-term consequences will be *to earn*. (We promise, no more Jesse Jackson imitations.)

Finally, children love to collect things—why not get them involved in creating a company scrapbook? They can flip through newspapers and clip stories about their favorite companies. Some of the news will be good, some bad, some even horrible. By doing so, they can build the skills they'll need for investing. They'll learn more about the world around them—good and bad. And they'll have a base of mathematical and business knowledge to support their other callings in the decades that lie ahead. Mind you, we're not suggesting this in place of seashells or baseball cards, without which many of our childhoods would have been so much the poorer. No, this is only in addition to those sterling pursuits.

Guiding your little guys and gals to buy one share of stock in a strong company that they know as a consumer will have them outsmarting MBA graduates in a matter of years (without dishing out the $80,000!). Try McDonald's or Disney or the Gap. Knowing that they have a stake in a company is a great incentive toward getting them to learn more. And again, it'll keep them from being persuaded by misleading credit card advertisements, misrepresentative claims by managed mutual funds, and misguided business models in the full-service brokerage industry.

Now, brainstorm some ideas of your own to get your kids, nieces, nephews, and grandchildren involved in stocks. May we start by suggesting a monthly investment club?

a monthly investment club
_____
_____
_____
_____
_____

If it's accessible to you, come share your ideas and enjoy those of other Fools in our family finance section online, named the Family Fool. The Family Fool is found at the Fool's main addresses—on AOL of keyword: FOOL, and on the Web at www.fool.com.

THE NEXT STEP IN YOUR GROWTH

Your family may now be set up, but *you* paid for this book! What about you?

Let's assume that you're saving money regularly. You've got clearly defined financial goals. You know how to choose your portfolio, how to manage risk, and how to take charge of your financial future without the hand holding and price skimming of the so-called experts. You've moved from financial dependence—on your parents, on your job, and on the financial establishment—to the early stages of independence. You are quickly becoming the master of your fiscal fate, the captain of your soul.

Now what?

In Fooldom, we sometimes like to talk of a way of life beyond independence, where you are not only seeing to your own needs, but also contributing to the advancement and improvement of others. Again and again we've seen shareholders, motivated by mutual self-interest, banding together to educate, enlighten, entertain, and inform one another. Rather than acting in isolation, investors are increasingly forming alliances and acting in consort to achieve their aims.

One perfect example of this online is our collective movement to block exclusive meetings between the financial industry and public companies via closed quarterly conference calls. Individual investors have been stepping up and making it known that they think such activity violates basic securities laws that legislate free flow of information for everyone, regardless of how much money they have.

Another perfect example is the autumn and winter rally in Fooldom to make charitable contributions. With sufficient privacy and the distance of a computer linkup, people are becoming social capitalists. Rather than building up chests of wealth and withdrawing from the world behind wired gates, they're diving into the community and working to solve problems that once seemed insurmountably huge.

The same options are open to you. Rather than pure dependence or independence, there is a growing interdependence because of the Internet. A financial community larger than anything the industry has seen is swarming around Fooldom, from Warsaw to White Plains, from Hong Kong to Helena. If one person has an idea about how to deal with the uncomfortable world of car buying and car dealerships, over the next few weeks everyone will have that idea, will be able to turn it over, improve it or reject it. For that reason, we can't recommend any more strongly that you join the community of investors online.

Joining the Community of Investors

Though the mission of this book is to make saving and investing an almost reflex reaction undertaken by any responsible adult, starting off on a life of investing can be pretty intimidating for a beginner. There are plenty of mistakes to be made out there, and if you've done any investing at all, you've undoubtedly already made a few. It's a daunting task to launch a financial program that will (one can hope) last a lifetime.

Fortunately, you do not have to face it alone.

All across America, thousands of investors are joining together in small investing clubs. Typically, each group comprises a dozen or so members who pay monthly dues and meet regularly to share the work of making investment decisions. They research stocks together, evaluate companies and industries, examine trends, and vote to decide what sorts of methods are best suited to maximizing the return on their investment dollars. The camaraderie that develops can be re-

warding far beyond the mere dollars and cents of investing.

Investment clubs might be associated with your place of employment, your school, or your church. You can start your own group, or join one already established in your area. What can you expect from an investment club? Some hard work, good friends, tough choices, contemplative thought, and some blunders. You can slap high fives when your investments are up, commiserate when your investments are down, and learn from varying and common perspectives.

Don't imagine for a second that you are too inexperienced to join the community of investors. We're all learning more every day. The authors of this book have benefited in countless ways from talking turkey with investors around the country. Dive in; your own perspective will strengthen those of others.

Cooperative Investing Online

Now, imagine your small town investors' club writ large. Instead of a dozen members sitting around a table in Ethel's parlor, you have thousands of investors working together in concert across the nation and around the world. Here you can share insights, alert one another to trends, pass on information and breaking news, and argue the finer points of investing technique, twenty-four hours a day, every day of the year.

It's happening right now, online.

Features of the Online Universe

So, you've got a cutting-edge computer with a powerful 56-baud modem (that'll seem weak soon enough, Buster Brown!). You're all wired up and ready to dive headlong into the online world. You point your mouse at the little box on the screen labeled "Click here to log on." But wait—where do you go to online? What should you be looking for? What exactly is out there? We don't have the space to be comprehensive here, but we can offer a brief overview of some of the features that make our online areas distinct from the culture of Wall Street.

1. Message boards. Think of an online message board as the analogue to a bulletin board in a school hallway or a company meeting room. You or anyone else can tack a message to that board, commenting on any subject you might wish. Others who pass by can read the message and leave messages of their own, commenting on yours or introducing a different matter altogether. The only difference between the two is that if you now look to your right, you'll find that this particular bulletin board stretches on into infinity.

That's messaging in cyberspace. At our Motley Fool Online Web site (www.fool.com), and in our area on America Online (keyword: FOOL), we have message boards devoted to thousands of different companies, each one housing its own community of investors devoted to the study and monitoring of that particular stock. Veteran investors rub elbows with absolute beginners. People's willingness to exchange information is astonishing, especially considering that up until only a very few years ago, such exchanges were entirely impossible and considered self-destructive. Pa-tooey!

Let's say you're interested in an intriguing new software company, but you don't know much about it and you're no programmer. Head on over to our message board for this company and you'll find lots of people who've never met in person discussing whether the stock is destined for greatness or for embarrassing anecdotes. You may hear from people checking out stores in their neighborhoods and reporting how well the company's products are selling. You may hear from people who live near the company, summarizing how busy the headquarters look on weekends. If, instead, it's a health-related company, you'll probably read the thoughts of doctors, who have a better understanding of the product than you do. And you're sure to always find messages from total beginners, asking basic questions and getting answers. The combination of unique perspectives has staggeringly positive consequences.

2. Unparalleled resources for research. In addition to the message boards (some have literally tens of thousands of postings), there are investment resources as vast as the whole of what you can get in print, but searchable and updated daily. There are databases filled with company news releases, pages devoted to individual industry analysis, and government libraries filled with information on every corporation that trades on the major stock exchanges. Increasingly, companies themselves are establishing their own Web sites; many of these have pages of information devoted to responding to the needs of individual investors. Online, you'll find access to earnings and revenue estimates, company profiles, industry analysis, and a lot more. Only historians many steps removed will be able to measure just how great the effects of this change will be, and the final, positive outcomes possible for individual investors.

3. Stock research and market quotes. The Fool provides users with instant access to market quotes. With the touch of a button, you can monitor your portfolio, check the latest value of your positions based on the day's trading, and see how your investments have been behaving—even on a minute-by-minute basis, if you're a compulsive, not too Foolish sort. Such information was formerly available only to those willing to spend their days standing in the lobby of their broker's office. You might choose to use that immediate information, but we hope you don't go nuts applying it! Though we love the increase in information, we do still prefer to avoid commissions and taxes by buying and holding.

In summary, there's so much out there that, at some point, any attempt to quantify it becomes inadequate. Of course you can do quite well for yourself investing and never get near a computer keyboard. But The Motley Fool has built a happy home in the 1990s in the digital world; please excuse our gushing enthusiasm for it. In fact, indulge us in one last rhapsodic effusion about the glorious online world—then we'll stop. Imagine a newspaper comprising mostly letters to the editor (with replies!). How about a radio station where all the listeners have microphones? Or a magazine with features that are updated minute by minute. A television set with as many channels as there are viewers?

The online universe is a communications revolution that will change not only investing but also the very structure of the way human beings communicate with one another.

The Dark Side of Online Investing!

Be careful out there online! Not everything is sunshine and flowers in the digital universe—dangers await investors who are not prepared!

The pitfalls fit neatly into three categories:

1. Hype! Believe it or not, not everyone you meet online is going to have your best interest at heart. The same thing is true when a cold calling broker reaches you during dessert! Some will try to spread rumors or incite panic in order to move a stock price. One should never take another's word at face value—always verify your facts before reacting.

2. Not all investors are Foolish! Many of those who haunt online forums are day traders and speculators at brokerage firms, moving in and out of stock positions sometimes many times in one day. Their arguments can be seductive, but are usually anathema to the sort of long-term, value-based investing that built tens of millions in profits for twentieth-century life investors in Coca-Cola, for example.

3. Self-hypnosis! The immediacy of the medium can be so mesmerizing, so compelling, so gosh-darned gripping that it can drive you to distraction. If your eyes are glued to the stock ticker all day, then whatever value you've gained from the return on your investment is lost in a life wasted staring at a cathode ray tube. Too much focus on each passing moment can drive you stark raving bonkers. Remember that there's a reason that your computer has an off switch.

A FOOLISH INVITATION

We hope this book has been a help to you in demystifying the world of investing. That world has been mystifying for a reason—everywhere the financial establishment stands to rake in a tidy profit by making both money and its management seem much more complicated and arcane than they ever need be.

We now live in an age where the tools to educate and empower ourselves are in our hands.

We are reaching out to you offline with this book and other books; we are also reaching out to you in cyberspace with The Motley Fool Online.

In addition to the message boards and chat rooms described above, we offer a dizzying array of features, from games to daily news features to exclusive stock research to educational materials to model portfolios managed with complete accountability in full public view. It's all part of our commitment to educate, enlighten, and inform—and to have a heap of fun doing it, too.

Join us—it's available to you free of charge, with just a point and a click.

On America Online, go to keyword: FOOL.

Or point your Web browser to http://www.fool.com.

Fool on!

APPENDIX I:

Extra Credit

Still reading?

We are quite flattered. Does this mean:

a. Joyous momentum has carried you into these back pages, thirsting for more sips from the clear, chilled spring of Foolishness?
b. You just thought we weren't done?

No matter how you answered this question, we have one final project for you to work on. Take a firm hold on the edge of this page. Give it a good tug once or twice to test for resistance. Then, gently tear it from the binding of the book, top to bottom.

Done? Good. Next, fold it up and tuck it in your pocket; throw on some shoes, walk out to your nearest bookstore, hand it to the helpful person behind the counter, and say, "I'd like to purchase these, please."

You Have More Than You Think
by David and Tom Gardner

Wherein you get your personal pocketbook hosed down like a dog, lathered up, rinsed off, and blown dry. Following a few simple steps, we can help you out of debt and give you a firm but friendly shove toward financial independence. If you aren't paying your credit card balance in full every month, this book will scare your pants off. Once you're properly clothed, this Foolish bestseller will lead you to your first investment—no matter who you are.

The Motley Fool Investment Guide
by David and Tom Gardner

Wherein we take you step by step through the Foolish investment approach. The bestseller includes full explanations of the pitfalls of mutual funds, the beauty of ugly Dow stocks, and the hazards of investing in a biotech company that manufactures lemons the size of Yankee Stadium.

RIGHT NOW you can get a full-color catalog online that is constantly updated with all the latest Fool products, including primers, e-mail services, Fool caps, Fool golf balls, and a full range of Foolish books. Online at AOL (keyword: FOOLMART) and www.foolmart.com.

APPENDIX II:

How to Get Online

Why bother visiting The Motley Fool Online? Is it really worth leaving the familiar comfort of books, magazines, newspapers, and TV? You betcha! Online we offer you a community of fellow investors, asking and answering questions, debating the merits of various companies or investment approaches, and learning together. You'll also find our Fool School, covering many basic investment and personal finance topics (like credit card debt and buying a car); our Hall of Portfolios, where we run several real-money portfolios, discussing their progress each day; and our News and Research Departments, which report on companies making news and companies worthy of a closer look by investors.

As you've probably assumed, entering the brave new world of cyberspace is an extremely complicated and difficult thing. One little mistake can damage your furniture or disrupt the neighborhood. The wrong approach can cause hypertension, leaf mold, ozone layer deterioration, and shingles.

We jest. Joining the online world is surprisingly simple. Here's all you need:

- A computer
- A modem (which often conveniently comes with the computer)

- Software to let you access cyberspace
- An electrical outlet and a phone line
- An account in good standing with your local electric company and phone company
- About $20 per month for access charges
- An interest in exploring, learning, and having fun

That's it! Either a Macintosh or a Windows machine will do. You probably want a modem that runs close to the fastest current available speed. For software, call an Internet access provider and have them send you a start-up disk. America Online has many good features and is remarkably easy to use. Other companies offering access include AT&T, CompuServe, Earthlink, Mindspring, and the baby Bells. The software they'll send you will come with instructions and customer-support telephone numbers. It will also probably include a Web "browser," to allow you to access Web sites on the World Wide Web. To find the easiest or nearest Internet provider, just check your newspaper. They're looking for you, so there should be plenty of ads for you to choose from.

Once you fire up your computer, turn on your modem, and get online, come see us! You'll find us at www.fool.com on the Web and at keyword: FOOL on America Online.

APPENDIX III:

Getting Started—Fifty Companies to Call

COMPANY	PHONE NUMBER	TICKER SYMBOL	COMPANY	PHONE NUMBER	TICKER SYMBOL
3Com	408-764-5000	COMS	Eastman Kodak	716-724-4000	EK
3M	612-733-1110	MMM	Eli Lilly	317-276-2000	LLY
Allied Signal	201-455-2127	ALD	Exxon	972-444-1000	XON
Allstate	708-402-5000	ALL	FedEx	901-369-3600	FDX
America Online	703-448-8700	AOL	Gannett	703-284-6000	GCI
American Express	212-640-2000	AXP	Gap	415-737-4333	GPS
Applied Materials	408-727-5555	AMAT	Gillette	617-421-7600	G
Barnes & Noble	212-633-3300	BKS	Harley-Davidson	414-342-4680	HDO
Bed Bath & Beyond	201-379-1520	BBBY	Hershey Foods	717-534-7552	HSY
Borders	313-995-7262	BGP	Hewlett-Packard	415-857-1501	HWP
Boston Market	303-278-9500	BOST	Hilton Hotels	310-278-4321	HLT
Bristol-Myers Squibb	212-546-4000	BMY	Home Depot	404-433-8211	HD
Chase Manhattan	212-552-2222	CMB	IBM	914-765-1900	IBM
Chevron	415-894-7700	CHV	Intel	408-765-8080	INTC
Chrysler	313-956-5741	C	Intuit	415-322-0573	INTU
Cisco Systems	415-688-8246	CSCO	Johnson & Johnson	201-524-0400	JNJ
Coca-Cola	404-676-2121	KO	Lone Star Steakhouse	316-264-8899	STAR
Compaq Computer	713-370-0670	CPQ	Marriott	301-380-3000	MAR
Dayton Hudson	612-370-6948	DH	Mattel	213-524-2000	MAT
Dell Computer	512-338-4400	DELL	Maytag	515-792-8000	MYG
Digital Equipment	508-493-5111	DEC	MCI Communications	202-872-1600	MCIC
Disney	818-560-1000	DIS	Merrill Lynch	212-449-1000	MER
Dole Food	818-879-6600	DOL	Microsoft	425-882-8080	MSFT
Dow Jones	201-938-4000	DJ	Monsanto	314-694-1000	MTC
Du Pont	302-774-1000	DD	The Limited	614-479-7000	LTD

Acknowledgments

The Motley Fool Investment Workbook sits in your hands as testimony to the collaborative efforts of a large number of exceedingly Foolish individuals. First, we thank Simon & Schuster editor Bob Mecoy for all the usual stuff. Blah blah blah—hey, you the MAN, Bob. We also thank our agent, Suzanne Gluck, of ICM, for occasionally trying to be Bob's worst nightmare while still managing to be a fine partner in the process. Back at Simon & Schuster we also thank Isolde C. Sauer and Chuck Antony who took on the unenviable task of making sense of our manuscript including a prodigious amount of marginal scribblings, scrawlings, and sprawling additions. And Deborah Feldstein deserves our thanks for a most un-Wise afternoon photo shoot.

A cheer for the home team as well. In this case, Team Fool! We are alphabetically grateful to the following Fools for their individual and team efforts in helping to research and write portions of this book: Barbara Eisner Bayer for

her Foolish spin on personal attitudes about money, Randy Befumo for his insights into the nuances of valuation, Jeff Fischer for his arduous work—fact checking, editing, and number crunching (and for his usual limitless display of good humor throughout), Brent Harris for his work building out the Messages Incorporated story, Joseph Hecht for finding the time in between seeing patients to share his portfolio-tracking expertise, Holly Hegeman for her eloquence on freeing oneself from debt, Donna Howell for her imaginative thinking about getting out of one's chair and into the neighborhood to scan for stock ideas, Roy Lewis for turning talk about taxes and tax ramifications into a pleasurable (!) experience, Gabrielle Loperfido for her graceful and outstanding work in managing this book from inception to completion, Selena Maranjian for her edits and her eminently Foolish "Fool Lib," Tony Miller for his sartorial metaphors applied to mutual funds and Dow strategies, Aristotle Munarriz for his Foolish twists on the mechanics of making trades and for his too-true "Number Love" section, Dave Neiman for his inventive M&M allocation model, George Runkle for conceiving of and introducing our "cases" in chapter 1, Erik Rydholm for his unfailingly Foolish humor, Jerry Thomas for his family-spirited personal finance navigation, and to Debora Tidwell for helping us frame the individual investor's limits and challenges in the proper long-term context.

We further thank Melissa Flaim who continues to bestow style and coherence upon the ever-changing arrangements of our lives. We thank our families for the richness of the lives we lead beyond the bounds of Fool HQ.

And finally, as always, we thank you, our reader. Without you there is no Folly. So many of you have touched our lives with your stories, your generous offers of aid, your calls for help. We work hard to be of the best service to you now and in the coming decades, too. We hope you'll fulfill your end of the deal by letting us know whenever you see a way for us to improve our business. We always look forward to hearing from those who haven't yet communicated with us as well as from those who have. Our e-mail address is: FoolWorkbook@fool.com.